CONVERSATIONS WITH
A SUFFERING SERVANT

CONVERSATIONS WITH A SUFFERING SERVANT

David W. Williams

t&tclark

LONDON • NEW YORK • OXFORD • NEW DELHI • SYDNEY

T&T CLARK
Bloomsbury Publishing Plc
50 Bedford Square, London, WC1B 3DP, UK
1385 Broadway, New York, NY 10018, USA

BLOOMSBURY, T&T CLARK and the T&T Clark logo
are trademarks of Bloomsbury Publishing Plc

First published in Great Britain 2021

A catalogue record for this book is available from the British Library.

Library of Congress Cataloging-in-Publication Data
Names: Williams, David W., (David Wyn), author. | Noel, Jared, 1981-2014.
Title: Conversations with a suffering servant / by David W. Williams.
Description: London ; New York : T&T Clark, 2020. | Includes bibliographical references and index.
| Summary: "A literary reimagining of the Suffering Servant through the lens of the work of Mikhail
Bakhtin offers insight into how the prophetic characterisation influenced Paul's construction of faith,
hope and love as epistemologies (in Corinthians). This book provides new insight into how faith,
hope and love act as a dynamic equilibrium of knowing that opens us up to lives of story, encounter,
and innovation-lives that resonate with the suffering servant, and which challenge contemporary
ideas of power, wisdom and prosperity"-- Provided by publisher.
Identifiers: LCCN 2020030106 (print) | LCCN 2020030107 (ebook) |
ISBN   9780567676108 (hb) | ISBN 9780567696885 (pb) | ISBN 9780567676115 (epdf) |
ISBN 9780567696878 (epub)
Subjects: LCSH: Suffering--Religious aspects--Christianity. | Suffering--Biblical teaching. |
Bakhtin, M. M. (Mikhail Mikhailovich), 1895-1975.
Classification: LCC BT732.7 .W536 2020 (print) | LCC BT732.7 (ebook) | DDC 248.8/6--dc23
LC record available at https://lccn.loc.gov/2020030106
LC ebook record available at https://lccn.loc.gov/2020030107

ISBN:	HB:	978-0-5676-7610-8
	PB	978-0-5676-9688-5
	ePDF:	978-0-5676-7611-5
	ePUB:	978-0-5676-9687-8

To find out more about our authors and books visit www.bloomsbury.com
and sign up for our newsletters.

Contents

Part II
Dialogue with Jared, a Suffering Servant

ACKNOWLEDGMENTS

This book was almost two decades in the making. The exegetical study of the Servant Songs of Second Isaiah is drawn from my doctoral thesis published in 2007, entitled *A Dialogic Reimagining of a Servant's Suffering: Understanding Second Isaiah's Servant of Yahweh as a Polyphonic Hero*. My supervisor was Dr Suzanne Boorer, senior lecturer at Murdoch University in Perth, Western Australia. I'm also grateful to one of my PhD examiners, David J. A. Clines, Emeritus Professor at the University of Sheffield, who was the first to recognise the potential of my research for publication.

The second phase of the book's development began late in 2014 when I was invited by Dr Jared Noel to ghost write his memoir, *Message to My Girl: A Dying Father's Powerful Legacy of Hope* (2015, Allen & Unwin). I interviewed Jared more than 20 times in the weeks leading up to his death, and that task was made easier by the support of his wife, Dr Hannah Noel, who gave her permission for those interviews to be used in this book. I am very grateful to Hannah for her key role in both projects.

Clinton Sanford made the current project possible in the latter half of 2019 with his mentoring and practical support. A great sponsor of theological conversation and learning, Clinton was determined that this project be completed and went above and beyond to ensure it happened. More works would be unearthed for the good of others if more writers and theologians had friends like Clinton.

I would achieve very little as a writer if it were not for the ongoing understanding and encouragement of my wife, Carolyn, and my daughters Beth, Meghan, Esther and Olivia. Whether in times of suffering or celebration, they continue to be voices of encouragement and love, and any work I produce is because they travel the highway with me.

Abbreviations

AB	Anchor Bible
ABD	*The Anchor Bible Dictionary*, ed. D.N. Freedman, 6 vols., New York: Doubleday, 1992
ANETS	Ancient Near Eastern Texts and Studies
ANF	*The Ante-Nicene Fathers*, ed. A. Roberts and J. Donaldson, Repr. ed. Grand Rapids, MI: Eerdmans
ASV	American Standard Version, 1901
BDB	*A Hebrew and English Lexicon of the Old Testament (abridged).* Based on *A Hebrew and English Lexicon of the Old Testament*, ed. F. Brown, S. R. Driver, and C. A. Briggs. Oxford: Clarendon, 1907
BETL	Bibliotheca ephemeridum theologicarum Lovaniensium
BKAT	Biblischer Kommentar: Altes Testament
BSac	*Bibliotheca Sacra*
BZAW	Beihefte zur *ZAW*
CBOT	Coniectanea biblica: Old Testament Series
CBQ	*Catholic Biblical Quarterly*
ESV	English Standard Version
FAT	Forschungen zum Alten Testament
GKC	*Gesenius' Hebrew Grammar*, ed. E. Kautzsch, trans. A. E. Cowley, Oxford: Clarendon, 1910
HALOT	*Hebrew and Aramaic Lexicon of the Old Testament*, ed. L. Koehler and W. Baumgartner, 2 vols., Study Edition. Leiden: Brill, 2001
HKAT	Handkommentar zum AT
IB	*The Interpreters Bible*, 12 vols., Nashville: Abingdon
ICC	International Critical Commentary
JBL	*Journal of Biblical Literature*
JETS	*Journal of the Evangelical Theological Society*
JPS	*Tanakh: A New Translation of The Holy Scriptures According to the Traditional Hebrew Text*, Philadelphia: The Jewish Publication Society, 1985, 1999
JSNT	*Journal for the Study of the New Testament*
JSOT	*Journal for the Study of the Old Testament*
JSOTSup	Journal for the Study of the Old Testament Supplement Series

JSS	*Journal of Semitic Studies*
KJV	King James (Authorised) Version
LXX	Septuagint
MT	Masoretic Text
NASB	New American Standard Bible
NIB	*The New Interpreters Bible*, 12 vols., Nashville: Abingdon
NICOT	The New International Commentary on the Old Testament
NIDOTTE	*New International Dictionary of Old Testament Theology and Exegesis*, ed. W. A. VanGemeren, 5 vols., Grand Rapids: Zondervan, 1997
NIV	New International Version
NJB	The New Jerusalem Bible
NLT-SE	New Living Translation
NRSV	New Revised Standard Version
REB	Revised English Bible
RSV	Revised Standard Version
SBL	Society of Biblical Literature
SBLSP	Society of Biblical Literature Seminar Papers
SBTS	Sources for Biblical and Theological Study
SJOT	*Scottish Journal of Theology*
TBü	Theologische Bücherei
TDOT	*Theological Dictionary of the Old Testament*, ed. G. J. Botterweck, and H. Ringgren, 15 vols., Grand Rapids: Eerdmans, 1977–2006
TLOT	*Theological Lexicon of the Old Testament*, ed. E. Jenni and C. Westermann, trans. M. E. Biddle, 3 vols., Peabody: Hendrickson, 1997
TWOT	*Theological Wordbook of the Old Testament*, ed. R. L. Harris, G. L. Archer Jr, and B. K. Waltke, 2 vols., Chicago: Moody, 1980
TynB	*Tyndale Bulletin*
Vg	Vulgate
VT	*Vetus Testamentum*
VTSup	Supplements to Vetus Testamentum
WBC	Word Biblical Commentary
ZAW	*Zeitschrift für die alttestamentliche Wissenschaft*

Introduction:
Dialogue with a Suffering Servant

THE PROBLEM OF SUFFERING

Religious Ideology and the Outsideness of Suffering

This is a book about dialogue, about discourse that shapes our self-awareness, about new ways of understanding dominant paradigms and old narratives, and about faithful response to God in spite of suffering, as opposed to faith that seeks to justify suffering. It's a book about suffering most of all, however. Or, rather, it's about conversations about suffering, as well as a challenge to some traditional ways of thinking about suffering, and a call to take a second look at certain scriptures that seem to focus on suffering. It's also a book about two "heroes" of the faith whose renown arose against a backdrop of suffering but who demonstrated that despite great adversity, suffering never tells the whole story, and rarely tells an enduring one.

Mikhail Bakhtin, a Russian literary philosopher whose work features prominently in what follows, used suffering to explain his theories of outsideness and otherness in his essay *Author and Hero in Aesthetic Activity*. He says that when we see a person who is suffering—suffering that is only ever really experienced from *within* that person—we can respond with an ethical action such as giving assistance or offering consolation, but afterwards we always return into ourselves. We can never fully experience the suffering as the other experiences it. We can never sit in the space that they occupy and see or feel the world as they see and feel it. We experience the suffering of the other—as we experience everything about the other—from *outside*. Which is why it is so appropriate to have conversations about suffering, and with people who are suffering. Suffering affects us all, one way or another, but it affects us all personally, in ways that reinforce the reality that we only ever fully experience suffering alone. If you have tended to a wife battling breast cancer you'll know how this feels, from *outside*. If you've tried to support a daughter wrestling with mental health issues you'll know how this feels. If you have watched the unfolding of a global pandemic from the safety of your self-isolation at home, you will be in no doubt how this feels. No matter how much love you show, how many words of comfort you offer, how many hours you spend consoling the sufferer themselves, ultimately all we can give is the affirmation that we hear them, respond to them, understand them…from *outside*. It's the reason we talk about suffering when we're in the midst of it. The reason we cry out. The reason we seek words of comfort from those we trust. Or why we ask for reassurance from a medical professional. Or hop online to read what other sufferers have experienced before us. Or tell close friends why we're not around as much. It's also the reason we seek comfort in ideological responses to suffering. Why we convince ourselves we live in a universe where it's possible to speak something negative and have something negative come back to us. Or why we repeat the mantra that everything happens for a reason. Or chastise ourselves for not praying more. Or try to learn the one thing God must want to tell us in our suffering. All because in the face of the knowledge that ultimately what we experience in suffering we do so in isolation, our words to ourselves, our words to others, and their words to us, as well as their words about us, matter. They shape us. And they shape us because that relational dynamic—the I for myself, the I for the other and the other for me—is what constitutes each one of us as a conscious *self*. So that despite experiencing suffering in isolation, words and responses and acts of comfort that are outside of me are nevertheless *transgredient*[1] to me; that is, they don't just inform me, they constitute me. And the other who is outside of me plays a vital part in how I'm constituted, by also *consummating* me. That is, at some point my suffering ceases to be felt as suffering by the other. At some point the other stops projecting themselves onto my suffering in order to feel it and understand it. They retreat back into themselves and my suffering becomes another object on their horizon. As Bakhtin says, describing how the other experiences this moment, "The position of his body which had first informed us about his suffering and which led us to his inward suffering now takes on a purely plastic value, becomes an expression which embodies and consummates the suffering expressed, and the emotional and volitional tones of this expressedness are no longer the tones of suffering" (Bakhtin 1990: 27). This consummation, the objectification of my suffering, far from making my suffering more isolating, is the other's gift to me. Without the other seeing me as part of what Bakhtin calls the "plastic and pictorial world," I am left with my own "inner affirmation of myself" in the midst of my suffering, and with no knowledge of my outward expressedness—how I am experienced or seen, not in a subjective sense, but objectively, as I exist in a world of objects and things. With no foundational experiencing

---

1. Transgredience is a Bakhtinian concept to describe elements that are constitutive of a self but originate from outside the self.

of what that is, I would remain incomplete, experiencing true isolation and true torment; the hell of not knowing myself *out* of the soul of the other and *for* the other; suffering alone with my "inner self-sensation" (Bakhtin 1990: 31).

My own questions around suffering were piqued not as a biblical scholar, initially, but as a journalist. I had been a newspaper journalist for 10 years when I was confronted by my "biggest story," the one that would make me realise I didn't have the epistemological framework for coping with or comprehending extreme trauma. I had witnessed death before; I had attended my share of car accidents and drownings, had witnessed communities of people grieving over people killed unexpectedly and tragically. But I was unprepared for how I would respond to the death of nine people, some of them friends, crushed to death by a collapsing cliff as they sheltered beneath it during a primary school surf competition on Western Australia's southwest coast. As one of the first on the scene I wasn't afforded the safe distance I typically enjoyed as a reporter. I had to roll up my sleeves and crouch on the fallen cliff like 50 or so other volunteers, scraping the sand away with our hands, or hauling limestone boulders away with old rope, in the unlikely event there were survivors beneath the tonnes of cliff face that had fallen without warning. As it happened, there was a survivor—a young girl, who had slipped into a tiny air pocket beneath two boulders and was still alive when we dug her out. Her mother didn't survive. She was crushed beside her daughter, along with eight others—five adults in total, and four children. My response was to sink into a form of the hellish subjectivity that Bakhtin describes— hiding the worst of the grief away from people so they wouldn't see the outward expression of the torment I was feeling. The grief was about the tragedy and the loss of life, absolutely, but it was also, and perhaps more so, about confronting the realisation that I was ill-equipped to process what I had seen. I'd heard fellow journalists speak about this moment but never fully comprehended it: when the depth of tragedy is so great it overwhelms the coping mechanisms you have been built up over the years to guard against life's darker moments leaving a lasting impact. For a journalist those mechanisms invariably involve alcohol, or any number of related addictive behaviours. I tried many of them, with no success. I simply didn't have the imagination to forge a path through this trauma.

I embarked on theological studies not to find answers to questions such as why we suffer, but, in hindsight, to construct an epistemological framework that would at least accommodate contemplation of such things as suffering, faith, hope, love, death, life, art, sex, desire…all the good things; the things that "make us human," as the cliché goes. Then in 2007, I completed my doctoral studies, submitting a thesis on a subject that even my examiners described as a "shopworn" topic—the nature and identity of Second Isaiah's Suffering Servant. It's fair to say I'd been intrigued by the figure of the Servant much earlier than my existential crisis at the beach. I'd pondered the Suffering Servant my whole life, at least as he was defined by the narrow ideology of my faith tradition. In the conservative, evangelical and, yes, fundamentalist faith community in which I was raised, the Suffering Servant of Isaiah 53, in particular, was pivotal for interpreting and understanding the redemptive and vicarious sufferings of Christ. Indeed, the "man of sorrows" who was "wounded for our transgressions" and "bruised for our iniquities" (KJV) was at the heart of the theory of penal substitution that informed our theology of atonement and grounded many of our beliefs and practices in scripture. Salvation just wouldn't have been the same without him.

They were unfair burdens to place on any portion of scripture, as I came to discover, especially one as beautiful as the poem which has become known as the fourth Servant song. I also discovered that actual life trauma is as unkind on the religious ideologies that have protected you since childhood, as they are on the ways you do life in general. It is not so easy to say that Christ, or the Servant of Isaiah 53, suffered so that we don't have to when you have seen mangled and twisted bodies pulled from beneath the sand. No wonder the atonement theories of my faith community had not been able to help me confront actual suffering. They were not designed to. They are designed to maintain a distance between us and trauma, much like a journo's Friday night session at the pub. It is far easier to contemplate suffering from a distance than it is to look it full in the face. I discovered that our worship of the man who had "borne our griefs and carried our sorrows" had somehow deflected from the horror that accompanies actual death, actual suffering, actual crucifixion. Not his fault, of course, but there was more truth to Isa. 53.3, "we hid as it were our faces from him," than I had realised. As Moltmann says, "We have made the bitterness of the cross, the revelation of God in the cross of Jesus Christ, tolerable to ourselves by learning to understand it as a necessity for the process of salvation…as a result the cross loses its arbitrary and incomprehensible character" (Moltmann 1974: 41). Religious ideology had enabled us—me, at least—to look away from suffering as if it were not nearly so traumatic as it is—like Myshkin in Dostoevsky's *The Idiot*, confronted with Holbein's painting of *The Body of the Dead Christ in the Tomb*, but instead of allowing ourselves to be disturbed by the reality it represents, turning away to gaze instead upon the beautiful saviour of more traditional (and favourable) religious art.

It's only when you have faced trauma and scrambled around in the darkness of religious ideology for something solid to hold onto that you discover just how frail it is.

"I'll pray for you," goes one such response. Or, "thoughts and prayers," a phrase that's become as political as it is religious; synonymous with the very worst responses of supposed people of faith to events as traumatic as mass school shootings. It's not for nothing that Twitter erupts in rage when yet another mass shooting is followed by even more "thoughts and prayers" from members of Congress who were elected to make legislative change in response to such events, not trite religious phrases.

"God's in control," goes another, typically in response to the confronting reality of suffering's caprice. If God is in control then nothing happens by accident, which in turn means that traumatic events are part of a bigger, unknown or unknowable design. This response is easier to maintain if it comes in response to a car running out of fuel. It's not so easy to maintain in relation to the deaths of 186 children in a school massacre in Beslan, Russia.

"Everything happens for a reason," goes the increasingly popular pat phrase. It isn't necessarily "God's" reason that's being touted. It's more often the Universe that's assumed to be in control; "God" in a different guise. The Universe moves all the pieces according to its purposes so that everything just works. It's so complex a machine that we can't possibly know why things happen the way they do. What we do know is that suffering is an inevitable byproduct of the Universe making sure everything moves forward according to its design.

"Everything works together for good." Or for God's glory, as seems to be the case in the death of Lazarus (Jn 11.14). Balancing the trauma of human suffering, according to this popular retort, is the knowledge that God will bring something good from the tragedy; his own glory, for example, or the salvation of the lost. A former student of mine had been troubled by this ideology for several years following the sudden death of her 17-year-old son during a football game, and the response of her well-meaning friends that focused on the number of people whose faith had been quickened *because* of the tragedy.

Religious ideological responses to human suffering are effective for only so long, and sometimes, if the trauma is great enough, they don't work at all. So why do they arise at all? It's true that, as Bakhtin points out, we project ourselves into the suffering of others to offer love and encouragement and consolation, because we're all aware of what we would need in the same situation. We all want hope. No one wants to capitulate to fear. And we have a great capacity to generate narratives and ideologies that serve us, that speak into the unknown, that maintain control or a semblance of it, that shield us from pain and meaninglessness, that bolster our faith, that prevent us from being cut adrift. We want things to make sense. We like certainty and purpose. We want our lives to have value, and, if we can, to make a long-lasting impact.

We are also wired for self-justification; for things to have ultimate value and validity; for life itself to affirm us and our decisions, to bless the things we want, to support the permissions we give ourselves. When things go well it's easier to believe that life, the Universe, God, has validated us. When trauma strikes, it's not so easy; in fact, we may even believe that the opposite is true—that we haven't been validated at all.

None of which was theoretical for me, following the Gracetown cliff collapse. It was with a personal agenda that I began a dialogue with the Suffering Servant to see whether he represented a different way of thinking about suffering beyond the security blankets of religious ideology.

The Polyphonic Hero

The Suffering Servant of Second Isaiah

Just as evangelical faith traditions have over-burdened the text of Isaiah 53 with their atonement theories, so scholars have seemingly exhausted the topic of the Servant songs of Second Isaiah, and particularly the question, Who was the Servant? It was pointed out to me too late that dissertation advisors generally want their students to steer clear of the subject. After all, what more could be said of the Servant and the songs that concern him? My research into the history of interpretation on the topic was to bear this out. Since Bernhard Duhm in 1892, scholars had been mining the topic in order to try and identify the anonymous figure whose story unfolds over numerous poems throughout Isaiah 40–55. What more, indeed, could be added to the field?

My thesis was that there was plenty more that could be said.

The issue with the Suffering Servant is this: his ambiguous characterisation has left scholars struggling to settle on who it is, or even whether the figure represents the nation Israel, or an individual, such as the prophet who is responsible for Isaiah 40–55 (referred to as Deutero- or Second Isaiah). Does it matter? It does to scholars, and if that was the end of the matter then we could, as suggested by my thesis examiner, Professor Carol A. Newsom, just move right along. But my thesis was that perhaps the ambiguity itself counts for something—that perhaps the difficulties concerning his ambiguous characterisation had arisen not because there were multiple Servants, as some scholars had suggested, but because the Servant—as an aesthetic work, a literary character—had been constituted differently to conventional literary figures. I also wondered whether his unconventional constitution was a literary device that might unlock the Servant's purpose in the text. I realised early in my research that the Servant is never described by the prophet, and his actions are never depicted. The author of the Servant poems never gives the reader an image of the Servant that they can hold onto, objectively speaking. The reader's only access to the Servant as a character is via utterances addressed to him, or those made by him, or those made by others about him—very much reflecting Bakhtin's *I-for-myself, I-for-the-other/the-other-for-me*. In other words, the Servant as a literary creation exists at the point of convergence of several crisscrossing discourses. He is constituted wholly by dialogue, in fact—by direct speech, by reflective thought, and by banter.

Why is this important?

I knew from my initial reading of the work of Bakhtin that such dialogically constituted characters have a particular ideological and aesthetic function in a text. Because they exist where lines of discourse meet, they uniquely represent an idea as much as they do an actual figure, whether historical or literary. Bakhtin's theories derived from the novels of Fyodor Dostoyevsky; his term "polyphonic hero" refers to a character who is constructed primarily by dialogue in order to achieve a particular effect in a text. The polyphonic hero is distinguished from the characters of a conventional, monologic work by his or her dialogic design. The hero is constituted primarily, if not wholly, by dialogue—by what he says, and by how he responds to what others say to him, and about him and his world. In Bakhtin's own words, the polyphonic hero isn't composed of "features of the hero himself or of his everyday surroundings—but rather the *significance* of these features for the *hero himself*, for his self-consciousness" (Bakhtin 1984: 48). In other words, the literary character digests discourse concerning himself the way we do in life; the way Bakhtin describes what happens when a person who is suffering is constituted by the consummating gaze of the other. Examples of a polyphonic hero in literary works include Dostoevsky's own Underground Man, and James Joyce's Leopold Bloom of *Ulysses*. A polyphonic hero represents what Bakhtin calls a "voice-idea," a unique and embodied ideological perspective on the world that cannot be represented in the same way by another character, just as in life no two people can ever share the same space, or, consequently, have the same view of the world around them.

Theories peculiar to Bakhtin, and to his unique evaluation of Dostoyevsky's work, provided a new framework from which to approach the Servant texts, and to examine their dialogic nature and the Servant's "multi-voiced" constitution. Bakhtin's theories are concerned with the worlds, and utterances, of both fictional characters, and flesh and blood people. Undergirding much of Bakhtin's thought is his concept of simultaneity—that identity is a relational achievement that doesn't encompass differences through a process of homogenisation, or by being the *same as*, but by being *simultaneous with*, thereby allowing for difference, variety, freedom and unpredictability. Bakhtin's idea was informed by Dostoevsky, whose artistic vision, Bakhtin observed, was not categorised by evolution, or progression along a temporal line, but by coexistence and interaction: "He saw and conceived his world primarily in terms of space, not time" (Bakhtin 1984: 28). Even so, it's counterproductive to search for an overarching idea in Bakhtin, whose wide-ranging thought emphasised variety, difference, heterogeneity, dialogue, performance, actuality, the carnivalisation of authority, unpredictability, uncertainty, unfinalisability, and the centrifugal forces of existence, which "compel movement, becoming, and history" and "long for change and new life" (Clark and Holquist 1984: 8). Bakhtin viewed existence as a struggle between these forces and the centripetal forces of stasis, homogenisation, sameness and death. He denounced monologism—the idea that truth can be contained in a single belief system, or god, or text or person—because monologic "truth" can be controlled and manipulated. He located meaning in the community. Bakhtin's development of dialogism, from within a Soviet system that was committed absolutely to the ideals of monologism, seems to have been both a reaction against that system and achieved in response to the uncertainties and heterogeneity of life. His belief was that these vagaries were not to be feared and managed, but acknowledged and celebrated.

Polyphony and Dialogism

Polyphony is the word used by Bakhtin to describe a literary design unique to the novels of Fyodor Dostoevsky. For a work to be polyphonic it must be composed of a dialogic conception of truth, and the author must assume a position relative to the novel's characters that enables a faithful expression of that sense of truth through the characters' individuality and unique perspectives on the world.

The best picture of dialogical truth is the conversation, in which several voices come together to create something that is quite separate from each of them, but nevertheless requires their participation. In the process their voices do not merge—they don't surrender their individuality or uniqueness. It's precisely the multiplicity of distinct voices that comprises and facilitates the conversation. Even when those voices are competing with one another, as in an argument, the dialogue retains its integrity—perhaps even more so, in Bakhtin's view. A multiplicity of voices is essential for dialogical truth to be generated because dialogism reflects multiple and distinct perspectives (ideologies) on the world. Another way of saying this is that dialogical truth requires a "plurality of unmerged consciousnesses" (Bakhtin 1984: 9). Bakhtin characterises the monologic world as "Ptolemaic": the earth, representing the author's consciousness, is the centre around which all other consciousnesses revolve. The polyphonic world is Copernican; as the earth is but one of many planets, the author's consciousness is but one of many consciousnesses (Morson and Emerson 1990: 240). So, a polyphonic work is one in which the author has intentionally created such a multi-voiced environment.

Dialogical truth has a personal, embodied and unrepeatable quality, since the utterances which comprise it are unique to the people who have made them. Indeed, for words to become an utterance, Bakhtin argues—to move beyond the logical and semantic relationships that constitute simple statements—they must be embodied; they must be uttered: "They must enter another sphere of existence: they must become *discourse*, that is, an utterance, and receive an *author*, that is, a creator of the given utterance whose position it expresses" (Bakhtin 1984: 184, emphases original). Bakhtin calls these utterances "voice-ideas," since they express a unique idea of the world. Voice-ideas represent "a unity of idea and personality: the idea represents a person's integral point of view on the world, which cannot be abstracted from the person voicing it" (Morson and Emerson 1990: 237).

In polyphonic works such as the novels of Dostoevsky, the character and their voice-idea are integrally bound together. They emerge from the dialogue itself. We come to know the characters as they come to know themselves, as their voice-ideas engage with other voice-ideas. Each voice-idea is ideologically independent, even from the author. Propositional statements are not voice-ideas, since they are monologic in nature. They are not embodied, since they can mean the same whether spoken by one person or by another. Propositional statements can *mean* outside a plurality of voices; they can be understood and expressed fully by a single consciousness. A conversation, on the other hand, can never fully be comprehended by a single mind. Dialogical truth cannot be systematised, since a system requires finalised propositions. What emerges from the dialogue is not a system but an event—the event of distinct voices interacting dialogically.

Dialogical truth is also open-ended. The final word can never be said, since each utterance or voice-idea that comprises the dialogue is both a response to an already existing word and in itself contains an implicit invitation to respond. The word "unfinalisable" is how Bakhtin describes this phenomenon, by which he means not consummated.

Fundamental to the design of a polyphonic work is the position of the author in relation to the dialogic event. The author of a polyphonic work intentionally retains no surplus knowledge over and above their characters. They know only what the characters are able to know and utter concerning themselves and their world. The author surrenders the conventional God view in order to encounter their characters as equal dialogue partners. Bakhtin doesn't suggest that an author isn't involved in the polyphonic design, only that they intentionally construct a dialogic event in which he or she is a participant, in the same way the characters are participants. In his earlier work Bakhtin described this process as a meeting of consciousnesses, the author's (the consciousness of the "I") and the hero's (the consciousness of the "other") (Bakhtin 1990: 89). The author of a polyphonic work is not hidden or voiceless, nor does he or she suppress their own self-awareness. But they do not allow their consciousness—of themselves, their world, or their characters and the world of the text—to objectify the awareness of the characters, or to attach finalised, objective definitions to them. The author does not stand at a distance from the characters and finalise them with personalities, hopes, ideologies and back-stories—frameworks within which they then construct dialogue. The author is aware only of that which enters the consciousness of the characters and is spoken by them. Therefore, the characters themselves have the power to *mean* directly, which is the reason why, Bakhtin argues, so many literary critics refer directly to the ideology of an Ivan Karamazov or a Grand Inquisitor (both characters from *The Brothers Karamazov*) (Bakhtin 1984: 5). In a monologic work this power to mean belongs only to the author. But polyphony subverts monologic conventions—it up-ends the world of the conventional text by making multiple points-of-view not only possible but as valid as those of the author.

The Polyphonic Hero

Dialogue is a fundamental component of the polyphonic hero. The hero must be spoken to, pressed to make himself known, both to himself and to others, since the reader only accesses the hero via his internal discourse. Bakhtin points out that this mirrors life itself, in which the depths of the human consciousness can only be revealed dialogically. He argues it is impossible to understand humanity by objectifying people—they must be spoken to, and they must speak, in order for their hiddenness to be revealed, especially to themselves.

Behind Bakhtin's understanding of the polyphonic hero is his particular model of the "self," which is divided between an "I-for-myself" and the two-sided coin of "I-for-the other"/"the-other-for-me." The "I-for-myself" is fluid, never able to rest in a finalised (or sculptured) picture of itself or anything the self has done (knowing that it could have been done in an infinite number of different ways). Any "security in time and space" (Emerson 1997: 213) can only ever be granted by others, who give us the gift of finalised versions of ourselves, and thereby sculpt our self-understanding. What the self is unable to form out of its own, fluid materials, it looks to others for: more contoured, finalised images—hence Bakhtin's "outsideness" and "outsided knowledge." Even these aren't fully finalised, since the "I-for-myself" reserves the ability to negotiate whatever images those outside perspectives give it.

What Bakhtin theorised about the self as a dialogically negotiated encounter between the "I-for-myself" and outsided knowledge granted by others maintained its currency in the field of aesthetics and informed his "polyphonic hero," a literary figure who is no more able to form a fixed image of himself than any real world person. So, for Bakhtin, there exists no firm, external or predetermined image of the polyphonic hero. The author does not begin with an image of the hero that is then fleshed out; the author engages dialogically with the hero in order to provoke a response by which he may become known. The hero doesn't answer the question "who is he or she?" but only "who are you?" and "who am I?" This doesn't mean that the author or another character cannot observe the polyphonic hero objectively—the opposite is true, in fact, since these objectifications are others' gifts to the hero. What it does mean is that those observations must become part of the hero's self-consciousness, thereby fulfilling the "other-for-me" component of the dialogically consti- tuted self.

The author is an active participant in this process. It's intentional. He or she purposely discards any surplus information they may otherwise want to retain regarding the hero:

> The author retains for himself, that is, for his exclusive field of vision, not a single essential definition, not a single trait, not the smallest feature of the hero: he enters it all into the field of vision of the hero himself, he casts it all into the crucible of the hero's own self-consciousness. (Bakhtin 1984: 48)

And so the polyphonic hero becomes self-aware, as an "I-for-myself" engaged with others, a fully realised individual. Nothing is said about him or his world that does not enter into his self-consciousness and become an element of his voice-idea. The unique ideological position that the polyphonic hero occupies in the text is the primary reason for his presence in the polyphonic work—to embody the idea, to flesh it out, to enact it and to enable others to engage dialogically with it.

My early observation was that the Servant of Second Isaiah shares some of the polyphonic hero's peculiar characteristics. He is constituted by dialogue; there exists no fixed image of him anywhere in the collection; and he remains unfinalised and open to fresh dialogic encounter, as demonstrated by a history of interpretation in which readers have consistently seen themselves and others in light of his voice-idea (even if they did not use that precise terminology).

Double-voicing

Bakhtin's term for an utterance that has appropriated the discourse of another, in order to restate it with the intonation of the new speaker, is double-voicing. Double-voiced discourse serves two speakers at the same time and expresses, simultaneously, two different intentions: the direct intention of the character who is speaking, and the refracted intention of the author. In such discourse there are two voices, two meanings and two expressions (Bakhtin 1981: 324).

In the event of double-voicing, two voices sound simultaneously, creating a multi-levelled dialogic text. The voices can be those of the author and a character, or a character speaking with words that have originated in other texts or traditions. The possibilities for double-voiced discourse are endless, because no word is spoken in isolation from other, competing words. Bakhtin argues that both voices in this dialogue—that of the original utterance, and the double-voiced discourse—know of each other. This means that in the event of double-voiced discourse the original utterance retains its semantic integrity even as it is being used in another, alien discourse. The heteroglossia—other, competing voices—that infuse the original utterance are embraced by the new discourse and are brought into direct dialogic encounter with not only the new utterance, but with the audience of that utterance, so that in one discourse two dialogic planes converge. Double-voicing represents "refracted" discourse, in that an author's intentions are served by co-opting the discourse of authors that had different intentions. So, double-voicing makes use of words that are already populated with the social intentions of others and compels them to serve his (the new author's) own new intentions, to serve a second master. Therefore the intentions of the writer are refracted, and refracted at different angles, depending on the degree to which the refracted, heteroglot languages he deals with are socio-ideologically alien, already embodied and already objectivised (Bakhtin 1981: 299-300).

This insight is helpful in an exegesis of the Servant poems, since, as Tull points out about Second Isaiah, it was created by a prophet who was trying to assert "a new understanding of the divine will in the exilic situation" with all its competing voices—the traditions, theologies and ideologies of both Israel and Babylon (Tull Willey 1997: 67). The Servant discourse was not created in a vacuum, but "in full awareness of the multiplicity of other possibilities, and it was designed to answer, anticipate, and overcome those alien words" (67–8). My thesis was this: the Suffering Servant of Second Isaiah was both a paradigmatic figure who called Israel to respond to Yahweh in a particular way, and at the same time was a voice-idea, the focal point of a quarrel between old, and not-so-old, ideological positions, and a new theological position opened up by the prophet's ministry during the period of Israel's exile in Babylon (586–539 BCE). The Servant was an ideological battlefield on which the prophet was challenging ideas from Israel's recent past, particularly the idea that the people had suffered unjustly for the sins of previous generations. Within the voice-idea of the Servant, this position experienced a radical overhaul. The suffering of the present generation was viewed not as a cause for lament and complaint, but as the catalyst for the redemption of the nations. But in the process, ideas around suffering and redemption experienced an overhaul too. It couldn't be said that suffering itself was redemptive, as was the case in the atonement theories of my childhood faith community. At least, not based on Isaiah 53. More is going on in that poem than the idea of vicarious atonement through suffering inflicted by Yahweh. It was my suspicion that Isaiah 53 was far from being the proof text my brothers and sisters in faith would like it to be.

The Meaninglessness of Suffering

Contemporary Dialogues with a Suffering Servant

The impact of the polyphonic nature of the Servant's constitution extends beyond the world of the text, and even further—beyond the world of the first readers/audience; the exilic and post-exilic communities. As Bakhtin says, characters constituted dialogically cannot ever be finished off, since they exist on the threshold of new dialogic encounter. A polyphonic hero exists to prompt a dialogic response, which means the conversation should continue beyond the scope of the work, beyond its epoch. The hero should discover new contexts in which to signify. More will be said about this in the concluding chapters of the exegetical component of this book, "Part I: The Suffering Servant of Second Isaiah." I refer to it here to introduce "Part II: Dialogue with Jared, a Suffering Servant," and to explain the presence of biography in a biblical studies book on Second Isaiah.

I met Dr Jared Noel some six years after the completion of my doctoral studies. I mention the time frame only to point out that I was already familiar with, and a proponent of, the voice-idea of the Suffering Servant and its capacity to signify beyond the scope of Second Isaiah. This is why, after all, the figure of the Suffering Servant remained open to being reinterpreted as Christ by the New Testament writers, one of whom, Paul, also understood his own ministry as the ongoing work of the Servant. The Servant is a paradigm, and, more than that, the figure is an open invitation to respond to God in a particular way. Emeritus Professor David Clines, another of my thesis examiners, was the first to suggest my dissertation should be published. He was also the first to say that he couldn't envisage what form the book would take. I shared his doubts—until I met Dr Jared Noel, a young aspiring surgeon who was in the final weeks of a five-year battle with bowel cancer. Jared embodied many of the themes that had arisen from my study of the text of Isaiah. I admit that it's a long bow to draw from the Suffering Servant of the exilic period to the death of a Kiwi in Auckland in 2014, and I'm well aware of the risks associated with applying ancient texts to contemporary contexts. But in my view Jared's story was precisely the type of reimagining of a polyphonic hero that I had proposed in my thesis, not to mention the embodiment of the Servant's voice-idea in a new epoch and in a new situation. What occurred in my conversations with Jared was totally consistent with the conclusions of my Bakhtinian reading of the Servant poems, as is borne out in the following book.

My first meeting with Jared was on Tuesday, August 26, 2014. He was alone, sitting upright in a bed in a room at a hospice in the western suburbs of Auckland, New Zealand. Although we'd never met, I knew him well. He'd been in the media spotlight for some time—first as a blogger writing about his five-year-long terminal diagnosis of bowel cancer, and then, as his sickness seemed to be reaching its conclusion, as the husband of a pregnant wife hoping to stay alive long enough to meet his unborn daughter. He made the front page of the *NZ Herald*, a daily metro daily newspaper twice, and a subsequent campaign to raise money to pay for powerful chemo drugs that would potentially grant him a stay of execution to see his daughter raised almost $200,000 in a few days—the most successful campaign of its kind in New Zealand to that point. New Zealanders had fallen in love not just with the drama of Jared's attempts to lock eyes with his daughter, but with Jared himself—a forthright, young aspiring surgeon who used his blog to break down taboos associated with cancer and dying; a Christian speaker who used his illness as an opportunity to speak about faith in the context of suffering; an "antihero" (his own description) who never tried to justify his suffering as the "will of God" or claim that his illness would be miraculously cured, but with honesty and authenticity wrote and spoke about the disappointments, doubts, sadness and sorrow that assailed him in the same ways they do anyone given a terminal diagnosis. His was not a triumphalist message. But it was a hopeful one.

We met in the hospice that day because Jared, aged just 33, wanted to write a book about his life, his writing, his battle against cancer, and the few months he had been able to spend with his daughter Elise (who had born in January of that year). He had, perhaps, eight weeks to live—probably less—so the task was daunting. Our initial meeting was primarily for Jared's sake, to see whether we connected well enough for him to trust me with his story. We talked generally about his illness and the struggles of the previous five years. Specifically, I was interested in his faith journey during that time, and what had sustained him as he stood on stage before thousands of people talking about his battle one week, then underwent another course of chemo treatment the next. His response was quite bizarre. He started to recite some theology he'd picked up, about suffering, and its meaninglessness, and how Christian ideology often overloads certain parts of scripture in order to derive value or purpose or meaning from suffering itself, in a way that often results in psychological and spiritual bondage for the sufferer. Jared, a medical professional, had discovered instead that suffering is arbitrary and capricious, not linked to some hidden divine intent, and that the appropriate response to suffering is to love, and in loving encounter with others to discover hope. It turned out Jared was echoing my lectures on suffering and hope without even knowing it. He'd picked up the teaching from a colleague of mine, who had shared the material at a symposium on theology and cancer. Without knowing it, Jared was double-voicing the Suffering Servant. And more than that, his own wrestle with human suffering had been shaped by the Servant's voice-idea.

So, this is a book about two conversations: one with the Suffering Servant of Second Isaiah; the second with Dr Jared Noel. It's also about a third conversation: Jared's dialogue with the Servant, a dialogue that transcends epochs and contexts, and which embodies themes around suffering, and love, and around redemption and purpose, disappointment and doubt, which ultimately is a conversation around the human dilemma: how to respond faithfully to God in the context of human suffering.

PART I

THE SUFFERING SERVANT OF SECOND ISAIAH

WHAT SCRIPTURE SAYS
ABOUT THE SUFFERING SERVANT

Mistaken Identity

The curious case of the identity of the Servant of Second Isaiah is at least as old as the dialogue by the desert road between the evangelist Philip and the Ethiopian eunuch (Acts 8.25-40). The eunuch's question, περὶ τίνος ὁ προφήτης λέγει τοῦτο; περὶ ἑαυτοῦ ἢ περὶ ἑτέρου τινός ("About whom does the prophet say this—about himself or someone else?," Acts 8.34) is sparked by his reading of Isa. 53.7c-8c,[1] and his confusion, as borne out by generations of scholars who have asked similar questions, is well-founded. The problem of the Servant's identity is not confined to the so-called fourth Servant song (Isa. 52.13–53.12). Indeed, the Servant's appearance throughout Second Isaiah only adds to the confusion. The title of David Clines' seminal 1976 monograph *I, He, We, and They* may refer specifically to the personal pronouns used in Isa. 52.13–53.12, but it also reflects the ambiguity of the Servant's identity in the larger collection. The Servant of Yahweh in the so-called Servant Songs of Isaiah 40–55 (the first three songs are 42.1-4; 49.1-6; and 50.4-9) is at times an *I*, at times a *he*, at times a *we*, and at other times a *they*. More often than not he is a *you*. For this primary reason interpreters of Second Isaiah have been unable to identify the Servant definitively or posit a consensus explanation for the ambiguity of his characterisation. On the face of it there are several servants in Second Isaiah: Israel, the prophet, an ideal "messiah" figure, or the group of Judahites (or some of them at least) who were taken into exile in 586 BCE. But there are other reasons for seeing behind the Servant references a sole figure, or at least a single collective. For example, the Servant makes no appearance in

---

1. For ease of reference to portions of a verse in poetic texts the line breaks of the JPS Hebrew text (1999, based on *BHS*) are followed, with a, b, c, and d referring to the first, second, third and fourth lines in a verse, and so on. JPS inserts line breaks between the poetic phrases in the *BHS* Hebrew text.

either First or Third Isaiah.[2] This suggests one of two things—that he is either a character whose activity is confined to the collection of Second Isaiah, or that the author/s of Second Isaiah had a penchant for using servant imagery. But the Servant also seems to undergo some character development: in the references that occur early in the collection he is presented to onlookers and assigned a task (e.g., Isa. 42.1-9), and later his mission is revised (Isa. 49.1-6). He experiences suffering (Isa. 50.6), and ultimately it seems that he dies (Isa. 53.8c). Indeed, Isa. 53.2-10 presents a biography of sorts, from the Servant's childhood (v. 2) to his demise (vv. 8-9), and even beyond.

But hindering attempts to characterise the Servant in a conventional literary sense is the fact that there exists no objective description of the Servant in the collection of Second Isaiah. He is not constituted in the way that characters are conventionally constituted—meaning that he is not described and his actions are not depicted. The author provides no image of the Servant that the reader can objectively assess. Our only access to the Servant is via discourse addressed *to* him and directly concerning him, spoken *by* him, or said *about* him in the form of confession (as in 53.1-10). In other words, the Servant is constituted at the intersection of several lines of discourse. Another way of saying this is that the Servant is constituted wholly by poetic dialogue, and, further, by dialogue that converges upon *him*, rendering any objective interpretation of him suspect, to say the least.

However, the Servant *is* named—as the nation, "Jacob"/"Israel" (e.g., Isa. 41.8; 44.1, 21; 45.4; 48.20; 49.3). Some scholars interpret the term "Jeshurun" (Isa. 44.2) as the Servant's name—this will be discussed later. But even so, identification is not as straightforward as it might be. Four of the main discourses that constitute the Servant suggest that he is an individual: 42.1-4, where the Servant is presented as a prophetic or royal figure; 49.1-6, where the Servant actually speaks; 50.4-9, where a figure who is generally taken to be the Servant recounts acts of abuse that appear to have been directed at an individual; and Isaiah 53 (Isa. 52.13–53.12), where the Servant is described in terms that are not immediately consistent with the experiences of Israel related elsewhere in Second Isaiah. Muddying these already murky waters is the strong historical

---

2. The plural "servants" of Yahweh is used predominantly in Third Isaiah (63.17; 65.8, 9, 13, 14, 15; 66.14). However, there is also a reference to the servants of Yahweh in Isa. 54.17e. This is seen as an anticipation of the development of the servants motif in Third Isaiah. On this see Beuken (1989, 1990). See also Sweeney (1997).

association between the Servant of Isaiah 53 and Jesus, an association that is, again, at least as old as the story of Philip and the eunuch in Acts 8. The association is so profound that it influences interpretations of not only Isaiah 53, but all the so-called Servant songs. Redressing the imbalance to some degree is the strong association historically between the Servant and Israel among Jewish interpreters, which tends to be equally myopic when it comes to the Servant's characterisation as an individual.

Even this cursory overview of the basic interpretive problems pertaining to the Servant of Second Isaiah generates a number of key questions: (1) How are we to understand the ambiguous, if not intentionally elusive, nature of the Servant's characterisation? (2) How are we to interpret a character who is constituted wholly by dialogue? (3) What advantages might the Servant's dialogical constitution have over more conventional styles of characterisation? (4) What is the function of the Servant within Second Isaiah's broader message? (5) Does a fresh approach that pays heed to the Servant's dialogical constitution enable us to better identify the Servant's identity and purpose in Second Isaiah? (6) Does any of it matter anyway?

These questions provide the focus and the framework for this book. And right off the bat it's worth saying that by the time we revisit the story of Dr Jared Noel in the later chapters, the answer to question 6 will be patently obvious. A fresh reimagination of the Suffering Servant that pays heed to the way he is constituted dialogically has massive implications for the ongoing application of texts such as the songs of Second Isaiah, as well as broader epistemological implications, particularly around the New Testament ways of knowing of faith, hope and love.

A History of the Servant's Interpretation

The history of the interpretation of Second Isaiah's Servant of Yahweh begins in the pre-Christian era and continues through the early church period, in the New Testament, the early Church Fathers and Jewish texts, down to the modern period. The questions concerning the ambiguity of the Servant's identity began with the earliest interpretive communities. From the earliest times, the Servant was open to reinterpretation, as different communities interpreted his identity and purpose in light of their own presuppositions and needs. Before the era of modern scholarship, during which critical methodologies have established some objective distance between interpreters and the Servant, interpretive communities often sought to understand themselves in light of the Servant, rendering their interpretations highly subjective from the outset. But it may be that such subjective reading strategies are more appropriate with a character that is constituted like the Servant. We don't see this type of reinterpretation with more defined biblical characters, such as David or Abraham or Paul, for example. Even so, in general terms, even among pre-critical interpretive communities, the Servant has been understood according to three broad categories: he is an individual (an historical or ideal figure); he is a corporate personality (representing either historical or ideal Israel, or elements of both); or, he is both an individual and a corporate personality—a fluid figure who in some texts is the nation Israel, and in others an individual who represents the nation, perhaps even the anonymous writer of Second Isaiah himself.

The Servant in Late Old Testament Texts

There are possible references to the Servant in Old Testament texts postdating Second Isaiah in the image of the gentle king who rides into Jerusalem on a donkey in Zech. 9.9 and the shepherd of Zech. 13.7b who is "struck" (נכה, cf. Isa. 53.4d), both of which would represent individualistic interpretations if the link was effectively demonstrated. Hengel and Bailey (2004: 85–90) note other similarities between the language of Zech. 12.10-14 and 12.9–13.1, and Isaiah 53. The scattering of the sheep in Zech. 13.7 evokes Isa. 53.6 (sheep going astray), and the image of "the one whom they pierced" (דקר) in Zech. 12.10 was influenced by the image of the Servant who was pierced (חלל) in Isa. 53.5 (see Hengel and Bailey 2004: 88–9).

The Servant of Isaiah 53 is possibly behind the image of the "wise" (משכלים) who lead many to righteousness (מצדיקי) in Dan. 12.3, 4 since the Servant is known as the one who "will act wisely" (ישכיל, Isa. 52.13) and is described by Yahweh as "my righteous (צדיק) servant" in Isa. 53.11. If the link is valid then it represents a collective understanding of the Servant. Fishbane, for example, argues that "quite certainly, the author of Daniel 11–12 wished to stress that his group was heir to the mantle of the suffering servant of YHWH. As that servant suffered, so do they; as he was later glorified (cf. Isa. 53.12), so will they be resurrected to eternal life; and in so far as this group read the 'servant song' as a description of the historical tribulations of the nation of Israel, the משכילים believed themselves to be the true Israel, the righteous remnant" (Fishbane 1985: 493).

Scholars also have seen in the servants of Third Isaiah (mentioned in Isa. 63.17; 65.8, 9, 13-15; 66.14) an attempt to interpret a righteous element of post-exilic Israel in light of the Servant figure, perhaps as the

Servant's offspring (Isa. 53.10). Also, Bastiaens (1997: 432) has argued that Job 16–19 contain traces of the Servant poems. The Servant poems provide a "frame of reference" for several images of suffering in these chapters, although they do not suggest an identification of Job with the Servant. More is said on the theme of suffering in Job later in this book.

None of these texts represents a direct interpretation of the identity and purpose of the Servant himself. At best they can be described as allusions or textual echoes of imagery associated with the Servant. They may suggest an idealistic interpretation of the Servant in pre-Christian times, in light of which contemporary figures are seen to fulfil Second Isaiah's hope—but this would have to be demonstrated in each case.

The Servant in Deutero-canonical Old Testament Texts

The possible allusions to the Servant figure in a number of Old Testament apocryphal books are suggestive, but they are as questionable as the canonical references. In the Wisdom of Solomon, the oppressed "righteous" who provoke repentance in the unrighteous in Wis. 5.1-6 suggest the suffering of the Servant and the "we" who look on in Isaiah 53. Hooker (1959: 53) also highlights possible parallels with the suffering Servant in Wis. 2.12-20, in which the unrighteous plot the righteous man's death and are therefore "led astray" (cf. Isa. 53.6); and in 3.1-9, in which the righteous are said to have been disciplined a little, and therefore receive great good. Hooker (19959: 54) also traces parallels with the Servant in *4 Maccabees*.[3] In *4 Maccabees* 1 the deaths of the aged philosopher Eleazar and his fellow martyrs are said to purify the land (v. 11), recalling the suffering of the Servant in Isaiah 53 which is said to "bring peace" and to "heal" (v. 5) the speaking "we" of the poem.

Hengel has drawn parallels between the Servant and the figure of Elijah in Sir. 48.10, where the prophet is given a task "to turn the heart of the father to the son" (cf. Mal. 4.6) and "to restore the tribes of Jacob" (cf. Isa. 49.6). Hengel argues the allusion to the Servant indicates an individual, even a messianic interpretation, but concedes that "it remains questionable whether Ben Sira wished to identify the Servant *directly* with Elijah *redivivus*" (Hengel and Bailey 2004: 83, emphases original). Hengel similarly sees a parallel with the Servant in the Son of Man figure of the Similitudes (chs. 37–71) of *1 Enoch* (Hengel and Bailey 2004: 101).

---

3. This text may not strictly belong in a section on pre-Christian writings, since it may date from as late as the middle of the first century CE.

Both figures share a number of traits. For example, they both function as a righteous judge of the ungodly; both share the element of concealment; both are given a name; and both are described as a "light to the gentiles."

The Servant in the New Testament

The uses made of the Servant passages by the New Testament writers, particularly Isaiah 53, range from the direct quotation (e.g., Mt. 8.17, quoting Isa. 53.4ab) to the allusion (e.g., Heb. 9.28, possibly echoing Isa. 53.12). Since our task is to ascertain how the New Testament writers viewed the Servant's ambiguous identity, we will concentrate on those passages that suggest an attempt has been made to evoke the character of the Servant and its related themes.[4]

It is in the New Testament era that we begin to see the Servant figure identified consistently with an historical figure (Stuhlmacher 2004: 149). The era is marked by an almost exclusive association of the Servant with Jesus, perhaps along the lines of the messianic interpretation of the Servant passages by early Judaism that is reflected in the Isaiah Targum, which inserts the words "the messiah" into Isa. 52.13: "Behold, my servant, the messiah, shall prosper."

The Servant in the Gospels and Acts

The New Testament texts that associate Jesus with the Servant are divided between those that claim the identification began with Jesus himself, and those that simply make the link without reference to Jesus' claims. Prominent in the former group are two passages in Mark's Gospel. In Mk 10.45 Jesus is recorded as saying, "The Son of Man will give his life as a ransom for many" (cf. Isa. 53.10), and in Mk 14.24 Jesus is portrayed as describing his upcoming death as the shedding of blood that is being "poured out for many" (cf. Isa. 53.12). The texts suggest that at the very least the author interpreted Jesus' death with reference to the Servant of Isaiah 53. However, there is no way of knowing whether the evangelist meant to suggest that Jesus fulfilled the Servant poem, much less that he was the Servant, or whether the author merely deemed the language of Isaiah 53 appropriate for describing Jesus' ministry.

---

4. For a thorough discussion of whether Jesus saw himself as the Servant, or whether the Evangelists sought to make the connection by having Jesus quote passages from Isaiah, see Hooker (1959) and Stuhlmacher (2004).

Likewise, the descriptions of Jesus' beating in Mk. 14.65 (Mt. 26.67; Lk. 22.63-64; cf. Jn 18.22) and Mk 15.15-20 (Mt. 27.26-31; cf. Jn 19.1-3) have been linked to Isa. 50.6, in which the Servant recounts physical abuse. Several words in these passages echo words in the LXX translation of the third Servant song (Isa. 50.4-9). Hooker (1959: 91) challenges the link on the basis that the gospel accounts do not conform precisely to the description of the Servant's suffering in Isa. 50.6: "If their aim had been to show clearly that Jesus was the Servant they would surely have kept more clearly to the original" (Hooker 1959: 91). Hooker argues a more compelling link to the Servant lies in the description of Jesus' silence before the high priest (Mk 14.61; Mt. 26.63; 27.12), Pilate (Mk 15.5; Mt. 27.14; Jn 19.9) and Herod (Lk. 23.9).

Some of the clearest references to the Servant in the gospels are in Matthew. Matthew 8.16-17 resonates with the MT of Isa. 53.4ab, drawing a link between the healing effects of the Servant's suffering and Jesus' healing ministry. One wonders why the author chose to link Jesus' ministry to this text, if it was not for the desire to link the person of Jesus with the figure of the Servant. Jesus' healing ministry is in the foreground again in Mt. 12.18-21, where Isa. 42.1-4 is quoted in its entirety to demonstrate that Jesus' healing of the sick fulfilled Isaianic prophecy.

The same Servant discourse is possibly echoed in two other key places in Matthew's Gospel—at Jesus' baptism (3.17) and at the scene of the transfiguration (17.5). Neither text quotes Isa. 42.1-4 directly, but both possibly allude to Yahweh's "delight" in his Servant (Isa. 42.1b). Leske supports the view that the Matthew passages parallel those in Isaiah:

> In this prophetic context it becomes clear that Jesus' mission is…to exemplify in himself the role of Servant Israel to be a people covenant and a light to the nations; thus he is identified as such in the references to and quotation of Isaiah 42. (Leske 1998: 165)

One of the few direct quotations of Isaiah 53 in the Synoptics is Lk. 22.37, which quotes Isa. 53.12d: "And he was numbered with the transgressors." Hooker has argued the reference is used as a proof text and has no bearing on whether Jesus' death was understood as a direct fulfilment of the Servant's sufferings (Hooker 1998: 92). But the references to Isaiah 53 continue in the second volume of Luke's work, the book of Acts. Acts 3.18 refers to the view that the prophets had foretold the suffering of the messiah; Acts 17.2-3 possibly alludes to the Servant's suffering and apparent rising to life; Acts 26.22-23 apparently repeats the allusion, and in its use of the "light to the Gentiles" motif alludes to the Servant texts in

Isa. 42.6 and 49.6. The clearest reference is that of Acts 8.32-33, which is referred to at the beginning of the chapter, which quotes Isa. 53.7c-8c in the story of the evangelist Philip and the Ethiopian eunuch. Clearly, by the time the book of Acts was written a firm association had been made between Jesus and the Servant.

It is important to note that the ministry of Paul, and on one occasion that of his fellow missionary Barnabas, is also interpreted in light of the Servant passages. In Acts 13.46-47 Paul uses Isa. 49.6ef to justify his mission to the Gentiles, taking the Servant passage as a personal divine imperative. This is an intriguing variation on the christological interpretation of the Servant figure, which, as we have just seen, features prominently earlier in the book of Acts. It is possible that Luke sees a salvation-historical continuation of the Servant's ministry through both Jesus *and* Paul. The motif of light from darkness, echoing Isa. 42.7 and 49.6, is repeated in Acts 26.17-18, again referring both to the ministry of Paul and to the ongoing ministry of the resurrected Jesus. It is evident that at this stage in the Servant's interpretation he was not exclusively associated with just one historical individual. Indeed, the work of the Servant was apparently being handed on to successive servants: "Jesus had suffered, and thus fulfilled the words of the fourth Servant Song, but Paul was called by Christ to be the 'light to the Gentiles', and thus to continue the work of the Servant which had been begun by Jesus" (Hooker 1959: 115, citing vol. 2 of Lucien Cerfaux's *Recueil Lucien Cerfaux* [1954: 439–54], "Saint Paul et le 'Serviteur de Dieu' d'Isaïe"). It's precisely the ambiguity of the Servant's characterisation that makes possible this reapplication of the Servant discourses to new situations.

The Servant in the New Testament Epistles

We find a number of allusions to and quotations of the Servant discourses in the New Testament epistles. Almost all of them draw some sort of parallel between the Servant and Jesus. But some also draw parallels between the Servant and the writers themselves, and between the Servant and sections of the early Church.

In Rom. 15.21 Paul quotes the last words of the LXX of Isa. 52.15 to both justify his preaching to the Gentiles, and possibly to draw a parallel between the subject of his preaching—Christ—and the subject of the original text—the Servant. It is difficult to be certain on this point, since Paul does not explicitly link the Servant of Isaiah 53 with Jesus here. As Wagner (2003: 334) concedes, it could be argued that Paul did not read Isaiah 53 christologically, especially since he does not quote the passage anywhere in Romans. Since Paul quotes from Isa. 52.7, 52.15 and 53.1

to justify his own mission to the gentiles, Wagner (2003: 335) proposes another possibility:

> In the context of Romans, the "him" of whom they have not heard or been told, but whom they shall see and understand (Isa. 52:15), is Christ (Rom. 15:20). The "good things" announced by the messengers of Isaiah 52:7 and the content of the rejected "message" of Isaiah 53:1, according to Paul, is the ῥῆμα Χριστοῦ (Rom. 10:17). Paul completes two stages of the equation: (1) Heralds of Isaiah 52–53 = Paul and other preachers of the gospel; (2) Message concerning the return from exile and the servant of the Lord = gospel of Christ. Though the last step of the equation, (3) Servant = Christ, remains unarticulated, it lingers behind the text as a virtually unavoidable implication of Paul's larger reading of Isaiah.

In other words, although Paul does not explicitly say so, he views Christ as the Servant of Isaiah 53. This view is supported somewhat by the possible allusion to Isaiah 53 in 1 Cor. 15.3, where Paul says that Christ died "according to the Scriptures." Scholars claim the reference can only be to Isaiah 53 and the death of the Servant.

Links have been drawn between Isaiah 53 and Rom. 4.25, particularly in the use of the verb παρεδόθη ("hand over"), which appears three times in the LXX of Isa. 53.6 and 12, and the preposition διὰ ("for"/"because of"), which appears three times in the LXX of Isa. 53.5, 12. Hurtado traces the utterance in Rom. 4.25 to circles of believers pre-dating Paul's mission (Hurtado 2003: 128–9), which suggests the reinterpretation of the Servant's identity in light of Jesus' ministry began fairly soon after that ministry came to an end. According to Hurtado, these believers were "people who naturally turned to the Old Testament Scriptures for an understanding of God's purposes, and who were sufficiently familiar with relevant biblical passages that this kind of allusive formulation was adequate" (129).

The LXX of Isa. 53.4a and 53.12 seems to be behind Heb. 9.28, which says of Christ that he had been "offered once to bear the sins of many" (RSV). The MT of Isa. 53.4a reads אכן חלינו הוא נשא ("Surely he bore our sicknesses"), while the LXX replaces חלינו with τὰς ἁμαρτίας ἡμῶν ("our sins"), echoed in Isa. 53.12: αὐτὸς ἁμαρτίας πολλῶν ἀνήνεγκεν ("he bore the sins of many"). These words are echoed in those of Heb. 9.28: εἰς τὸ πολλῶν ἀνενεγκεῖν ἁμαρτίας ("to bear the sins of many").

The most obvious reference to the Servant in the New Testament epistles, and possibly the clearest indication of how Jesus' ministry was interpreted with reference to the Servant of Second Isaiah, is 1 Pet. 2.21-25. Hooker argues this is probably the only text in the New Testament that interprets Isaiah 53 the way it has been used in the Christian tradition: "Is this perhaps *the* significant moment in the exegesis of that passage, when it was first interpreted of the *meaning* of Christ's death?" (Hooker 1998: 92, emphases original). It is worth noting again that in this passage, although Jesus' suffering is interpreted with reference to the suffering of the Servant in Isaiah 53 (LXX), it is not so exclusively. The parallel between the Servant and Jesus is drawn in order to encourage slaves, inferring that when they are unjustly beaten they too become like the Servant. Verses 24-25 draw further parallels between the purposes behind Christ's suffering and those of the Servant, and also parallel the sheep-like behaviour of the epistle's recipients with the behaviour of the speaking "we" in Isaiah 53.

There is another possible allusion to the Servant, particularly as described in Isa. 42.1-4, in the pastoral epistle, 2 Timothy. In 2 Tim. 2.24 the young pastor is instructed that the "Lord's servant" (δοῦλον δὲ κυρίου; cf. Isa. 42.19, οἱ δοῦλοι τοῦ θεοῦ, LXX) "must not quarrel; instead, he must be kind to everyone, able to teach, not resentful." If the parallel is legitimate, then it indicates a continuing application of the Servant beyond Jesus, to ministers of the Church.

The Servant in the Church Fathers

The Servant continues to be reinterpreted in the period immediately following the New Testament era, as indicated by mentions in the patristic literature. The identification of the Servant with Jesus continues into the writings of the Church Fathers, as one would expect. However, another important tendency is evident—that of interpreting the life of the Christian in light of the Servant's mission and sacrifice. Christoph Markschies has labelled these dual approaches to the Servant's interpretation the "exemplary model" and the "Christological model" (Markschies 2004: 225). Markschies' focus is Isaiah 53, and not the broader Servant texts, but his observations appropriately describe the patristic use of the Servant texts in general:

> In the first model the Servant is taken as an example of the true Christian and the text [Isa. 53] is taken, so to speak, as instruction in ethical behaviour. In the second model Isaiah 53 is understood as a statement about a singular saving act of Christ. (Markschies 2004: 231)

The *First Epistle of Clement* (ca. 97 CE) contains one of the earliest extant interpretations of Isaiah 53 after the New Testament writings. In ch. 16 Clement apparently attempts not only to demonstrate that Jesus has fulfilled Isaiah's prophecy of a Servant who would humble himself for his followers, but also to impress the same humility upon divisive elements in the Church:

> For Christ is of those who are humble-minded, and not of those who exalt themselves over His flock. Our Lord Jesus Christ, the Sceptre of the majesty of God, did not come in the pomp of pride or arrogance, although He might have done so, but in a lowly condition, as the Holy Spirit had declared regarding Him. (*ANF*: 9)

Clement then goes on to quote Isaiah 53 in its entirety, and ends with an appeal for the Church to imitate Jesus' behaviour: "Ye see, beloved, what is the example which has been given us; for if the Lord thus humbled Himself, what shall we do who have through Him come under the yoke of His grace?" (*ANF*: 9)

The *Epistle of Barnabas* (ca. 100 CE) likewise draws attention to the exemplary nature of Jesus' humility. In ch. 5 of the epistle the writer makes reference to Isaiah 53. Interestingly, Barnabas preserves the awareness that the text was written to Israel before it was made significant for the Church:

> For to this end the Lord endured to deliver up His flesh to corruption, that we might be sanctified through the remission of sins, which is effected by His blood of sprinkling. For it is written concerning Him, partly with reference to Israel, and partly to us. (*ANF*: 139)

Barnabas then quotes from Isa. 53.5 and 7, in order to show that "the man perishes justly, who, having a knowledge of the way of righteousness, rushes off into the way of darkness" (*ANF*: 139).

Markschies notes that following a number of allusions to the Servant figure in the *Martyrdom of Polycarp* (ca. mid-second century CE) and other martyrologies, the interpretation of the Servant becomes overwhelmingly christological. Markschies explains this by arguing that "Christians wished to avoid relativising the exclusive claims of Christ evident in the christological use of [Isa. 53]" (Markschies 2004: 244).

Justin Martyr (100–165 CE) is one of the few early interpreters of the Servant figure to link a variety of Servant texts from Second Isaiah with Jesus—although Isaiah 53 is his overwhelming favourite. In chs. 49–51 of his *First Apology* (*ANF*: 179–80), written around 150–155 CE, Justin draws a direct parallel between the passion of Jesus and the suffering of the Servant in Isaiah 53, clearly interpreting the text as prophecy. He draws the same parallel in ch. 13 of his work *Dialogue with Trypho*

(*ANF*: 200–201), written around 155–160 CE. In ch. 121 (*ANF*: 260) he draws a parallel between Jesus and the Servant of Isa. 49.6, and in the following chapter (260–1) interprets the "witnesses" of Isa. 43.10a to be Jesus, since Jesus continues, argues Justin, to witness to his believers. In ch. 123 (261), and again in ch. 135 (267), he interprets the Jacob and Israel of Isa. 42.1-4 as parabolic names for Jesus.

Eusebius (260–340 CE), in his *The Prophetic Selections*, likewise interprets the Servant passages of Isaiah 42, 50.1-9 and 52.13–53.12 as prophecies of Jesus (cited in Childs 2004: 82). As Childs points out, Eusebius assumes that Isaiah 53 is only intelligible as a prophecy of the person and purpose of Jesus.

To these patristic writers who take up the motif of the Servant we can also add Jerome (345–420) and Cyril of Alexandria (378–444), both of whom wrote commentaries on Isaiah and interpreted the Servant passages as prophecies of Christ. Likewise, Origen makes a direct link between the Servant as a prophetic figure and Jesus. In *Against Celsus* (ch. 54), Origen argues that Isaiah 53 was a "prediction" not only of Jesus' suffering, but also of his reputation among the Gentiles.

> It was predicted, moreover, that some from among the Gentiles would come to the knowledge of Him (among whom the prophets are not included); and it had been declared that he would be seen in a form which is deemed dishonourable among men. (*ANF*: 420)

Elsewhere Origen links the role of Isaiah's Servant and the servanthood of Jesus. In ch. 37 of his commentary on the Gospel of John, Origen paraphrases Isa. 49.6 to describe the work of Jesus: "For if He had not become a servant, He would not have raised up the tribes of Jacob, nor have turned the heart of the diaspora of Israel, and neither would He have become a light of the Gentiles to be for salvation to the ends of the earth" (*ANF*: 316).

The Servant in Jewish Literature

In contrast to the dominant Christian interpretation of the Servant texts as prophecies of Jesus, the dominant Jewish interpretation, at least since the Middle Ages, has been that the Servant represents suffering Israel in exile. There is no standard Jewish interpretation of the Servant, since, as Schreiner correctly observes regarding Isaiah 53, even within Jewish scholarship "opinions about the 'correct interpretation' can differ just as much as the Christian interpretations do" (Schreiner 2004: 419).

Although there have been notable exceptions to the general rule, particularly in the Isaiah Targum (as noted above), the dominant Jewish interpretation of the Servant's identity has not dwelt upon his apparent ambiguity, but has seen him as quite unambiguously the Jacob-Israel of the early Servant discourses. This is certainly the interpretation of renowned French scholar R. Solomon ben Isaac, otherwise known as Rashi (1040–1105 CE). Rashi tends to view the Servant as a corporate personality representing both the nation as a whole and a righteous element within Israel. Paraphrasing Isa. 52.13, Rashi inserts the name Jacob after the reference to "my servant" and describes him as "the righteous who are in him" (cited in Driver and Neubauer 1999: 37). But concerning Isa. 53.3, which speaks of the suffering of the Servant, Rashi says, "This prophet speaks constantly of the whole people as one man," and links this description of the Servant with Isa. 44.1, 2, where the Servant is explicitly named Jacob and Israel. Rashi claims that Israel suffered "in order that by his sufferings atonement might be made for all other nations: the sickness which ought to have fallen upon us was carried by him" (cited in Driver and Neubauer 1999: 38). Rashi also argues that the image of the Servant being led like a sheep in Isa. 53.7 refers to Israel being led to freedom from exile by Cyrus:

> The prophet here publishes the glad tidings of Israel's release, representing the Gentiles as announcing it in the latter days when they see him *taken from the confinement* in which he had been kept by their hands... (cited in Driver and Neubauer 1999: 38, emphasis original)

Rashi again has the exile in mind when commenting on Isa. 53.9, which says the Servant was "assigned a grave with the wicked." He argues the "wicked" are the Gentiles, among whom the Jews in exile were buried: "He gave himself over to whatever burial the wicked Gentiles might decree: for the Gentiles used to condemn the Israelites to be murdered and then buried like asses in the bellies of dogs" (quoted in Driver and Neubauer 1999: 38).

R. Abraham Ibn Ezra (1093–1168) similarly identifies the Servant with the nation Israel in exile, but is more polemical than Rashi, arguing against the Christian interpretation of the Servant on the basis that it does not take into account aspects of the text that seem to contradict the identification of the Servant with Christ:

> Our opponents say that it refers to their God, supposing the 'servant' to signify his body: this, however, is not possible, for the body cannot 'understand' even during a man's lifetime. (quoted in Driver and Neubauer 1999: 43)

Ibn Ezra also disputes the view that references to the Servant "seeing offspring" and "prolonging days" (53.10), as well as "dividing spoil with the strong" (53.12), can be said of Christ. Rather, the proof of the Servant's identity, at least in Isaiah 53, lies in the passage's context. Immediately before the passage, in 52.12a, "you" refers to Israel, and immediately afterwards, in 54.1a, the "barren woman" also designates Israel: "Similarly *my servant* means each individual belonging to Israel, and consequently God's servant, who is in exile" (quoted in Driver and Neubauer 1999: 43, emphases original).

Likewise, R. David Kimchi, otherwise known as Radaq (1160–1235), argues that Isaiah 53 refers to the captivity of Israel, which is called "my servant" as it is in Isa. 41.8a. Jewish interpretation of the Servant represented by Kimchi and those who came before him does not allow for two different servants, an individual and a collective. Neither does it allow for the so-called songs to be isolated from their literary context.

The Aramaic translation of Isaiah, the Targum, is a notable exception to the generally accepted Jewish interpretation of the Servant figure. Written prior to the debate between the early Church and Jewish interpreters regarding the perceived links between Isaiah 53 and Jesus (see, for example, the aforementioned *Dialogue with Trypho* by Justin Martyr), the Targum interprets the Servant, at least the Servant of Isaiah 53, messianically. The Targum of Isa. 52.13 reads "Behold, my servant, the Anointed One (or, the Messiah), shall prosper. He shall be exalted and increase, and be very strong" (cited in Stenning 1949: 178). However, this is where the identification between the Servant and the Messiah ends. The rest of Isaiah 53 identifies the figure that suffers as Israel, not the Messiah. It is "they" who are despised and of no account in Isa. 53.3, which is at odds with the "he" of the MT. And it is "we," and not the "he" of the MT, who are accounted smitten, stricken and afflicted in 53.4cd. The distinction between "us" (i.e., Israel) and "he" (the Messiah/Servant) runs throughout the poem—"we" suffer, while the Servant is victorious for our sake.

What Scholars Say
about the Suffering Servant

Introduction

Attempts to come to terms with the Servant's ambiguous characterisation have been as divergent among scholars over the past two hundred years as they have been between Christian and Jewish interpreters since the days of the early Church. In his extensive review of the history of interpretation of the Servant since the 1800s, North (1956) is able to delineate two clear lines of interpretation: the Servant is either an individual, or he is a corporate identity that represents Israel or a section of it. There are complexities to the arguments on both sides, but those who argue for a corporate identity generally emphasise the Servant discourses outside the Servant songs, where the Servant is clearly identified as "Jacob-Israel." Those who argue for an individual interpretation tend to emphasise the songs, which appear to not only describe him as an individual, but as an individual who stands over against Israel (e.g., Isa. 49.1-6 and Isa. 53).

The case for an individual Servant associated with the songs is usually attributed to the publication in 1892 of Bernhard Duhm's commentary on Isaiah, *Das Buch Jesaia: übersetzt und erklärt*, in which Duhm argues the songs originated independently of Second Isaiah. There is a clear attempt by Duhm to minimise ambiguity in the Servant's characterisation by isolating those discourses that most contribute to it—the seemingly individualistic poems, Isa. 42.1-4; 49.1-6; 50.4-9; 52.13–53.12. Duhm's thesis had its desired effect—it removed ambiguity by positing not only two discrete servants (the collective Servant, Jacob-Israel, and the individual Servant), but two discrete sets of discourses. So axiomatic was Duhm's thesis that North's history of interpretation distinguishes between pre-Duhm and post-Duhm interpretations of the Servant. Still, even before Duhm's work, scholars differed markedly on their theories regarding the Servant's identity and purpose.

What is gained by reviewing how academics have interpreted the ambiguous nature of the Servant's characterisation? Apart from laying out the long history of the difficulties associated with identifying the Servant, it demonstrates and contributes to the polyphony of voices that have contributed to the Servant's "voice-idea" and opened the character up for the likes of Jared to see themselves in his light.

Pre-Duhm

The idea prevalent among Jewish interpreters, that the Servant is a corporate personality representing the nation Israel, persists into the modern era. North traces the argument among modern scholars back to Heinrich Stephani in 1787, followed by J. C. Döderlein in the third edition of his commentary *Esaias* in 1789. In his previous two editions Döderlein presents a traditional messianic interpretation—the position that the servant passages are predictive prophecy referring to the coming Messiah (for many readers Jesus fulfils this messianic hope). In the third he says Isa. 42.1-4 is speaking of Cyrus, and that 49.1 and 52.13–53.12 speak of the entire Jewish people. In his 1794 work, C. G. Schuster describes Isaiah 53 as an allegory of the fortunes of collective Israel. To this group of scholars North also adds J. F. Telge (1816–18), J. Wellhausen (1883), who famously states "There is no God save Yahweh, and Israel is his prophet," and B. Stade (1888).

A variation of the corporate personality interpretation views the Servant not as the entire nation of Israel, but as Israel as it should be—in other words, ideal Israel. This is one of a number of ways of accommodating the distinction in some of the Servant discourses between the Servant and empirical Israel. J. C. R. Eckerman (1790) distinguishes between the state of Israel and its citizens—the citizens have sinned and the state has suffered. W. Vatke (1835) argues that the Servant is Israel "according to its higher religious unity and divine calling," H. Ewald (1840) that he is Israel according to its true idea. The first British critic to break ranks and abandon the traditional messianic interpretation was Samuel Davidson in 1863. Davidson describes the Servant as ideal Israel. T. K. Cheyne followed in 1870 by describing the Servant as the "personified ideal of the Israelitish nation."

Another variation of the corporate theory in the pre-Duhm era finds expression in H. E. G. Paulus (1792), who argues the Servant represents a pious minority within Israel. This group "suffered because of the rest of the Jews." C. F. Ammon (1794) says the Servant is the "nobler part" of Israel. This theory seemed to lay dormant until 1832 with Otto Thenius, followed by F. J. V. D. Maurer (1836), D. G. C. von Cölln (1836) and August Knobel (1872). The latter work argues the Servant is "the theocratic *Kern* of the people." A. Keunen (1877) is more explicit: the Servant is "the better portion, the flower of the Israelitish people."

A further variation of the corporate theory sees the Servant as the order of the prophets. This was first suggested by E. F. C. Rosenmüller (1799), who later abandoned the view in favour of the full collective theory. Nevertheless, the theory took hold. W. Gesenius (1821) argues that in the figure of the Servant "the prophets are…viewed as a corporate body or moral person." F. W. Umbreit (1828), clearly recognising the ambiguity of the Servant's characterisation, combines a number of theories, seeing in the Servant the prophets, the Messiah, and Israel: "In some passages of the prophecy…the Servant is Israel as a whole, in others the better elements in Israel, and in yet others the prophets" (cited in North 1956: 38).

Throughout this period it is evident that the identity of the Servant is bound up with the question of his purpose—a point that is key to my own argument later on. If the Servant is deemed to be Israel, then his purpose is to suffer on behalf of the world, to bring God's justice to the nations. If the Servant is a righteous element within Israel, then his purpose is to restore the relationship between Yahweh and the nation of Israel. If the Servant is "ideal Israel" then his purpose is to call Israel to what it should be: a witness to God's saving power, and one who suffers on behalf of the Gentile nations.

Alternatively, a number of theories linking the Servant with historical individuals also proliferates among scholars pre-Duhm. The Servant is Hezekiah, Isaiah, Uzziah, Jeremiah, Second Isaiah, Zerubbabel, or an unknown individual (see North 1956: 39–42). The traditional messianic interpretation of his person and purpose continues unabated in this period. However, North notes that from the mid-1800s interpreters took a more liberal approach to messianic interpretations by, for example, attempting to fuse them with the collective interpretations. The classic expression of this is by Franz Delitzsch (1890), who describes the idea of the Servant as a "pyramid." On one level the Servant is the whole people (the base of the pyramid), on another he is Israel "according to the spirit" as well as the flesh (the mid-section of the pyramid), and on a third level he is the person of the redeemer (the summit of the pyramid) (cited in North 1956: 44). Delitzsch is acknowledged for drawing attention to the Servant's "fluidity"—albeit with a model that was too "static"—in an era when Duhm's sharp contrast between the individual and corporate Servant would misconstrue the issue (see Childs 2001: 385). George Adam Smith (1890) puts forward a similar view, arguing that Second Isaiah holds "dissolving views" regarding the Servant's characterisation: he is at first the nation, then a distinction between the nation and the real Servant is introduced. But, ultimately, the "personification of previous passages is at last…presented as a Person" in Isaiah 53 (cited in North 1956: 45). This explanation of the Servant's fluidity underscores a number of recent commentaries. My own reading reflects a certain type of "fluidity" but without the element of "dissolving" characterisation.

Duhm to Mowinckel, 1892–1921

Following Duhm it becomes commonplace to interpret the Servant in the four songs as one figure. North notes that the period from Duhm to Mowinckel (1921) is "notable for strong reaction…against the collective interpretation, and the advocacy of a number of theories identifying the Servant with some historical individual" (North 1956: 47). Duhm himself argues the Servant is a "disciple of the prophets, a teacher of the law and a pastor of souls" (cited in North 1956: 48). Other theories continued to suggest the Servant was one of a variety of historical individuals, some of whom had already been posited—among them Eleazar the scribe, Zerubbabel, Jehoiachin, Moses, an anonymous contemporary of Second Isaiah, and Ezekiel. One writer suggests the Servant is, at different places in the text, three figures, Hezekiah, Jeremiah and Uzziah, and another that he is Cyrus (see North 1956: 48–57).

Despite the reaction in this period against the collective interpretation it does persist, most notably in Karl Budde (1899) and F. Giesebrecht (1902). Budde's argument for a collective interpretation is based on his conviction that Second Isaiah is a unity (cited in North 1956: 58). Indeed, throughout the history of the Servant's interpretation there is a strong correlation between theories espousing the fragmentary nature of Second Isaiah and individualistic interpretations of the Servant. Giesebrecht's explanation for the differences between the Servant's presentation inside and outside the songs is that the songs are written for the prophet's close circle of disciples, with whom he can be more esoteric (cited in North 1956: 59). A different spin is put on the collective interpretation by Henri Roy (1903), who says the Servant is always empirical Israel, but that certain passages—42.1-7; 49.1-13; 50.4–51.8 (excluding 50.10-11); 52.13–53.12—were interpolated in the post-exilic period of the diaspora, and therefore reflect a different understanding of Israel's relationship to the world and to God (cited in North 1956: 61).

Among interpreters who continue to defend the collective interpretation in the period from Duhm to Mowinckel are those who argue for a narrower understanding of the Servant's identity and purpose—that the Servant is not the whole of Israel, but a pious minority, or that the Servant represents Israel only in its ideal state.

The messianic interpretations also continue. Julius Ley (1893) is recognised as the first to mount a reasoned defence of the messianic approach against modern interpreters, followed by L. Laue (1898), Gerhard Füllkrug (1899), and Ernst Ziemer, who, North notes, advocates the position along strictly conservative lines. This position, which has continued to be defended unabated by conservative scholars throughout the modern period, defends Isaianic authorship of the whole book, and reads the Servant passages, particularly the individualistic songs, as predictions of the Messiah, Jesus. The historical context of the book of Second Isaiah, in this view, is irrelevant.

Mowinckel to North, 1921–1956

North assigns the 1921 monograph *Der Knecht Jahwäs*, by Norwegian scholar Sigmund Mowinckel, a place of prominence in the history of the Servant's interpretation that it no longer holds. Nevertheless, it is remembered as a landmark work, one that at the time was described by Otto Eissfeldt as one of "outstanding importance" that "exercised an influence comparable with that of Duhm's commentary" (cited in North 1956: 72). The importance of the work from my perspective is that it introduced the autobiographical interpretation of the Servant songs. Mowinckel argues that the speaker in the second and third songs has to be either Yahweh or the prophet. Since the Servant of Yahweh cannot be Yahweh himself, he concludes he must be the prophet, Second Isaiah. But Mowinckel is also typical of scholars who see no ambiguity in the Servant's characterisation at all, a position that is reaffirmed strongly in his seminal work *He That Cometh*:

> The Servant is regarded and described as a specific individual. This is clear, not only from all the purely individual and personal traits in the picture, but also indirectly, since every collective interpretation leads to absurdities. (Mowinckel 1959: 213–14)

Mowinckel's view immediately attracted the attention of a number of scholars, some of whom abandoned previously held views to expand upon Mowinckel's thesis. Among them is Gunkel (1921; rev. 1929):

> This explanation of the Servant of Yahweh as the Prophet himself gives a picture so uniform, historically intelligible, and impressive, that we may well take it for granted that, after some lapse of time, it will be widely accepted. (cited in North 1956: 75)

The view certainly caught on. Gunkel's monograph was supported in 1923 by two separate essays endorsing the interpretation. Both were included in a collection of essays presented to Gunkel on his sixtieth birthday. A commentary by P. Volz in 1932 attempted to support Mowinckel's theory and get around the sticking point of Isaiah 53, which cannot be autobiographical since the Servant is already dead. Volz says Isaiah 53 is eschatological and originated in the fourth or third century BCE. The difficulties of fitting Isaiah 53 into the autobiographical theory are also tackled by E. Sellin (1930), Mowinckel himself (1931), Karl Elliger (1933) and Joachim Begrich (1938), who finally brings the argument full circle by saying Second Isaiah did compose the last song, in anticipation of his own death.

The messianic interpretations continue their prevalence in this period, but with some variations. W. Rudolph (1925) proposes a merging of the historical and messianic approaches by suggesting the Servant, a contemporary of Second Isaiah, was a messianic leader of the exilic people: "The task to Israel is thus, on the one hand, that of a military leader, statesman, and ruler, and, on the other, that of a teacher and prophet" (paraphrased by North 1956: 86). According to Rudolph, the autobiographical nature of the second and third songs eventuated because Second Isaiah became so united spiritually with the Servant that he could identify completely with him (see North 1956: 87). Rudolph's view is supported by that of W. O. E. Oesterley (1937), who proposes that the Servant is an historical, as opposed to an ideal, individual, who Second Isaiah believed to be the Messiah.

The traditional messianic interpretation, which sees the Servant as a forerunner of Jesus Christ, also continues in this period, in the work of H. Gressmann (1929), Johann Fischer (1939), J. S. van der Ploeg (1936), J. Schelhaas (1933), A. H. Edelkoort (1941), Otto Procksch (1938) and Ivan Engnell (1945).

Other individual interpretations that continued to be defended were those of the ideal figure (North 1956: 100–101), and a mythological interpretation that had first come to prominence with Hugo Gressmann in 1905. Proponents of the latter view attempt to link the figure of the Servant, particularly as he is presented in Isaiah 53, with the myth of Tammuz, the dying and rising Mesopotamian god. F. M. Th. Böhl (1923) resurrects discussion concerning the commonalities between Tammuz and the coming Messiah, of whom the Servant is a "shadow" (see North 1956: 102). Lorenz Dürr (1925) develops an earlier theory that the Servant is linked to a Babylonian new year festival, and is presented as a contrast to the Babylonian king. Finally, proponents of the collective interpretation continued to defend the position, often espousing new theories to explain old difficulties. One of the main obstructions to the collective interpretation has been Isa. 49.3-5, in which the Servant is named Israel, but then is sent on a mission *to* Israel, on its behalf. H. Wheeler Robinson (1926, 1936) seeks to find a way around the problem by arguing the individual and collective interpretations do not actually stand over against one another. Robinson's main argument, which is helpful to my own later in the book, is that to set the two interpretations over against one another is a modern rationale, and is not necessarily true to ancient modes of thought:

> We are to think of the prophet's consciousness as capable of a systole and diastole, an ebb and a flow, so that though he utters his own experience in the service of Yahweh, it is always with the sense implicit or explicit that these things are true of all the devout disciples of Israel, and that they are Israel. (cited in North 1956: 105)

Eissfeldt's (1933) explanation of the problem is that "Israel" is distinct from "Israelites," as Zion is from her children; "Israel" is an ideal that "makes demands upon succeeding generations" (cited in North 1956: 107).

North's own position has proved remarkably resilient in the years since the publication of his work. His observations are based somewhat on Delitzsch's theory of the Servant as a pyramid. There is a "fluidity" in the character of the Servant (1956: 215) and a shift in his identity, from collective Israel to an individual. However, North argues that the individual who is represented in the later songs is not an historical identity as such. He is grounded in the historical context of the prophet and the people, but as expectation and hope. The Servant is the Messiah, an individual who is neither the prophet nor anyone else who has lived to that point. North acknowledges the difficulties with the traditional messianic view, namely that it is wedded to a too-mechanical doctrine of inspiration (207), and that the prophet becomes a mere conduit for a message that will bear no relevance for several hundred years. He argues for a more realistic interpretation, namely that the Messiah-Servant concept is grounded in Second Isaiah's personal and historical circumstances, and there need not be total correspondence between the prophetic writings and their fulfilment in Christ (208):

> The essential likeness between the Servant and Jesus lies in this: that whereas prophets like Jeremiah suffered in the course of, or as a result of, their witness, for both the Servant and Jesus suffering is the means whereby they fulfil their mission and bring it to a triumphant conclusion.

The casting of the suffering of the Servant in Isaiah 53 in the perfect tense is a stumbling block to predictive messianic views. North argues that the suffering is past only in relation to a future that has not yet happened, and not in relation to the prophet's present (1956: 211). The Servant songs, argues North, are "myth—provisional or anticipated history—not allegory" (216). Second Isaiah fully expected the Servant to come.

Collective Interpretations

Interpreters have continued to defend the major positions in the time since North's survey. The following are some of the representative voices of each position, together with a brief discussion of any major deviations from the standard views.

The collective interpretation has continued to attract a large number of proponents. In the same year as North's work was published (1956), Muilenburg defended the position on the basis that the Servant songs were an integral part of Second Isaiah's composition. Therefore, the Servant was consistently Israel-Jacob, as identified in a number of passages. Muilenburg's commentary is significant because it marks a new era of literary approaches to the book of Isaiah.[1] Muilenburg's own approach is categorised as rhetorical criticism, since it seeks to discover how the text is able to persuade by its use of structure and stylistic patterns of words and phrases. Muilenburg argues that while a variety of individuals have been linked with the Servant,

> when all is said, the fact remains that no single person is sufficient to bear the burden of what is disclosed in the songs… For the reality that lies within and behind the songs is infinitely greater than any person could exemplify. (Muilenburg 1956b: 409)

This is an important point, and one I will take up later—it is key to understanding how the idea of the Servant's role continues to be taken up by individuals through history. Muilenburg argues the Servant's mission could not have been carried out by any historical individual, and the Servant's sufferings as described in Isaiah 53 could hardly have applied to any single person (1956b: 409). However, he says, what cannot be said of any one individual can be ascribed to the community of Israel.

---

1. Muilenburg's epoch-announcing *Form Criticism and Beyond* is widely credited with giving credence to the fledgling rhetorical critical school. It was first published in *JBL* 88 (1969): 1–18, but originally delivered as the presidential address at SBL's annual meeting on December 18, 1968, at the University of California. It was included in a 1992 volume of works dedicated to the (then) new literary methodologies (see House 1992).

There's another key contribution from Muilenburg that I want to note here, since it sets up my own case for appreciating the poetic construction of the Servant with new literary tools. Muilenburg argued that the forms of oral communication known to the prophetic writers were already well-suited to poetic literature, with its repetitions and parallelisms. However, the poems of Second Isaiah are of such a complexity that they are clearly written, rather than spoken—or at least they are elaborations of spoken utterances. The poet/prophet is "the proclaimer of the Word of God as the other prophets were. But he transfigures the prophetic forms into great artistic compositions" (1956b: 386). Muilenburg also says that many of the poems were composed in order to be effective when delivered orally, as the presence of assonance bears out, for example in the forms of onomatopoeia, paronomasia and alliteration. Assonance is only one of the stylistic features of Second Isaiah's poems studied by Muilenburg. He also notes the regular use of parallelism, particularly in repetitions, climaxes, and the more traditional rhetorical features of exclamation and question, and the use of triadic forms. He notes that the language of Second Isaiah is highly dramatic, and argues that the composition intentionally culminates the "dramatic quality of biblical faith" (387). The point I want to stress in this is that it isn't far-fetched to think the writer of the Servant songs was aware of the type of impact his poetic construction of the Servant character would achieve—or that its "fluidity" was intentional.

I've already made the point that the isolation of the Servant songs from their context has become a fundamental aspect of the argument that the Servant within the songs is an historical individual. Norman H. Snaith (1977) argues against the foundational presupposition of a collection of Servant songs, thereby countering the individual interpretation. He argues there is no main body of prophecy in Isaiah 40–55, merely a collection of oracles—how then can there be a special, distinct group of oracles that should be separated from the rest? Are they not all distinct? Accordingly, Snaith argues the Servant represents the first batch of exiles who were taken with Jehoiachin in 597, with a tendency to include the 586 exiles (1977: 170).

R. J. Clifford (1984) echoes H. Wheeler Robinson (1926, 1936) in his interpretation of the Servant. He argues that the Servant is Israel "obedient to the divine word" (Clifford 1984: 153). However, Clifford's apparent collective interpretation is by no means rigid:

> The Servant can of course be an individual but all Israel is called to obey the word through him, and the concept can include those Israelites who are associated with the servant in obedience to the present task.

Clifford tackles the ambiguity of the Servant's characterisation in terms of Israel's dialectical understanding of servanthood. Servants were understood in relation to those to whom they were sent: "People and servant were profoundly orientated to each other" (Clifford 1984: 153). This is why Second Isaiah was able to speak of the Servant Israel having a mission to Israel. That mission is to call Israel back to the word of Yahweh.

John F. A. Sawyer (1989) favours a collective interpretation because of the parallels between the figures of the Servant and the Daughter of Zion in Second Isaiah. Sawyer argues that, like the Servant, the Daughter of Zion can be interpreted both individually and collectively (1989: 101). However, the Daughter of Zion most frequently represents the exiled people of God. Sawyer argues that, logically, the "same collective interpretation must surely be dominant in the story of 'Israel, my servant, Jacob whom I have chosen' throughout these chapters [Isa. 40 onwards]" (102). With reference to Isaiah 49 and the difficult issue of the Servant being given a mission to Israel, Sawyer argues that in Isa. 40.9 Zion appears to be given a mission to Zion, and yet there is no doubt that Zion represents the nation, or at least a section of it.

Within the collective interpretations, the theory that the Servant represents "ideal Israel" has continued to attract its proponents as well. Antti Laato (1992) has argued that the Servant's purpose in Second Isaiah as the ideal Israel is to lead the people into a right relationship with Yahweh. Laato makes a clear distinction between loyal and disloyal Israel, and it is only the former that is depicted in Second Isaiah as the Servant (1992: 111).

> That the ideal Israel is described in Isa. 40–55 as the group which will inherit the promise of YHWH given to David…indicates that the word of comfort in 43:1-7 is connected with the common tendency in Isa. 40–55 to describe the ideal Israel as playing the role of the Davidic Messiah. (1992: 96)

Following the exile the "ideal community of Zion" (1992: 130) includes "ideal Israel" now returned from Babylon, and their purpose is to draw other nations to Yahweh and "the plan of salvation which he has begun to carry through by means of the return of Israel" (130). This includes spreading the law and the justice of Yahweh throughout the world.

Patricia Tull (1997) has taken up the argument that the Servant songs should be read in their literary context, and therefore sees the Servant as a single, collective figure. Tull also takes a literary approach to Second Isaiah, and recognises in the Servant's characterisation an openness that invites the community to understand its experiences of suffering in light of the Servant's perseverance. This is another key position for my own approach—Tull, one of my PhD examiners, is also a Bakhtin scholar. With reference to the apparent contradictory depictions of the Servant, Tull acknowledges they are not easy to account for: "Hyperbole and paradox, and the logical tensions that result from them, permeate not only this character, but the entire text of Second Isaiah, and are not easily resolved on a rational level" (Tull Willey 1997: 177). However, these logical tensions do not stand in the way of a collective interpretation, but alter the nature of the questions interpreters should be asking. Such questions ultimately leave the interpreter pondering a Servant who is Israel:

> While modern scholars (and interpreters throughout the centuries) have posed the question as "who is the servant of YHWH?" the question the text seems bent on answering rather is "who is Israel in relation to YHWH?" The oft-repeated answer in Isaiah 41–45 is, "Israel is YHWH's servant." (1997: 176)

More recently, H. G. M. Williamson (1998: 143) has argued the Servant is Israel but with a new, messianic spin. Williamson argues, with reference to Ps. 89.4, 21, 40 [3, 20, 39], that the designation "Servant" in Isaiah is a royal title that is transferred to the people.

The regular designation of Israel as God's servant in Deutero-Isaiah is also a deliberate transfer to the people of a title once ascribed especially (though of course not exclusively) to the person of the king (1998: 129).

Williamson has a foot in more than one camp, however, since he also allows for a fuller traditional messianic interpretation of the Servant in light of Jesus, who, he argues, "fulfills, but does not thereby exhaust, the prophecy" (1998: 143). This is an important point, and my own approach will echo this idea—that it's an aspect of the Servant's composition that multiple people can see themselves in light of the Servant's role. Williamson betrays a more individualistic interpretation of the Servant, but continues to argue that in the text of Second Isaiah, and even in the difficult discourse of Isa. 49.1-6 the Servant, at least in principle, is a group (152). Williamson ultimately argues that the focus is not so much on who the Servant is, but on the task he/they will perform. And that task is one that was "previously deemed to be suitable for royalty" (154).

Individual interpretations

With the continued widespread acceptance among modern scholars of Duhm's Servant song theory it is no surprise that the individual interpretations of the Servant, at least within the songs, has continued. A quick review of the different positions within this approach: that the Servant was, or was going to be, the Messiah; that he was an historical individual—most likely a contemporary of Second Isaiah—or, that he was Second Isaiah himself. The Servant's task varies depending on who he is viewed to be. The traditional Christian messianic interpretation views the Servant as someone who will atone for not only the sins of Israel, but for the world as well. The view that the Servant was a contemporary of the prophet usually leads scholars to understand his suffering as the means of Israel's liberation from Babylon. Those who suggest the Servant was Second Isaiah himself generally argue that he suffered as a result of his preaching (at the hands of either the Babylonians or the exiles), and that only later was it acknowledged that his ministry was for the sake of the people.

John L. McKenzie (1968) seeks to build a bridge between the corporate and individual interpretations of the Servant. Firstly, McKenzie takes the position that the songs are not related to their literary context, except where the first three songs are responded to in the verses immediately following them (1968: XXXIX). Secondly, McKenzie traces a progression of thought from one song to the next but argues each is intelligible (or "difficult") in itself. He discounts suggestions that the Servant is a fluid figure who is first the nation, then an individual. Thirdly, he argues against seeing the Servant as a definite individual who would arise in the future. However, the Servant is an ideal figure, and a corporate personality, and an individual, though McKenzie disagrees with scholars who say the Servant is clearly an individual in some poems and a corporate figure in others:

> The corporate personality resolves the tension between the individual and the collective traits. The Servant is conceived as an individual figure, but he is the figure who recapitulates in himself all the religious gifts and the religious mission of Israel... Such a figure is not exactly a "fluid" type, as the Servant is sometimes called. The Servant remains an individual, but an ideal who reflects the genuine character of all Israel. (1968: LIII, LIV)

> While the Servant songs are not predictions of the future, they are "insights" into the future: "Unless Israel accepts the Servant as its incorporation, it cannot keep faith with Yahweh." (1968: LV)

Likewise, Westermann (1969) takes the position that the Servant songs form a special strand within Second Isaiah, but argues they originated with Second Isaiah himself, rather than a disciple, as is argued by McKenzie. And, like McKenzie, Westermann takes something of a middle ground in his interpretation of the Servant's identity and work, associating the Servant with the prophet himself, thereby leaning towards an individual interpretation, while stressing the cryptic language of the text, which he deems deliberate:

> On principle, their [the songs'] exegesis must not be controlled by the question, "Who is this servant of God?" Instead, we must do them justice by recognising that precisely this is what they neither tell nor intend to tell us... The cryptic, veiled language used is deliberate. This is true of every one of the songs alike... (1969: 93)

Writing of Isa. 49.6, which he says seems to rule out the collective interpretation, Westermann argues that it is only here that the particular Servant, most likely the prophet himself, can be spoken of as the Servant, among a whole series of servants (1969: 211). The third song, Isa. 50.4-9, seems to back this up, since it is clearly a confession by a minister of the Word: "While this does not prove that the Servant is the prophet Deutero-Isaiah, it does show that he regarded his task, his sufferings and his relationship to God as those of a prophet" (228).

Harry M. Orlinsky likewise favours the view that the Servant was not only an individual but the prophet Second Isaiah (1977: 77). His mission was to Israel in exile, and it was the Jews in Babylon who proved to be the cause of his suffering. Orlinsky admits that some of the references to the Servant in Second Isaiah are to the nation, but that the songs are definitely concerned with an individual. His work includes a close reading of each of the songs, the first three of which constitute "a statement by the prophet himself...in which he rebukes his fellow Judean exiles for not having more faith than they do" (90). Orlinsky argues against one popular reading of Isaiah 53, which views the Servant's suffering as vicarious:

> Once it is realised that the person in 53 did not die but would live to see grandchildren...that his career was essentially the same as that of so many other prophets in the Bible...and that he suffered (but not vicariously!) at the hands of the very Israelites to whom he was sent by God to admonish and persuade, then it is only natural that it is our prophet himself, Second Isaiah, who is that person. (1997: 92)

R. N. Whybray (1983) takes a position similar to that of Orlinsky. Not only was the Servant the prophet Second Isaiah, his death was neither a sacrifice, nor was it vicarious. His suffering came as a direct result of his prophetic call, which included a politically explosive message in the historical context—that Babylon was about to fall. According to Whybray, the prophet bore the sins of many "not in the sense of suffering instead of the many…but of enduring additional and exceptional suffering" (78). Whybray also notes the ambiguity of the Servant's characterisation, but flattens it by arguing that instead of treating each description as equally valid, only one of them, that of the Servant as an individual, should be treated as normative:

> It may be that of the various features of the Servant portrayed here only one set is directly descriptive, while the others are allusive and intend to present him as embodying in his person all that was positive in Israel's earlier traditions. (1983: 69)

Others from this period who interpret the Servant as an individual, though for different reasons, include F. Duane Lindsey (1985), W. A. M. Beuken (1990), and Rikki Watts (1990). The latter, while acknowledging the merits of the argument that the Servant is Second Isaiah, actually returns to the view that he is an ideal figure who is yet to come. Watts points to the difference between the clear identification of Cyrus (in Isa. 44.28, 45.1 and 45.13) and the obscure depiction of the Servant as an indication that he is not an historical figure. He is an "unknown individual" with a mission to "turn the remnant back to God" (Watts 1990: 54):

> Who is this deliverer? The prophet simply does not know, but he recognises that he will need to be an exceptional figure, which may account for the idealistic portrayal. (1990: 58)

Anthony R. Ceresko (1994) takes the position that the Servant was Second Isaiah, though Isaiah 53, the work of the Servant's disciples, is "a thanksgiving hymn celebrating the vindication of the prophet's preaching" (Ceresko 1994: 43). R. Bergey's (1997) emphasis is on the Servant as an individual who prefigures Christ. Bergey points to the parallels between their missions—the Servant is crowned with success, while Christ is elevated to the highest position, namely, the right hand of God (Bergey 1997: 188).

One of the richer interpretations of the Servant to emerge in recent times is that of R. E. Clements (1998), who seeks to understand the fluctuation between individual and collective depictions of the Servant in Second Isaiah by finding parallels in the roles of kingship, prophecy and the Deuteronomic portrayal of Moses (1998: 42). Firstly, Clements rejects the idea that the Servant is a literary creation that is meant to personify the nation. He argues that the language of the fourth Servant song, in particular, is "too exceptional" and the details of the Servant's suffering "too precise, for a straightforward poetic device to have led to its creation" (42).

Clements seeks to clarify the significance of the Servant's suffering to the speaking "we" of Isaiah 53, and suggests that it was related to the absence of the temple in exile and the inability of the people to make sin-offerings to maintain their relationship with Yahweh:

> Now Deutero-Isaiah introduces his boldest of assertions, that God will accept the sufferings of the Servant-Israel, perhaps largely focused on the specific sufferings of the unnamed prophet himself, as the *'ašam* by which the restored nation will be purified. (1998: 51)

John N. Oswalt (1998) represents the continuing conservative evangelical position on Isaiah 53—namely, that the Servant, of the songs at least, is an individual, the Messiah, who represents Israel, and whose purpose Christ fulfils. Oswalt argues that the Servant of the songs is distinguished from the Servant outside the songs by purpose—the Servant outside the songs plays a passive role, and is called only to "witness" to Yahweh (Oswalt 1998: 109), while the Servant of the songs is actively obedient to Yahweh, and through his service "Israel will be enabled to perform the service of blessing the nations" (108). The presence of the term Israel as a designation for the Servant speaks against the theory that the Servant is the prophet himself, since "no prophet ever thought of himself as the ideal Israel" (291). Pointedly, Oswalt concludes that the Servant is no mere human individual. While Oswalt's interpretation, and the traditional approach that he represents, is widely attacked by many modern scholars, Oswalt does make a point about the servant that is generally agreed upon:

> If the expending of so much scholarly effort has produced so little agreement, there must be something about the text itself that resists overneat conclusions. (1998: 377)

I agree with this, but also argue that there's a specific intention behind it that is also key to understanding the Servant's role. This precise point was made by David J. A. Clines in *I, He, We and They*, in which, after reviewing the "multiplicity of interpretation" surrounding the Servant, he argued that ambiguity itself was the key to understanding the most well-known servant song, Isaiah 53:

> What if the force of the poem—to say nothing of the poetry of the poem—lies in its very unforthcomingness, its refusal to be precise and to give *information*, its stubborn concealment of the kind of data that critical scholarship yearns to get its hands on as the building-blocks for the construction of its hypotheses? (Clines 1976: 25, emphasis original)

Another scholar who leans towards an individual interpretation, Michael Barré, also highlights a significant aspect of the Servant's role—that in the last song he does not speak. Barré (2000: 24) essentially argues that the Servant is presented as a wisdom figure in Isaiah 53, in contrast to the other songs where he is presented as a royal or prophetic figure. However, when it comes to the question of the Servant's purpose, Barré notes that what is in focus in Isaiah 53 is not what the Servant does, but what Yahweh does through him:

> No speech of any kind is attributed to him in this song… His "teaching"—or rather, Yahweh's teaching through him—consists of what God does to him rather than anything he accomplishes. (2000: 24)

Finally, Hermann Spieckermann (2004) has given voice to another aspect of the Servant's depiction—that of his "namelessness." Spieckermann argues for an individual interpretation, but with some reservations. He argues that the collective interpretation of the Servant is tied up with the "collective consciousness that soon began to develop in the postexilic period" (2004: 15), but which, significantly, leaves no redactional traces in the final Servant song, Isaiah 53, where the Servant is clearly depicted as an individual. Spieckermann argues that the Servant's "namelessness" throughout Second Isaiah has had certain interpretive consequences that may not have been part of the text's original intention:

> Just as it is true that a precise identification of the Servant is avoided in view of the prophetic background (no individual prophet fits the bill), so also it is true that the Servant's namelessness could misleadingly imply that the Servant's task can always be taken up afresh by particular persons in the future. (2004: 15)

My position is the opposite of Spieckermann's. What Spieckermann describes as "misleading"—the idea of the Servant's openness to being reinterpreted in light of future "servants" who take up his mission afresh—becomes a defining characterisation for those who understand the Servant as a "fluid" character who cannot be defined by either individual or collective interpretations, but must accommodate both.

Fluid Interpretations

A stream of interpretations that have attempted to accommodate the various depictions of the Servant has flowed alongside those of the collective and individual interpretations throughout the modern history of approaches to Second Isaiah. I have grouped these interpretations under the title "fluid," since, while they approach the ambiguous characterisation of the Servant differently, they have in common the belief that the Servant is changeable—that he is both a group and an individual, though not necessarily at the same time.

H. H. Rowley's (1965) suggestion represents the most popular approach in this category—that the Servant began as a personification of the nation, but became a person. This approach sees a linear development in the characterisation of the Servant, from the early Servant passages that depict him as Jacob-Israel, to the later passages, culminating in Isaiah 53, which depicts him as a full-fledged individual. This view generally regards Isaiah 49 as the pivot on which the Servant's identity turns. Rowley notes that the first Servant song is the closest of the four in style to the Israel passages outside the songs, but in the second song the prophet recognises that Israel must be purified—there must be a mission to Israel (1965: 53–4). In the fourth song the prophetic writer realises that suffering will be central to this mission, and that it will focus on an individual. In Rowley's view this individual was still to come at the time of the text's composition:

> In so far as the thought of these songs is of an individual Servant, in whom the mission of Israel reaches its supreme point, it seems incredible to me that it can be other than a future figure. To describe in these terms any figure of earlier history of whom we have knowledge seems utterly out of the question; to suppose that some nameless contemporary of the prophet was imagined to justify such language, yet left no ripple on the course of history, is equally beyond belief. (1965: 54–5)

Rowley is keen to highlight the differences between his approach and that of Christopher North, who, as I pointed out earlier, views the Servant as a "pyramid" whose foundation was the nation and whose peak was the person of Jesus. Rowley's position is that the Servant figure oscillates between both the collective and individual characterisations:

> I find development from the thought of Israel as the Servant to the thought of an individual Servant par excellence, without abandoning the thought of Israel as still the Servant. (1965: 56)

Morna D. Hooker's (1959) approach is similar. Hooker argues that the Servant represents a number of concepts at any one moment—he is Israel, the prophet, and the Messiah all at once, and although one concept may be dominant the presence of the others cannot be denied:

> This fluidity is not…a "linear" development, which moves from one idea to another, rejecting one figure and choosing a new one: there is, on the contrary, a continual oscillation between one concept and another, so that various images may be in the poet's mind at one time. (1959: 44)

John Goldingay (1976, 1984, 2005, 2007b) has consistently argued for a more linear development of the Servant figure. What begins as a calling to Israel becomes a calling to the individual because of Israel's intransigence (Goldingay 1976: 99). This shift is seen most vividly in Isaiah 49, where the prophet is named Israel. Yahweh points to the prophet and says, "You are the one true Israelite who is responding to me, you are the one through whom I will win Israel back to myself and then bring light to the nations" (100). In his later work Goldingay argues there is a development within the calling itself. What began as reassurance of Israel's status with God (Goldingay 1984: 90) becomes a mission to bring Yahweh's judgment and a covenant relationship to the world (94).

Peter Wilcox and David Paton-Williams (1988) note that the development of the Servant as a character reflects the shifts in the text of Second Isaiah. Their detailed study of the Servant songs, which Wilcox and Paton-Williams relate to their literary context, contra Duhm, highlights not only that outside the songs the Servant is always Israel, but that only from ch. 49 does the Servant's identity become an issue. In chs. 40–48 the Servant is unambiguously associated with Israel. After ch. 49 it is the prophet himself who lies behind the Servant (1998: 81).

Henning Graf Reventlow (1998) also sees a development in the figure of the Servant, but not in a linear or literary sense. The growth takes place from one redactional development to the next. For example, in the first layer the Servant is identified with Cyrus the Persian king (1998: 32). A second redaction interprets the first two songs collectively, associating the Servant with Israel or Zion. Ultimately, the Servant of Isaiah 53 is an individual. This, the fourth song, is a commentary on the third, and the Servant's mission described here is congruent with the commission the Servant received in the first two.

Christopher R. Seitz (2001) reads Second Isaiah as an unfolding literary drama and perceives the Servant's development in light of it. His position is similar to that of Goldingay. The Servant is announced as Israel-Jacob in the earlier chapters, but is presented by God as an individual from ch. 49 onwards. In this chapter the prophet himself, while never explicitly adopting the title "prophet," accepts the purpose that had been Israel's:

> It is a recommissioning in the light of developing circumstances at this particular juncture in the discourse, involving the role of Israel, the servant-author, and the nations... Language once applied to Israel is now applied to the servant, whose task (though once hidden) has been and remains to Jacob-Israel. (2001: 429)

Seitz pays special attention to Isaiah 53 where, he argues, there is a congruence of the Servant's various roles, a coming together of his identities:

> The servant's death is reckoned as representative of Israel's death and suffering at the hands of the nations. Whatever justice was required in God's judgment of the people, it is also true that, as with Zion (40:1-2), they bore a punishment at the hands of the nations that was overfull...and misunderstood and misinterpreted by the nations themselves. (2001: 461–2)

Seitz argues that Isaiah 53 depicts the death of an individual Servant, whose own servants then describe the realisation among the nations that the representation of Israel in the Servant's suffering has effected the removal of sin (2001: 462).

Childs takes a similar position (2001: 385). His commentary takes the now unusual step of tackling the book of Isaiah as a whole. By doing so Childs makes no claim for a single authorship—his canonical approach leads him to exegete the text as a unified work, whose final word is that which resonates with the canonical intentions of the interpretive community that accepted the text as scripture. In that light, Childs also views Isaiah 40–55 as a unified work, and treats the Servant on the basis of both his literary and diachronic development. Like Seitz, Goldingay and others, he argues that while the Servant was Israel in the earlier section of Second Isaiah, from Isa. 49.3 he is the prophet. The prophet carries not only the title "my servant" but also its office (384). From ch. 49 the "metaphorical usage" of the corporate image of the Servant becomes "more and more strained" (384).

Blenkinsopp (2002) also sees development in the identity of the Servant, but he identifies the Servant of 42.1-4 as Cyrus (2002: 118). The remaining twelve occurrences of the term "servant" in chs. 40–48 refer to Jacob, as ancestor and representative of the entire nation, and the references from ch. 49 on are to the prophet. Blenkinsopp argues the idea of the prophet taking the place of the nation in its divine commission goes back to the Deuteronomists, for whom Moses "the protoprophet is the pre-eminent Servant of God" (118). Blenkinsopp shares with Clements

(1998) the idea that the purpose of this individual Servant who now stands in for the nation is as one who suffers violence and death as a substitutionary sacrifice:

> The idea would be that now that the temple is in ruins and sacrifice no longer possible, the Servant serves as a substitute for the sacrificial guilt offering, one that is accepted by God. (Blenkinsopp 2002: 120)

Hans-Jürgen Hermisson's (2004) approach echoes the dialectic approach of Clifford (1984) when he argues that one-sided interpretations of the Servant as "individual" or "corporate" are too simple (Hermisson 2004: 16). Accepting as axiomatic the presence of Servant songs, Hermisson follows the modern line that the Servant within them is an individual, the prophet himself. However, the prophet cannot complete in himself the mission that Yahweh has given the nation:

> The individual prophetic Servant Second Isaiah cannot fulfil his worldwide mission of being a light to the nations without God's Servant Israel, whom he calls back to God and prepares to be the prime exhibit before the world of God's saving power. (2004: 16)

It is only in the cooperation between God's Servant the prophet and God's Servant the nation that the Servant's purpose is fulfilled. Similarly, Hengel and Bailey argue in the same volume that the apparently contradictory depictions are different aspects of the same Servant: "Interpretations that seem to us to compete with each other, such as the collective interpretation and the one focused on an eschatological redeemer figure, can stand side by side as different 'aspects' of the same text and topic" (Hengel and Bailey 2004: 79). Hermisson further argues that what modern interpreters see as contradictions or paradoxes (or ambiguities) in the text's depiction of the Servant is a sign of the history of interpretation of the Servant himself, already under development in Second Isaiah, and throughout the book of Isaiah. The collective interpretation is that of the third or fourth generation of readers:

> One must therefore speak of both servants in order to do justice to the phenomenon of a Servant who is spoken of both inside and outside the Servant Songs, with the same predicates applied to figures with different tasks (Hermisson 2004: 19).

These servants include the nation Israel, which is called to follow the highway home, and the prophet, who brings exilic Israel together and gets the journey underway.

Interpretive Streams

There has been a developing awareness in Isaiah scholarship that the old polarities concerning the Servant are not adequate for a full discussion of his identity and purpose. To say that he is either a collective body or an individual, when clearly the text presents him as both, is to risk imposing presuppositions upon the text that skew the final reading and even obscure the interpretive key that could unlock the exegetical treasures of the Servant figure and the purpose of his presence in the text.

Two discrete interpretive streams have emerged from this review of the history of the Servant's interpretation. The first comprises scholars who argue that the Servant can only be a corporate identity, such as the nation Israel or a section of it, or an individual, such as the prophet himself or some other historical or ideal figure. The second stream comprises scholars who want to account for the apparent contradictory or ambiguous depictions of the Servant by accepting them as aspects of the one character—they understand the Servant as both Israel and an individual. These scholars disagree on the nature of this relationship. Some, such as Childs and Seitz, argue for a linear or synchronic development (that also embraces diachronic developments) associated with the Servant's calling, while others see a dialectic or oscillating relationship in which the "Servant" as an office can only be fulfilled by the prophet and the nation together. This "fluidity" in the Servant's characterisation is not a new observation, but it seems to have become the preferred starting point in many recent studies, perhaps as a direct consequence of the prevalence of literary approaches to the book of Isaiah—such as my own—which are more accommodating of concepts such as ambiguity, contradiction and dialectic.

The fluid interpretation of the Suffering Servant is my own starting point.

THE SERVANT AS A POLYPHONIC HERO

Defining the Task

If Second Isaiah had been written by Dostoevsky then the Servant, as a polyphonic hero, would literally reflect on the words spoken to him and about him. He would take all such words into his consciousness, even anticipate them in his own thinking, and subsume them within his own internal discourse. Nothing would be said that the Servant would not make part of his own self-reflection. Even the objective world around him would be drawn into his introspection. In this way the Servant would remain outside the consummating influence of others' words. But Second Isaiah is not literature like the works of Dostoevsky, and the Servant does not reflect on every single utterance that is addressed to him, or that is said about him. However, that he is constructed entirely by discourse implies that all that we know about him he also knows about himself. Just as in the novels of Dostoevsky, in which the author's discourse about the hero is actually oriented toward the hero, so in Second Isaiah all that is said about the Servant is oriented toward the Servant. Although we are not given the Servant's response to each utterance, we are told nothing that the Servant himself does not have access to—except perhaps in Isaiah 53, where it is implied that the Servant is dead, and therefore has no chance to reflect on what is said about him. Where we are given the Servant's response to the discourse is obviously of prime importance, since it gives us a window into his dialogic response, and his unique voice-idea.

An imaginative reading of the Suffering Servant involves paying special attention to how the discourse seeks to constitute the Servant. My primary observation that the Servant is constituted dialogically requires a reading strategy that is fundamentally different to how we might read a conventionally constituted literary character. Traditional approaches to the Servant have been based on monologic reading strategies—that is, they have asked the question "Who is he?" on the assumption that the "author" of Second Isaiah has in mind an individual or group. The assumption has been that an objective reading of the available textual data should reveal the Servant's identity and purpose. Or, in a quite separate, though still monologic approach, some commentators have concluded that the texts comprising Second Isaiah are so disparate that an identification of the Servant is impossible. Neither approach takes seriously the Servant's dialogical constitution.

A reading strategy that pays heed to Bakhtin's theories explores what the discourse suggests to the Servant about himself and his world—and therefore how he is to understand his role in it. This is essential, since a polyphonic character, as discussed above, does not project a fixed image that we are meant to view objectively. A polyphonic character has been written in such a way that he represents a very specific point of view on the world that is unique to him. He is less a fixed image, and more a doorway to this world—a doorway that is constructed dialogically. Only by engaging with the dialogue that constitutes the hero can we hope to view the world as he sees it. As we engage the dialogue we must constantly ask, What does this discourse suggest to the Servant's unfolding voice-idea? For Bakhtin there is a higher form of reading that seeks to break down the monologic world that is conventionally erected by an author and shared by the reader, in which they both view the characters from a privileged position and make judgments on a finalised image of a character they have constructed in their imagination. But the hero as a voice-idea, "as an opinion on the world and on himself, requires utterly special methods of discovery and artistic characterisation. And this is so because what must be discovered and characterised here is not the specific existence of the hero, not his fixed image, but the *sum total of his consciousness and self-consciousness*, ultimately *the hero's final word on himself and on his world*" (Bakhtin 1984: 48, emphases original).

Bakhtin suggests a method of reading (with specific reference to polyphonic texts) that seeks to dialogue with the consciousness of others:

> Every true reader of Dostoevsky, who perceives his novels not in the mono-logic mode and who is capable of rising to Dostoevsky's new authorial position, can sense this peculiar active broadening of his consciousness, not solely in the sense of an assimilation of new objects (human types, character, natural and social phenomenon), but primarily in the sense of a special dialogic mode of communication with the autonomous consciousnesses of others, something never before experienced, an active dialogic penetration into the unfinalisable depths of man. (Bakhtin 1984: 68)

My reading of Second Isaiah seeks to apply such a strategy to the discourse that constitutes the Servant. The following reading pays close attention to the discourse, in terms of who is speaking, what they are saying, and what impact are they seeking to have on the Servant. It also pays close attention to instances of double-voicing, where the discourse seeks to make use of ideas from the Servant's era, as well as ideas from past eras. This requires close attention to what the dialogue suggests to the Servant from the place he occupies in the textual world of Second Isaiah; to re-examine his voice-idea from within the discourse itself. Although Bakhtin does not set out a formula for reading polyphonic texts, this method is consistent with his approach in *Problems of Dostoevsky's Poetics* (Bakhtin 1984: 47–77). It is a creative and imaginative reading strategy—a dialogic imagining of the Servant and his function in Second Isaiah. It is not a literary flight of fancy. My reading still grapples with the text according to established exegetical practices, which is vital, since the text is where the Servant is (dialogically) constituted.

The possibility that the Servant has been drawn as a self-aware literary character in the vein of Dostoevsky's polyphonic heroes offers new insight into the Servant, his identity, and his function in Second Isaiah. It is not conventional practice to ask what the discourse concerning the Servant suggests to his self-consciousness—but this is what sets a Bakhtinian approach to the question of the Servant's fluid nature apart from other methods.

Ultimately, it asks not "Who is he?" but "Who am I?"

Defining the Discourse

The Servant of Yahweh makes a number of appearances throughout Second Isaiah, and never outside it. Some scholars have also highlighted the peculiarity that he is referred to as the nation, Israel-Jacob, only within chs. 40–48. In chs. 49–53 he both speaks, and is addressed, apparently as an individual, as he is in 42.1-4. There are two ways of approaching this peculiarity, and the methodology chosen determines how the Servant texts are exegeted. The first way is to approach the text of Second Isaiah as a unified work, thereby attempting to trace within the collection a structural logic and a development of literary and theological themes and motifs. Muilenburg, for example, sees Second Isaiah as a "continuous series of poems by a single author" in a work that has "epic qualities" (1956b: 382). The Servant, in this approach, is likely to be understood as a character that develops in the course of the work. The Servant texts are understood as having some chronological and thematic shape to their arrangement, so that the Servant in the latter poems is a more developed figure than the one that is introduced early in Second Isaiah. But the assumption that Second Isaiah is a unified work is debated, as is the issue of the unity of the whole book. Form critics have approached Second Isaiah on the basis that it is a collection of short, generic textual units that may or may not be related thematically. The task of determining how the Servant is constituted in this approach is made quite difficult, since the Servant who is addressed in chs. 40–48 may not be the same Servant who speaks or is spoken about in later chapters. Indeed, the identity of the Servant may change from unit to unit, so that it becomes impossible to speak of his "constitution" by Second Isaiah.

The question that arises is whether it is possible to build a unified picture of the Servant from the whole of Second Isaiah, while at the same time paying due regard to the work by form-critical scholars on the smaller units that comprise the final form. Bakhtin offers a way of reconciling both approaches—though "reconciling" is perhaps misleading, since a Bakhtinian reading holds both discrete approaches in dialogic tension. A Bakhtinian reading welcomes the view that multiple textual units, genres, voices, traditions and ideologies have gone into forming the final work, since this reflects multi-voicedness, the presence of multiple voices that each reflect their own socio-political, cultural, traditional and ideological contexts. In dealing with the text's final form a Bakhtinian reading would seek to avoid flattening the text or reducing its multivocality to a final, overarching editorial voice. It would also hope to avoid disengaging the diverse voices in the text so that they no longer dialogue. It would hold diverse voices in dialogic tension, and would welcome the interplay that is introduced only when multiple voices are brought together in a single work. From a Bakhtinian perspective, we only see the complete picture when we recognise the uniqueness and the individuality of the voices in the text, while also attempting to hear the dialogue they generate. Applying Bakhtin's theory to Second Isaiah, we can say that a Bakhtinian reading acknowledges that while this or that text makes mention of the Servant, quite different traditions may be behind the use of the term in each one. However, it attempts to hear the dialogue that those texts, heard simultaneously, generate. A Bakhtinian reading does not support a purely synchronic approach, since such an approach would muffle the individual voices and traditions in the text. A diachronic awareness is also required, since only then are we in a position to overhear and engage[1] with multiple voices.

1. Unless otherwise stated I work with the JPS translation (alongside the Hebrew text, *BHS*). Where other translations are preferred, it is usually where the Hebrew is in dispute.

My reading seeks to honour the different voices that speak of the Servant in Second Isaiah—and then let them dialogue with one another. This is a literary exercise for heuristic purposes that takes the final form of the text as a starting point, since only in the final form of the text do we find the multiplicity of voices that are necessary for the text to be polyphonic. The Servant discourses upon which my approach focuses are those passages in Second Isaiah that refer to a Servant explicitly. On that basis my focus is on ten discourses. In the first seven of the ten discourses constituting the Servant in Second Isaiah (Isa. 41.8-16; 42.1-9; 42.18–43.7; 43.8–44.8; 44.21-22 [23]; 44.24–45.7; 48.20-21 [22]), Yahweh speaks to the servant, who never responds. The discourses also share the peculiar feature that they exclusively use the names "Israel/Jacob" of the Servant. He isn't referred to this way outside of Isaiah 40–48. He is referred to as Israel in Isa. 49.4, which will be addressed later.

Then, in Isa. 49.1-6 the Servant finally responds. He speaks again in Isa. 50.4-9, and 10-11. And finally, in Isaiah 53, the nations respond to Yahweh with their own testimony about the Servant, who doesn't speak again. The following reading will take each block of discourse in turn.

WHAT GOD SAYS TO THE SERVANT

The Worm that Turns

When we encounter the Servant for the first time in Second Isaiah (in 41.8-16), with the words "But you, Israel, my Servant," we're immediately made aware of the broader context of the dialogue between Yahweh and the Servant. Both the coastlands and the Servant are afraid. But while the coastlands are called to judgment (41.1d), the Servant is called to fear (41.10a). Yahweh is seeking to comfort his Servant with words of reassurance, resonating with the command to the prophet that begins the collection in 40.1: "Comfort, comfort my people." What is causing Israel's distress? In 40.27 the prophet echoes a complaint by Israel in order to dispute its validity: "My way is hidden from Yahweh" and "my justice is passed over by my God." The complaint cuts to the heart of Israel's crisis during the period of exile in Babylon (587–539 BCE): Where is Yahweh? And the prophet's response to the people is: How can you doubt a God who is worthy of praise like Yahweh. It must be cold comfort to the people, at least initially, who might be excused for believing God has reneged on his Davidic promises of temple, king and land. But rather than uphold the people's complaint, Yahweh responds with words of comfort, a response that seeks to correct the narrative by which Israel has come to frame its contemporary experience in exile. Reading Yahweh's response through a Bakhtinian frame, we might say the Servant's other in the dialogue—Yahweh—destabilises the Servant's self-awareness, not allowing the Servant's "I-for-myself" to get too carried away with its self-pity. In fact, all the way through the discourses Yahweh is reframing the Servant's self-understanding with reference to his socio-political circumstances.

When the Servant hears himself addressed as Israel, Jacob in 41.8ab for example, Yahweh seems to be locating the exilic community's self-identity within the broader context of the nation as a whole and its history of covenantal relationship with Yahweh. It is the Babylonian exiles who Yahweh is addressing in this way. That the exiles are being assigned names traditionally attached to the nation as a whole is important, since in this designation alone the Servant hears that he is truly Israel, and not some minor portion or version of it. Second Isaiah uses the dual name more than any writer of the Hebrew Bible (17 references, all between chs. 40 and 49). Why? I think it's safe to say that it's precisely because the names have a history—and specifically a history in which Yahweh was free to choose the figure of Jacob and assign him the name Israel, and is therefore free to choose (and name) Israel-Jacob again. A solidarity is established between the people of the past and the exilic community in the present. Which is highly significant for a community that believes it has been abandoned by Yahweh. Not so, Yahweh is effectively saying. You are the still the people I once designated Israel-Jacob. There's no benign doctrine behind the names; there's a long-held belief that the nation has been chosen.

In the words of Yahweh to the Servant, the names "Israel" and "Jacob" are no longer locked in the narratives associated with the past. They're brought refreshingly to life and given new and powerful significance in the circumstances in which the Servant, Israel-Jacob, now finds himself. They're spoken to the Servant at a time when the remnant nation needs to know that it is bound to the people of the past, the people of promise, and to the God who called those people into being.

The term "my Servant" itself reinforces the relationship. It, too, is bound to the knowledge that Israel-Jacob has been chosen by Yahweh, effectively binding the concept of servanthood to election. This reference to the servant in 41.8a is the first time the designation is used by Second Isaiah, and also the first time Israel-Jacob is described as such. What does it communicate to an exilic community whose empirical evidence supports its suspicions that Yahweh has rejected the nation? It communicates both consolation and reassurance—that the Servant has not, nor is he about to, lose his standing, since his election as Servant is grounded in Yahweh's free choice. This motif is repeated throughout Second Isaiah, underscoring its importance to the prophet's message. Perhaps more than anything, the Servant is reminded by these words that he continues to be defined not by the exilic situation in which he finds himself, but by the utterance of Yahweh; that an actual encounter and the uttering of words can override observable realities when it comes to knowledge of self.

Any ambiguity over Yahweh's election of the Servant is removed by his qualifying of the designation Israel-Jacob with "offspring of Abraham," which in turn is complemented by "my friend." It's an effective strategy, to shift attention from your circumstances to the ancestor with whom Yahweh has a long-established friendship, and a firmly grounded covenant (Gen. 12.2-3; 17.1-21). Particularly significant to a nation that's convinced it's been abandoned are the commitments in the original covenantal promises of offspring, land and deity (Gen. 17.8). A question has been raised concerning all three in exile.

The relevance of the reference to Abraham becomes more acute when the Servant is addressed as "you whom I seized from the ends of the earth, and called from its remote parts (Isa. 41.9ab). As Abraham once was (Gen. 12.1), the Servant is now being called from afar. We can't avoid the parallels between the nation that is sent into exile in Babylon, and the patriarch who went from Canaan to Mesopotamia and spent 20 years in servitude.[1]

"Ends of the earth" is a preferred phrase of Second Isaiah to represent the reach of Yahweh's creative and redemptive power.[2] In Isa. 40.28, the prophet responds to the people's lament by reminding them that Yahweh is the "creator of the ends of the earth." The use of the phrase in 41.9a echoes that reference to reinforce that the one who *creates* the ends of the earth is more than capable of *calling* his people from the ends of the earth—as he did with Abraham.

The purpose of Yahweh's discourse to the Servant isn't realised until 41.10, with the command to "fear not." The backdrop is the corresponding fear of the aforementioned coastlands, representing the nations, who are afraid because Cyrus is on the march, conquering all before him. What is this to the Servant? The implications of Cyrus's campaign are ominous—having survived the decimation of Jerusalem by the Babylonian king Nebuchadnezzar, the remnant now faces certain extinction at the hands of another, more terrifying force. The Servant is no longer afraid of his exilic captors—he's afraid of the one Yahweh has stirred in the East. As Goldingay says, the purpose of the "fear not" oracle is "to address an enemy within, the people's low self-esteem, as well as an enemy without" (2005: 112–13).

In the face of fear, the Servant is given two parallel assurances, "I am with you" and "I am your God," followed by the threefold promise of enacted commitment: "I will strengthen you"; "I will help you"; "I will uphold you with my righteous right hand." Yahweh, the very one who has stirred Cyrus into action, is committed to the Servant—Yahweh is his God, and Yahweh will uphold him during the coming onslaught, however unlikely that seems.

Even so, what is the value of Yahweh's words to the Servant when his promises haven't held up in the past? Is there any wonder Israel-Jacob has been complaining "My way is hid from the LORD, my cause is ignored by my God" (Isa. 40.27)? What's the value of being likened to Abraham,

1. See Sommer 1998: 133.
2. 40.28; 41.5, 9; 42.10; 43.6; 45.22; 48.20; 49.6; 52.10.

the "friend" of God, if that friendship failed to prevent the Babylonian onslaught? I suppose the real question in the context of the prophet's activity on behalf of the exilic community is whether they can hear the words of Yahweh and take them at face value in the context of the events of 587 BCE and the approaching threat from Persia.

As if realising that the promise of aid alone will not be enough to assuage the Servant's fears, in vv. 11-12 Yahweh draws the Servant's attention to the plight of his enemies. Their perishing will only add to the miraculous nature of the Servant's liberation, suggesting to the Servant that *anyone* who stands against him—or anyone who causes him to fear—will be reduced to nothing. The utterance is ambiguous enough to suggest that this could as easily apply to the Persians as to the Babylonians.

In summary, Yahweh's imperative to "fear not" addresses two of the Servant's fears. The first is that he has been abandoned by Yahweh, a fear linked to the lament that is echoed in Isa. 40.27. The reality that Yahweh is addressing Israel-Jacob *as* his Servant is an attempt to calm that fear. The command itself has a creative force to it—it is illocutionary, in that by the command itself Yahweh achieves his purpose, which is to realign the Servant's beliefs about Yahweh, about the world, the future, and of course, himself. As Westermann says, "It is the cry which banishes the fear" (1969: 71). The second fear is that the Servant's enemies will overwhelm him. Yahweh's assurance that this will not happen remains to be demonstrated, but the promise of his presence with his people, which is prominent in other exilic texts also, suggests that the fear is not so much that they face a formidable enemy, but that they will do so alone.

In v. 14a the Servant is described by Yahweh in peculiar terms, anticipating a fundamental turnaround in his status and prospects. Yahweh calls him a worm. A variety of explanations are possible. It may be that the insignificance of Israel in relation to powers such as Babylon and Persia is being highlighted. It could be that the term refers to the remnant of Israel as distinct from the nation as a whole, some of whom still remain in the land of Judea, as well as others who are scattered elsewhere. It probably highlights the contrasting fortunes that have and will befall the nation, which ultimately will become a "threshing board" (v. 15a). But as we know from Bakhtin, it's unhelpful to ask what a designation means in the abstract—we need to ask what it means dialogically, in its particular usage between Yahweh and the Servant.

The Servant hardly needs to be reminded of his lowly state by Yahweh, since he is undoubtedly well aware of both his current circumstances and the way he is perceived by the surrounding nations. Israel's own laments make reference to itself as a worm (e.g. Ps. 22.7). Whybray makes this very point.[3] Yahweh's words, rather than seeking to convince the Servant who he is, actually reflect back to the Servant how he is perceived already, not least by himself. In terms of literary devices, it's an example of a character being to revealed to himself as well as to the reader via dialogue. It's also an example of Bakhtin's double-voicing—echoing Israel's own words in order transform its self-understanding, which is the purpose here. The point is that the Servant will not see himself as a worm forever. Indeed, its usage seems only for the sake of magnifying the significance of the Servant's turnaround. It's another case of the utterance addressed *to* the Servant having more formative weight than the observable reality with which the Servant is contending. The "worm" is the reality; Israel has been brought low. But the worm will turn.

The Servant's fortunes will change not because of his own strength, however, but because the one who helps him (echoing v. 13d) is Yahweh. Contrasting "worm" is the description of the Servant as a threshing board (v. 15a, JPS), a new thresher with many spikes (v. 15b) that will thresh mountains to dust (v. 15c). Whether the mountains are an allusion to enemy forces or world powers (as in North 1964: 99) or top geographical elements that lie in the Servant's path home, or even to obstructions to the coming of Yahweh that is referred to in Isa. 40.4-5, is not the main point. It appears that what the Servant will achieve as a thresher is of more significance than the fact of his *being* one. Only in threshing the figurative mountains will the Servant know himself *as* a thresher—and only then will he know himself as something other than a worm. In other words, the emphasis is on the transformation, a transformation that can only occur as the Servant responds to the call of Yahweh. Is the transformation primarily psychological? Does it happen only in the story that the Servant tells himself? It's certainly the case that the transformation occurs dialogically, since only in his self-awareness in response to Yahweh's words does the Servant actually change. As yet, he has achieved nothing. For all intents and purposes he remains the worm. But does the dialogue correspond to externals realities? Or is it merely mind over matter? Or does the word of Yahweh create a new ontological reality? As in any self-other relation, any finished image that the other provides will be repurposed by what Bakhtin calls the "I-for-myself," whose very nature is to process everything within his horizon in line with his own subjectivity. Meaning, the Servant hears Yahweh describe his transformation from worm to thresher, but we are yet to see evidence of how the Servant responds.

3. Whybray 1975: 65.

A Commissioning

A natural reading of the Servant discourse in Isa. 42.1-9 depicts Yahweh in the process of commissioning the Servant in the presence of witnesses, then turning to address the Servant directly. There are two discrete units (42.1-4 and 42.5-9) that are linked not only by their juxtaposition in the final form of the text but also by the fact that Yahweh is the speaker in both and the subject of his discourse is a figure who is being commissioned for a task. The first scene evokes the commissioning of Israel's kings before witnesses (see, e.g., 1 Sam. 9.17; 16.12). It's not primarily for their sake, however, but the Servant's. It broadens what the Servant knows of both his relationship with Yahweh and the purpose behind the reassurances he was given in the previous discourse. What he now learns is that those assurances weren't ends in themselves but were given in order to prepare the Servant for his task.

The opening words of Yahweh concerning the Servant are stunning: "This is My servant, whom I uphold, My chosen one, in whom I delight." That's some reversal. And of course this pronouncement to unnamed witnesses is of the highest significance. Not only is Israel-Jacob no longer the one whose sacrifices Yahweh refuses to accept, as in Jer. 14.12, he's the one on whom Yahweh has placed his favour—and declared so publicly. In his very public declaration, Yahweh is obligating himself to the Servant.

The setting of Yahweh's declaration already suggests a royal designation of the Servant. Westermann argues exilic Israel is being invited to imagine itself in the unique position of discharging the offices of king *and* prophet. These two lines of mediation, which were combined in the one figure of Moses but had since diverged, have again been combined in the office of the Servant. This comes at a time when Israel is very aware that the throne is vacant. The Servant's fear of the coming onslaught from the East is likely exacerbated by the reality he is without leadership and without representation—it's the loss of the king that has partly convinced Israel-Jacob that Yahweh has abandoned him. Presumably the royal imagery of First Isaiah, with its promise of a leader in the mould of David, is known to the people.[4] The Servant might well ask: Where is that leader when the nation needs him the most? Guess what, says Yahweh—you're the man.

The calling is heightened by Yahweh's declaration in v. 1c that he has given the Servant his spirit, and then that the Servant is to bring justice to the nations, or the "true way" (JPS). The giving of the spirit

---

4. See, e.g., Isa. 9.6-7; 11.2-5; 16.5.

is traditionally an action that identifies the king,[5] as it is the mark of the prophet (see, e.g., Num. 11; 1 Sam. 10.6; 11.6). This echoes Westermann's view that the Servant has been assigned a dual role. But Yahweh's words also define for the Servant the manner in which that role will be carried out. In other words, the giving of Yahweh's spirit enables the hero to perform in a particular way—as it does in Isa. 11.1-9, where the giving of the spirit to the royal descendent of Jesse will ensure he has "wisdom and insight" (11.2b), that he receives divine "counsel and valour" (11.2c), and that he possesses "devotion and reverence for the LORD" (11.2d).

The call to bring the "true way," or "justice," to the nations is stated three times—in 42.1d, 42.3c, and in 42.4b. And the three-fold repetition creates a framing device around a series of ironic statements that define, by affirming what is perhaps contrary to expectations, how the Servant will act. Another way of saying this is that the Servant is given limitations. Yahweh's spirit is a restraining force that will prevent the Servant from acting in certain ways. Stating the same thing positively, Yahweh's spirit is a liberating force that prevents the Servant from making certain errors. The utterance of these limitations in the Servant's hearing (Yahweh refers to the Servant in the third person) becomes an invitation for him to respond accordingly. Specifically, the Servant hears that in his dispensing of the "true way" the Servant will not treat heavy-handedly those who are weak or diminished (e.g., he won't "break even a bruised reed, or snuff out even a dim wick," 42.3ab). In turn, the Servant himself won't become weak or crushed ("He shall not grow dim or be bruised," 42.4a). In other words, the same spirit that prevents the Servant from crushing the oppressed will also protect the Servant, who will not be crushed in return.

To summarise what the Servant has heard concerning himself from Yahweh to this point. Firstly, he's been prompted to remember that he has not been abandoned, despite the evidence and despite his laments. Secondly, the Servant has discovered that Yahweh has stood by him for a purpose. As Goldingay says, "Here the position of being Yhwh's servant is a matter of task not just privilege" (2005: 155). Thirdly, the Servant has been reminded that he is being upheld by Yahweh, who will continue to uphold him as he goes about his task. Fourthly, Yahweh has given his spirit to the Servant in order to prevent him from becoming weary or crushed—but also to prevent him from crushing others. This might come as a surprise to the Servant, who has previously been told he will become a threshing board. Taken alone, the image of the threshing board

5. See, e.g., the giving of Yahweh's spirit to Saul (1 Sam. 10.10); and the giving of the spirit to David (1 Sam. 16.13).

could be used to justify aggression against Israel's enemies. It might suggest to the Servant that his hope lies in becoming a mighty nation able to match its enemies on the battleground. But Yahweh's designation of his Servant, before witnesses, as one who will not break a fragile reed radically questions that interpretation. It's said within the Servant's hearing but to the witnesses, so that they can hold the Servant to account. It's on their behalf as much as it is the Servant's. Finally, the Servant has been commissioned in terms that evoke First Isaiah's oracles concerning a future king. In the knowledge that Israel no longer has a king, the Servant is invited to see himself fulfilling the king's tasks—specifically the role of bringing justice, or the right way, to the nations. A mighty commissioning indeed for a fledgling exilic community facing possible extinction from the Persian force headed towards Babylon.

It's on the word "justice" that the Servant's complete turnaround pivots. In 40.27 Israel-Jacob has lamented that "My way is hid from the LORD, my cause (justice) is ignored by my God." This is the whole cause of Israel's despair. But in the Servant discourse of 42.1-9 Yahweh echoes the term "cause" (Bakhtin would say the word is double-voiced by Yahweh) in order to fill it with new meaning. Justice is not something Israel-Jacob is owed, but something the Servant himself will establish. It's worth imaging how Israel might respond to this reframing of its complaint. How does the Servant reconcile Israel-Jacob's lament at being abandoned by Yahweh with the discovery that he will be the means by which justice will go out to the nations? And even that it's he, the Servant, who will judge righteously the nations of the world?[6] If he accepts Yahweh's commissioning, the Servant is called to imagine the re-establishment of the course of history "as determined by God's will and by his insight" (Beuken 1972: 10), and not by the natural contingencies of the socio-political circumstances in which he finds himself. Again, we can only surmise the Servant's astonishment at the magnitude of the task before him, particularly on the basis that the course of the nation's history seems to have been so badly neglected by Yahweh.

6. The equity and righteousness by which the king of Isa. 11.1-9 (see vv. 3-4) was said to judge seems to have taken its meaning from and extended the application of the traditions concerning David's role, seen in his dispensing of justice in 2 Sam. 8.15: "And David administered justice and equity to all his people." David's role resonates also with the actions of Yahweh, who, according to Ps. 37.6, brings forth righteousness like the light, and justice like the noonday—four terms by which the Servant hears his role described in 42.1-9.

If the Servant doubts that he has the strength or capabilities to carry out the task of establishing the "true way" (and why would he not?), Yahweh reminds him that he does not do so in his own strength. This is stated not to the assembled witnesses, as in 42.1-4, but to the Servant directly. Yahweh doesn't leave room for the Servant to object to his appointment on the grounds that he has nothing to contribute—instead, he calls the Servant to a role far greater than what he would have imagined for himself, at least in his present state. What is that role specifically? To be a "covenant to the people, a light to the nations" (42.6d). These are qualified further: "Opening eyes deprived of light" (42.7a) and "Rescuing prisoners from confinement" (v. 7b). The prisoners currently dwell in a "dungeon," "in darkness" (v. 7c). Who is being referred to here?; who is the beneficiary of the Servant's mission, Israel or the nations? The answer isn't straightforward because of the similar ways Israel-Jacob itself is described by Second Isaiah. But the reference to the nations in 42.1d, the reference to the earth in 42.4b, the coastlands in 42.4c, and the nations in 42.6d, clearly suggests that those who are blind and in the dungeon are the nations, not Israel. Yet it can't have escaped the Servant that in his depiction of the nations as blind and imprisoned, Yahweh has echoed discourse in which Israel is depicted in the very same ways. For example, the imagery of "light to the nations" suggests an echo of Isa. 9.1: "The people that walked in darkness have seen a brilliant light." For context, 8.22 describes the distress and darkness, straitness and gloom that have befallen the people. This replaced with the brilliant light that increases the nation's joy (Isa. 9.2). In Isaiah 6, the prophet has had a vision of Yahweh on the throne of the heavenly court and hears the instruction to make the hearts of the people dull, their ears heavy, and their eyes blind. But now, in the dialogic constitution of the Servant, from the mouth of Yahweh and in the hearing of assembled witnesses, a huge shift has taken place, whereby the nations now occupy the place of darkness that has been Israel's, while Israel-Jacob, who was blinded by the prophetic ministry of First Isaiah, has been called to administer freedom and justice.

These are some of the first signs of the transformative event that is the Servant's "voice-idea"—the unique perspective on the world that is embodied in the Servant who is constituted at the intersection of multiple crisscrossing lines of discourse, and which overhauls other perspectives. This is the purpose of the "new things" (42.9b) now spoken to the Servant—the mind-blowing commissioning of the Servant that says, "Stop wallowing in darkness and bring light to the world." Having already been commissioned in a way that revises the nation's hope for a king (and the associated desire for justice), the Servant learns that he will occupy the king's place and will himself administer justice. Now his commissioning (and dialogical constitution) revises the nation's hope for light in the midst of darkness—the Servant will *be* a light for the nations.

And yet the reality is that exilic Israel is no more liberated than the nations themselves, and this is impressed upon the Servant in the following discourse, 42.18–43.7. So, 42.1-9 introduces some complexity into the characterisation of the Servant. Using Bakhtin's terminology it can be described this way: while the Servant knows himself to be Israel-Jacob, and while the Servant and Israel exist simultaneously, it is becoming apparent that they do not occupy the same semantic space. In 42.1-9 we see the first signs that a gap has opened between Servant Israel-Jacob and empirical Israel. We've seen already that the Servant has been invited to see himself fulfilling a royal office. That idea can be expanded to say the Servant, Israel-Jacob, is himself a paradigm by which empirical Israel is invited to see itself. This does not mean, however, that there are two Servants; there is only one Servant—the character that is being constituted by the discourse of Yahweh in the poems of the prophet Second Isaiah, and the character who knows himself as such.

As Israel responds to the words of Yahweh it will discover that it has always been the Servant, the offspring of Abraham. As it responds by *being* the Servant, it will discover that it has been made a "covenant for the people," which I take to mean that he embodies the assurance of Yahweh's intention to bring light to the nations. Through the Servant the promise to bless the nations will be realised. How will this happen? While the discourse is not explicit, the following can be posed on the basis of what has been revealed so far: if the Servant is a paradigm by which Israel is invited to know and comprehend itself—and empirical Israel is still wallowing in darkness, as are the nations—then the response of Israel-Jacob to the voice of Yahweh is itself a sign of liberation, a "covenant" sign to the nations that Yahweh has pierced the darkness. The key to this is the Servant's response: if no one responds to Yahweh's call then there is no Servant. However, if only one person comes to know himself or herself as the Servant then he or she is the one who will act in the way Yahweh has described. The hope, however, is that all of exilic Israel will respond, since, as pointed out already, there are not two servants, just the one: Israel-Jacob.

A Love Story

The Servant discourse of Isa. 42.18–43.7 comprises two discrete units, 42.18-25 and 43.1-7, that are more often than not taken together, not only on the basis of their juxtaposition but also on the grounds of shared language and themes. Muilenburg says the judgment of the first "clearly anticipates he redemption" of the second (Muilenburg 1956a: 475).

At least two voices can be heard in the first unit—that of Yahweh (vv. 18-20) and that of the prophet (vv. 21-25). The subtle distinction between empirical Israel and the Servant that we saw developing in the previous discourse is heightened here, in that Yahweh directly addresses the "deaf" and the "blind" in the plural (42.18ab), and yet refers to his Servant/ messenger, who is also blind and deaf, in the singular (42.19). Even so, there is an expectation that the blind and deaf people will associate with the Servant who is also blind and deaf. Yahweh opens with imperatives calling for a response, apparently from the very people who are unable to respond. The first is directed to the deaf ones, and it's to "listen." The second is to the blind ones, and is to "look up and see." The immediate context suggests Yahweh is being ironic, since the blind, clearly, are not able to see and the deaf are not able to hear. However, v. 20 indicates that this is not strictly the case. The Servant *can* hear and see, but does not do so. Yahweh's imperatives in 42.18 are illocutionary—the command itself enables the deaf to hear and the blind to see. This is a vital component of the dialogical constitution of a character—the words of others, entering the awareness of the self. In this case, those who hear Yahweh and whose self-awareness is shaped by his words have already become the seeing ones and the hearing ones.

The imperatives not only demand a response, they provoke a question— to whom are they addressed? They are uttered so broadly they could be addressed to anyone who is blind and deaf. In the previous discourse, the "blind" to whom the Servant is commissioned to provide light represents the nations, not Israel. Certainly, as Yahweh begins his speech in 42.18 the Servant would not be expected to believe that *he* is among the blind and deaf. But the interrogative voice by which Yahweh speaks in v. 19 challenges this. The Servant is no different to the blind and deaf whom Yahweh commands to hear and see. He is, indeed, a deaf messenger, suggesting that despite his calling he is incapable of discharging his duties.

How the Servant Israel-Jacob might interpret this requires some thought, which begins with the link between this passage and Isa. 6.9-10, and Yahweh's commissioning of Isaiah of Jerusalem to "Dull that people's mind, stop its ears, and seal its eyes—lest, seeing with its eyes and hearing with its ears, it also grasp with its mind, and repent and save itself." Harsh words indeed. Isaiah 6 is pivotal in First Isaiah and it resonates loudly with 42.20. Both discourses speak of senses that are frustrated rather than defective. If the Servant hears Yahweh's discourse in the light of First Isaiah's commission, then he understands his blind and deaf state to be a direct result of Isaiah's prophetic mission—and not purely the result of his own disobedience. If sixth-century Israel-Jacob is indeed blind and deaf then the Servant is evidence that the prophet's preaching to eighth-century Israel-Jacob had its desired effect. This in turn suggests that the exile has not happened because Yahweh has abandoned Israel. Rather, it is an episode in a history very much directed by Yahweh. In other words, Israel's "justice" has not been neglected at all. The opposite is the case. Israel's misfortune has been brought about by Yahweh's very close attention.

Yahweh's imperatives in v. 18 double-voice his original commission to Isaiah of Jerusalem in order to reverse its outcome, as if Yahweh is now saying to Israel, "Your period of blindness and deafness, which I insti-gated, is over." The Servant has already heard that he is the exiled people of Yahweh, Israel-Jacob, the descendants of the very people to whom Isaiah of Jerusalem was sent. Now he discovers that the spiritual darkness suffered by that entire generation continues *in him*—the Servant is made to identify with the original recipients of Isaiah's message, but also to hear the command of Yahweh to see and to hear.

Despite his blindness, and despite his deafness, the Servant is left in no doubt that he remains the Servant. But the one who hears and knows himself to be Yahweh's Servant must also acknowledge that he is blind and dead. He cannot be one and not confess to the other. But in seeing and hearing, the Servant also sets himself apart from the blind of Israel and the nations—those who do not respond. In other words, only the exiles who hear and respond to the imperatives of 42.18 can know themselves as the Servant who is called to free those in darkness. This distinction is reflected in the Targum, which describes the addressees of Yahweh's disputation as the "wicked" who are required to repent before they can be called the Servant.[7]

Empirically, Israel-Jacob knows full well that it is experiencing dark times—it doesn't need to be told. On the surface, the prophet's discourse communicates nothing new. But again in 42.22-25 it does challenge the Servant's belief that his situation has gone unnoticed by Yahweh. Indeed, the reverse is the case—Yahweh not only sees Israel-Jacob's condition, he caused it to happen. There is a real element of futility in Israel's situation.

---

7. Spykerboer makes a similar distinction: "On the one hand, it is clear that the servant is blind and that the messenger whom Yahweh will send is deaf. On the other hand, the servant-messenger can only fulfil his function when his eyes and ears are opened. There is here a fluidity which must not be disturbed by neat distinctions" (1976: 99).

The prophet argues that Yahweh gave Jacob to the looters because the nation wouldn't walk in his ways, here paralleled with not obeying Yahweh's law. But now Israel's situation—as a result of its punishment—is the very thing standing in the way of Yahweh's law being glorified through the Servant. This double-edged judgment is as binding as the divine hardening that resulted from Isaiah of Jerusalem's commission. Israel-Jacob's blindness, like its captivity, is both a consequence of the nation's sin and the very reason the nation has been unable to respond to Yahweh's call.

It's true that the nation has also been blind and deaf to its own culpability in the situation in which it now finds itself. That's why the prophet must now appeal to the Servant. The judgment that came upon Israel-Jacob in the events of 587 was intended to make the nation understand its part—and yet it failed to see it, according to what the prophet now charges. As the disputation ends the Servant's dilemma is clear—but, in a sense, so is the solution. If Yahweh brought about the conditions that keep the Servant in darkness, then Yahweh can liberate his Servant. As Goldingay says, "At the threshold of chapter 43 the logic of the charge is that Jacob-Israel has everything to fear" (2005: 177). But logic collapses. Yahweh provides the Servant with a way of escape. In place of a word of judgment, the Servant hears a voice of mercy.

Yahweh re-enters the discourse in 43.1 with a declaration that is not only unwarranted but, in the context, mystifying: "Fear not, for I will redeem you." When the oracle of 43.1-7 is viewed in its chiastic structure, with v. 4 in the centre, what stands out are the radical words at its heart: "you are precious to me," "you are honoured" and "I love you." The root (אהב) is used in the whole of Isaiah only four times, and only here is it used of the Servant. The utterance could not be made more directly: I (Yahweh) love you (my Servant). Westermann sums up perfectly the striking nature of Yahweh's declaration:

> Here we also have one of the most beautiful and profound statements of what the Bible means by "election." A tiny, miserable and insignificant band of uprooted men and women are assured that they—precisely they—are the people to whom God has turned in love. (Westermann 1969: 118)

It's a message of love in the context of suffering. A love that is forming, liberating, assuring, shaping, engaged, embodied, dialogic. Not a principle, but a promise. But, in light of all that has happened to the Servant already, is this in actual fact gaslighting? It's fair to ask the question considering the context. And the answer depends on the outcome. For the moment,

Yahweh declares that the Servant belongs to him. From the moment of his formation, through the period of darkness in which Israel-Jacob was convinced that he had been abandoned by Yahweh, to the here and now and his call to mission, the Servant has always belonged to Yahweh. And as Muilenburg says, "This belonging is the source of (Israel's) confidence and hope" (1956a: 481). In other words, it's on the basis of Yahweh's spoken commitment to the Servant, Israel-Jacob, that he will be able to respond to the call Yahweh has given him.

Without the profound declaration of love, the disputation of the preceding unit is a bleak pronouncement of judgment. But together they generate an incredible dialogic truth that ultimately is embodied in the Servant's unique voice-idea—not as a general principle, but as a lived experienced—that out of the fire of judgment the nation will be redeemed in the one of the greatest miraculous acts ever witnessed in history. The Servant may no longer labour under the misapprehension that he is cast off by Yahweh, as claimed in the citation of 40.27. The opposite is the case, for good and bad. When the Servant wakens to this he discovers the incredible truth that Yahweh loves him, that he is precious, and that he is honoured.

But can the Servant trust even this? It's a fair question, and seems to be behind Yahweh's assurances in 43.3-7. The Servant's call, his belonging to Yahweh, and Yahweh's love for the Servant, will not remain mere words—they will find historical fulfilment in the act of redemption Yahweh is about to initiate. The Servant hears that Yahweh's words of assurance are no mere lip service; it is love in action, which in the context will prove to be the trading of "more valuable" nations for this band of exiles whom Yahweh loves. Specifically this will be the exchange Yahweh conducts for the sake of his chosen one: "I give Egypt as a ransom for you, Ethiopia and Saba in exchange for you" (v. 3). The strong national-istic tone of this discourse no doubt appeals to the Servant who has been stripped of his national identity. Some commentators have difficulties with this very point. Childs, for example, argues the imagery is meta-phorical, representing the high cost required for Israel's deliverance and the value of Israel to God: "Duhm's interpretation of the exchange as an abandonment of Africa to Cyrus because of disregard for the worth of other nations badly distorts the metaphor" (Childs 2001: 335). But metaphors need a referent and if the purchase of Israel's freedom with the giving of Egypt as a ransom is unthinkable the metaphor breaks down. We need to hear the oracle as the Servant heard it, not with modern sensibili-ties. There could be no greater expression of Yahweh's commitment to the Servant, in the face of the laments we have heard echoed in 40.27 and 42.25, than the surrender of other nations to Cyrus for the Servant's sake.

But there is a greater purpose to Yahweh's words of assurance—the Servant must make the journey home, which is probably the backdrop of the exhortation in 43.2. Words of salvation are accompanied by images of the return, not just from Babylon but from all points of the compass. Yahweh's discourse echoes the theme of diaspora, shifting the emphasis from those who were called in order to bring the nation into being ("I have singled you out by name," v. 1e) to those descendants of Israel-Jacob who will be gathered from afar—indeed, from the East, West, North and South. The prophet contextualises the Servant against the larger history of Israel-Jacob and the bigger problem. But the overwhelming message that will be embodied in the historically grounded response of the Servant is that in the here and now, when there appear to be so many reasons to fear, there are actually none.

The Trial

The prophet's rhetorical strategy ramps up in the discourse framed by 43.8–44.8 as he uses multiple generic voices to shake the Servant into action. But whether disputing with the exiles, or addressing them as if they are on trial, or speaking to them with words of reassurance and promises of salvation, the prophet attempts to impact how Israel-Jacob sees itself as a Servant of Yahweh. The generic voices draw from discourses that have significance to Israel-Jacob in that time and place—the trial, the dispute, the promise of salvation to a ruler in distress.

It begins with a dramatic turn in 43.8 when the prophet commands an unnamed individual, perhaps a bailiff, to "bring out" the blind and the deaf (ESV). The irony of the blind Servant being called to bring light to those in darkness has already been pointed out—the irony is echoed here, where the Servant hears that before he can bring anyone out of the dungeon, he himself must be brought out (from his metaphorical darkness/dungeons). The Servant is indeed brought out, into an imaginary judicial setting, where the nations have gathered to answer the prophet's challenge in 43.9 to produce witnesses and be vindicated in his accusation that they were not able to predict the "former things" as Yahweh did. It's the nations who are on trial here, and the Servant will be Yahweh's key witness. This is the first time the word "witness" has been used in Second Isaiah, and though it is used initially with reference to the nations, in Yahweh's discourse from v. 10 the term is attached to the Servant.

The structure of Yahweh's initial utterance to the Servant in v. 10 binds the voice-ideas of *witness*, *servanthood* and *election* together in the one dialogical partner: the Servant. In other words, the Servant hears that his service is his witness, and his witness is the purpose of his election. His testimony before the nations is his response to Yahweh. This is a key moment in Israel-Jacob's developing belief in who it is before Yahweh, and in terms of the aesthetics of the text it's an equally key moment in the Servant's developing self-awareness. It's here that the Servant discovers why it is that he *is*. The knowing, believing and understanding referenced by Yahweh are the very reason and basis for the Servant's calling and purpose. This is why his blindness and deafness was so tragic; the very purpose of the Servant's election had been thwarted by his disobedience. It was both an epistemological and an ontological challenge to the Servant. As Seitz says, "Knowing and believing and understanding were what failed, leaving a previous generation blind to God's ways" (Seitz 2001: 377).

That the Servant is now being told that he is Yahweh's witness, to know, to understand and to *trust* him, is a significant reversal. He knows that he is blind and deaf (42.19-20) despite being able to use his ears and eyes. Now he is being called to see again; and it is precisely in his role as "witness" that the Servant will discover his sight. Seitz has a wonderful way of summing this up: "No wonder the poet makes persistent reference to the calling of Abraham and the ancestral election; for all intents and purposes, *this generation is meeting God as if for the first time*" (Seitz 2001: 377, emphasis mine).

What Yahweh reveals about himself to the Servant is no abstract theology, but a lived-through, embodied truth: the involvement of Yahweh in Israel's history, its "right way." What the Servant has discovered about Yahweh—with more to come—is unique to the Servant. Again, no abstract theological principles, but impressions of the self, of the other, and of their interaction in the sacred space between. The specific content of Israel's witness will be: that before Yahweh no god was formed (v. 10f); that apart from Yahweh there is no saviour (v. 11b); that only Yahweh, and not some foreign god, has declared and saved and proclaimed (v. 12a-d); that no one can take the Servant from Yahweh's hand (v. 13b); that he is Yahweh, Israel's holy one, creator and king (v. 15). The Servant surely understands that these are realised only in him—that what Yahweh declares concerning himself also fundamentally concerns Israel. The Servant is not only the theatre of Yahweh's self-revelation, but also its key player.

The Servant is confronted with this sobering thought: that far from being neglected by Yahweh, he is now crucial to Yahweh's plans. The trial is an ideal setting for such a dialogic realisation, since in the trial a charge is upheld or dismissed on the basis of a single, crucial testimony, given in a face-to-face encounter with the one making the charge. The dramatic intensity of such an encounter is implicit in this discourse, as it should be. It's precisely in this dramatic setting that Israel discovers just how crucial its testimony is; those to whom Israel will witness must see the Servant's belief in action if Yahweh is to be truly vindicated before their nations and their gods. In the world of the Servant, at least as we have it in the Servant discourses of Second Isaiah, Yahweh's unique ability to fulfil a prophetic word has been most clearly demonstrated in his involvement in the Servant's history. It was Yahweh who made Israel blind; it was Yahweh who brought destruction upon the nation; now it is Yahweh who announces and promises salvation. The Servant is in the unique position to hear and trust this, and then will have the crucial role of paying witness to it. Westermann's oft-quoted statement on this goes to the heart of the issue for the Servant's understanding of his role and identity:

> What here decides a religion's title and claim is neither its spiritual or ethical or religious value, nor its enlightenment or high cultural level; instead, it is continuity in history and this alone, the power of a faith to throw a bridge over a chasm torn open by the downfall of a nation. (Westermann 1969: 122)

Westermann adds: "This, however, requires witnesses to testify to it, that is, those who confess the divinity of the god in question."

The Servant's role as witness to Yahweh's unique ability to speak to things before they happen is emphasised in 44.8, in a disputation that concludes the discourse, forming an inclusio with 43.10 around the phrase "You are my witnesses" and the theme of Yahweh's foreknowledge. Polemic frames the entire discourse, since to this point the Servant has not yet responded to Yahweh's call and therefore his witness to Yahweh's uniqueness remains unfulfilled.

But the nations are not the only ones on trial in this discourse. Where the truth or falsehood of the nations' gods is at issue in the trial scene of 43.8-13, in vv. 22-28 the issue is guilt or innocence—not that of the nations, but of Israel. Yahweh indicts Israel-Jacob (v. 22) and by the conclusion of the trial Israel's plight is adjudged to have been deserved (v. 28). But the trial establishes the guilt of Israel only in order to highlight the radical nature of the pardon at hand. Everything that is said about the Servant confirms his culpability, but in place of judgment he receives mercy. This is a startling moment of realisation for the despondent Servant, and it's a crucial point in his journey of self-discovery. The discourse constructs a matrix of judgment around the Servant only in order to dismantle it and demonstrate that he's actually forgiven. The result is that the Servant comes to know himself not in direct correspondence with his historical circumstances and what they signify but in relation to the promise of redemption and what that denotes. This is achieved dialogically—nowhere else for the time being. In reality, nothing has changed—not yet. The liberator Cyrus has not yet come. But Yahweh's words call for an internal response from the Servant initially. Only later will he be called to act. And when he is called upon to act, it will signify an even greater reversal, because the God who blots out Israel's sins will call the Servant to bear the sins of others. The link between this Servant discourse and that of Isaiah 53 did not escape Westermann:

> What here is the momentary sounding of a note, is to be taken up again in the poems about the *'ebed*, the servant of God: there is to be a servant who, at God's behest, is to take the sins of the others upon himself. (Westermann 1969: 132)

The Servant's new, sinless state is reaffirmed in the short Servant discourse of 44.21-22 (23). The purpose of Yahweh's exhortation to "remember these things, O Jacob" is two-fold: to inform the Servant that his transgressions have been blotted out and, on that basis, to urge his return to Yahweh. The indicative of Yahweh's forgiveness is prior to the imperative of the Servant's repentance. Another way to say this is that the knowledge the Servant gains about himself from Yahweh is what precipitates any action the Servant might make in response. The Servant's knowledge of self must be challenged before he can return.

The imperative to remember indicates a watershed moment in Yahweh's dialogue with the Servant. To this point, Israel hasn't been instructed to remember, in fact the opposite—to "not remember" the former things (43.18). Here is that imperative's counterpoint. In letting go of his idealistic memories of former acts of salvation the Servant is encouraged to remember the new thing—that he has been formed to be the Servant.

The news, in 44.22, that the Servant's sins can be wiped away as easily as a cloud, is profound. Throughout these discourses it has been impressed upon the Servant that certain things prevent him from responding *as* the Servant—his blindness and deafness in particular. But here the way has been cleared, the mist has been banished. The obstacles that seemed so indelible are actually no more than vapour. It's a return to the theme of the Servant's transformation that we see for the first time in 41.14-16, in which Israel the worm becomes a threshing board. Here again, the Servant stands at the threshold of a new beginning.

Cyrus

The central discourse of chs. 40–48 and the high water mark of the disputations that characterise this section of Second Isaiah is 44.24–45.7. It's somewhat different to those I've outlined so far since ostensibly it's addressed not to the Servant but to the Persian leader Cyrus, the one stirred up from the East (Isa. 41.2). The discourse is comprised of two literary units (44.24-28 and 45.1-7) and it's in the latter that Cyrus is addressed, who is also named at the end of the former. Everything that is said in the first unit is to prepare the Servant for the introduction of Cyrus. My discussion on this discourse is brief because it doesn't strictly comply with the others in their dialogical constitution of the Servant. However, it's a pivotal moment in the narrative of Israel-Jacob's demise and restoration—the Servant's faith in Yahweh, which is tied also to the Servant's knowledge of himself *as* the one formed from the womb to be his Servant, gains an historical foothold. The righteousness of the God to whom the Servant is dialogically tied will be measured not only by words but also by the success or otherwise of his chosen liberator. In other words, Yahweh puts his cards on the table and his reputation on the line. In Yahweh's scheme, it's imperative that the Servant accepts Cyrus as Yahweh's anointed; to reject Cyrus is to reject Yahweh (45.4cd).

The Servant's prophetic office has risen to prominence over several discourses but here, in 44.26ab, it undergoes some revision. In 42.19 the Servant/messenger hears that he is blind and deaf—by implication unable to perform his role of witness. In 44.26 the Servant hears that his word is confirmed by Yahweh and that his proclamation of Yahweh's plan is fulfilled—the plan being that Jerusalem will be rebuilt and the land of Judea inhabited again. This implies the Servant has already been liberated to fulfil his calling. This is the theme of 43.8-13—that the blind and deaf would be brought from their holes and serve as witnesses in Yahweh's trial with the idols of the nations. According to 44.26 this is occurring. What may come as a surprise is the specificity of the content of his message, which to now has only been alluded to: that the agent of Yahweh's redemption will be Cyrus whose restoration of Jerusalem is integral to Yahweh's plans (44.26cd, 28cd).

I'll reiterate that the Servant, Israel-Jacob, and empirical Israel, do not occupy the same semantic space. The Servant is a calling waiting to be answered, a mantle waiting to be put on. Or, in Bakhtin's terms, an utterance waiting for a response. The servant office has an active role in Yahweh's salvific plans but that role is not fixed to an historical entity—it is no more, but certainly no less, than an open invitation addressed primarily to Israel-Jacob. This doesn't mean the Servant ceases to be Israel-Jacob. Muilenburg comes close to the position I am advocating when he says that the Servant in 44.26 is "prophetic Israel" (1956a: 518). Hermisson, who believes the prophetic servant of the songs is Second Isaiah himself is nevertheless helpful when he describes the characterisation of the Servant in 44.26 as "not simply 'individual' or even 'autobiographical'. It seeks to do justice to the collective and supra-individual traits in the Servant Songs and to the correspondence between the two Servants" (Hermisson 2004: 46). I agree that the Servant addressed by Yahweh is both supra-individual and collective. However, there are not two Servants—there is one Servant whose dialogical constitution is able to resonate with multiple consciousnesses. In other words, many people can quite validly say, "I am the Servant." The Servant denotes anyone whose internal discourse resonates truly with the discourse of Yahweh that is addressed to the Servant in Second Isaiah.

In the final Servant discourse before the Servant responds, 48.20-21 (22), Yahweh does not speak. It's a short hymn containing a call to praise Yahweh, but it's also a call upon the exiles of Israel-Jacob to be willing to be known among the nations as the Servant who has been redeemed. It's the prophet who addresses the exiles on Yahweh's behalf. Indeed, he emerges from the text of Second Isaiah as another consciousness on the same plane as Yahweh and the Servant. Apart from his speech, we know no more about the speaker than we do about Yahweh or the Servant—all we know is what we hear him say, which is part of the reason so many scholars conflate the prophet with the Servant. His "role" in Second Isaiah is to address discourse to others, in this case the Servant. When I say that the prophet doesn't exist on a different plane to the Servant I'm referencing Bakhtin's idea of the polyphonic hero, who, as a character, exists in the same world as the author, meaning the author possesses no knowledge that the hero has no access to. Here, the prophet doesn't stand over against the Servant as an all-knowing author who treats the Servant as a tool for his own discourse. He respects the Servant as another consciousness alongside his own, and in counterpoint with him. This is essential to the polyphonic "atmosphere" in which a multiplicity of voices are able to dialogue on the same plane.

So, the Servant's call to action in this hymn, coming at a critical juncture in the history of Israel-Jacob, brings to mind all that constitutes "Servant" in chs. 40–48. It anticipates a moment of crisis in the Servant's self-knowledge since unless the exiles heed the prophet's imperatives the Servant Israel-Jacob, as he has been constituted by the discourse of Yahweh, will likely cease to exist. The call upon the Servant is no less than a call to reimagine his future as a nation reborn, fleeing Babylon as it proclaims that Yahweh has redeemed his Servant (48.20).

But how will the Servant respond? As yet, we haven't heard his voice. All that we know about the Servant has come via the speech of Yahweh and the prophet. Little of it has been *about* the Servant, in what Bakhtin describes as "finishing" a character, but *to* the Servant in a way that leaves the way open for the Servant to know speak back. Yahweh's discourse has respected the Servant as a "thou"—his words have anticipated an answer. And by the end of Isaiah 48, having heard so much addressed to this mysterious figure, we are left unable to really describe the Servant as one might a character in a monologic text, because we have not yet seen or heard his witness. We are blind and deaf, like the nations, needing the Servant to speak in order to know whether Yahweh will be vindicated or not.

We—along with Yahweh and the prophet—are still waiting for a response.

WHAT THE SERVANT SAYS TO GOD

"I Am the Servant"

From Isaiah 49 onwards we finally get the full dialogue we've been anticipating since the prophet began calling out Israel-Jacob in ch. 40 and Yahweh addressed his Servant. In Isa. 49.1-6 the Servant finally responds. Then immediately following the Servant's speech in 49.1-6, Yahweh responds to the Servant, in 49.7, 8-12. In 50.4-9 the Servant speaks again, and in vv. 10-11 someone, possibly Yahweh, responds. Then in 52.13-53.12 we encounter an entirely different type of discourse, the introduction and conclusion to which are voiced by Yahweh to an unnamed third party in a manner reminiscent of 42.1-4. But the heart of the poem, 53.1-10b, is spoken by a group whose identity is somewhat veiled. Their discourse is not directed to the Servant, and its content is a confession regarding the Servant's significance upon their own self-knowledge. The question will be what that confession signifies to the Servant, if anything at all, following his response to Yahweh in these initial songs.

But first, we encounter the Servant's response to the utterances of Yahweh from the preceding eight chapters. My reading of the Servant's response is that the poem is a piece of literary imagination that functions as the Servant's faithful answer to Yahweh's call. As such it has echoes of the "voice" of the generic call narrative, particularly that of Jeremiah. I'm not alone in this reading, by any means. Wilson, for example, says the form of Isa. 49.1-6 is dependent upon Jer. 1.4-10, but he also relates it to the prophetic call narratives generally, as well as the calls of Moses and Gideon (Exod. 3–4; Judg. 6.11-17; Isa. 6.1-13; Jer. 1.4-10; Ezek. 1–3) (Wilson 1986: 271).

Essentially, the Servant's speech demonstrates that he is awake to Yahweh's call and that he is ready to answer it faithfully. The many affinities between the poem and the utterances of Yahweh in Isaiah 40–48 highlight its nature as a response. Some scholars argue this doesn't prove anything in terms of the identity of the Servant who responds, only that the allusions demonstrate the language is Deutero-Isaianic. I have no problem with this, since my argument is that the reading strategy must always be dialogic, and avoid engaging with discourse on *a priori* assumptions. Let the dialogue be a check on our assumptions. The alternative approach is that taken by Seitz, who, having decided that the speaker is the same figure who is commissioned in ch. 40, describes the function of this discourse as a "recommissioning" of the Servant, "in the light of developing circumstances at this particular juncture in the discourse, involving the role of Israel, the servant-author, and the nations" (Seitz 2001: 429). I agree the discourse takes place at a critical juncture in the collection but I disagree that it's a recommissioning of the Servant. Since the discourse imitates the call and response of Jeremiah, it seeks to be understood as the first dialogic response of a prophetic figure, alluding to how the Servant understands his call.

The Servant's response is not directed to Yahweh, as we might expect, but to the coastlands, which in Second Isaiah are synonymous with the nations, representing the islands and coastlands to the west, the "people from afar" (49.1b). The Servant's speech to the coastlands begins with his credentials, "He named me while I was in my mother's womb" (v. 1d). While it's true that the phrase evokes the call of Jeremiah, "from the womb" has become synonymous with the Servant in Second Isaiah.[1] The phrase has always signified Yahweh's commitment to his Servant, Israel-Jacob, which began before his "birth." It has also signified the Servant's kinship bond with Yahweh. The significance here is that it is the Servant who is confessing this bond to the nations. The Servant is acknowledging that he belongs to Yahweh, and in doing so his speech is a proleptic fulfilment of Isa. 44.5cd: "Another shall mark his arm 'of the LORD' and adopt the name of 'Israel.'"

The content of the Servant's discourse is self-referential, meaning it's about his own speech. This is expected since in Isa. 48.20 he is commanded to *proclaim*, four times and in four different ways. In 49.2 the Servant likens his speech to a weapon sharpened by Yahweh—in other words, enabled by Yahweh. This acknowledgement is self-consciously dialogic. According to Bakhtin, such knowledge of the significance of others' discourse is a vital aspect of the polyphonic hero:

> Everything must touch the character to the quick, provoke him, interrogate him, even polemicize with him and taunt him; everything must be directed toward the hero himself, turned toward him, everything must make itself felt as discourse about someone actually present, as the word of a 'second' and not of a 'third' person. (Bakhtin 1984: 64)

---

1. For example, in Isa. 44.2, 24.

So we see with the Servant—when he responds in Isaiah 49 it's not with abstract words but with words and images provoked by the discourse of 40–48. By making reference to how Yahweh's utterance has impacted his own discourse, the Servant is highlighting precisely what has provoked his response.

The phrase "He hid me in the shadow of His hand" (v. 2b) draws attention to the Servant's coming to consciousness of his call. It connotes the revelation of the Servant to the nations and possibly even to the emergence of Israel-Jacob from the shadows of exile. It certainly refers to the Servant's response to Yahweh's command to speak to the nations, as he now is. In Isa. 42.22 the Servant is described as a people plundered and despoiled, trapped in holes and imprisoned (hidden) in dungeons. But here the Servant days that he was hidden not in prisons but in Yahweh's hand, transforming the narrative of his captivity and allowing Yahweh his agency. At the same time it builds on the reversal of the idea that Yahweh had abandoned his people (40.27).

Then the Servant quotes Yahweh, and explicitly brings Yahweh's discourse *to* the Servant within the Servant's self-knowledge. This is significant in the particularly dialogical emphasis of our reading strategy so far. When a polyphonic hero double-voices the discourse of an other who has expressed a point of view about the hero—as Yahweh has done regarding the Servant in chs. 40–48—it brings that discourse within the transformational dialogic field of the "self" and eliminates any finishing influence that discourse has had. In other words, the utterance of Yahweh concerning the Servant is dialogised by the Servant, altering its nature. For us the readers—or audience—the knowledge we have built up concerning the Servant from the words of Yahweh is no longer objec-tifying discourse, but knowledge that is now processed by the Servant himself who, having heard it and responded, makes it his own. This is no more but also no less than what occurs in life. It's more than a liter-ary device, but the aesthetics do reflect the way things are when others outside of our consciousness see us, encompass us with their perspec-tives, finish us with their gaze. It's a key observation of Bakhtin in his formative essay *Author and Hero in Aesthetic Activity*:

> All these moments that can consummate us in the consciousness of the other lose their consummating power by being anticipated in our own conscious-ness, and as such they merely extend our consciousness in its own direction. Even if we succeeded in encompassing the whole of our consciousness as consummated in the other, this whole would not be able to take possession of us and really consummate us for ourselves: our consciousness would take that whole into account and would surmount it as just one of the moments

in its own unity (which is not a unity that is given but a unity that is set as a task and, in its essentials, is yet-to-be). The last word, that is, would still belong to our own consciousness rather than to the consciousness of another, and our own consciousness would never say to itself the word that would consummate it. After looking at ourselves through the eyes of another, we always return—in life—into ourselves again, and the final, or, as it were, recapitulative event takes place within ourselves in the categories of our own life. (Bakhtin 1990: 16-17)

In that vein, it's no surprise that the words of Yahweh that the Servant double-voices first are "You are my Servant, Israel in whom I glory" (49.3ab). This utterance by Yahweh is a vital component of the Servant's awakening but, ironically, it also has the most potential to consummate or finalise him, in Bakhtin's terms. Unless the Servant subsumes Yahweh's call within his own consciousness it remains an image thrust upon him from the outside, and risks *defining* him. But by double-voicing it the Servant owns the utterance as an element of his own self-knowing, where we are never capable of speaking the final word concerning ourselves, whether it's spoken to us by God or not. All words spoken to us, any consummating image of ourselves that is directed towards us, is always reconstituted by our self-consciousness, since I never stop experiencing myself from within myself (see Bakhtin 1990: 37). As Bakhtin says,

My own consciousness...I experience as encompassing the world, as embracing it, rather than as fitted into it... In other words, the outward image of a human being can be experienced as consummating the *other*, but I do not experience it as consummating and exhausting *myself*. (1990: 39, emphases original)

As if to press the point, the Servant specifies that his designation is not just as *a* Servant but as *the* Servant, Israel (v. 3b). The title and the name are synonymous and dialogic—spoken by Yahweh, heard by the Servant, then spoken outward to the nations to whom the Servant has been commanded to speak. The Servant *is* Israel, Israel *is* the Servant, and here the Servant Israel responds to Yahweh's call with obedience and self-knowledge, which echoes Isa. 44.5: "This one will...name himself by the name of Israel." I maintain a position on this that remains different from how scholars have addressed the Servant's identity previously. It matters not who actually speaks as the Servant here. What matters is that Yahweh's call has found a respondent, a faithful dialogic partner— Yahweh's word has been fulfilled, and in this very act the task of witnessing to the nations regarding Yahweh's faithfulness and worthiness has been achieved.

Having double-voiced Yahweh's speech to him, the Servant in v. 4 recounts his response to Yahweh. Significantly, the Servant recalls how he resisted Yahweh's call. This is important since it highlights the Servant's independence from the potentially finishing discourse of Yahweh. As in life, the polyphonic hero doesn't merely accept the objectivising discourse of others—he or she argues with it, responds to it, reconstitutes it, voices an opinion on it. In other words, subjectivises it. So it is with the Servant: "I thought, 'I have laboured in vain'" (v. 4a). It echoes the "labour" (יגע) of 40.27-31, where the inability of Yahweh to grow weary is compared to the propensity of even youths to grow "weary" (יגע). In 49.4a the Servant is confessing that his own labour has been in vain, double-voicing Israel's complaint and by doing so acknowledging that Israel has previously failed Yahweh.

But the recounting of past failures is not the ultimate purpose of the Servant's confession. It merely emphasises the Servant's proclamation of Yahweh's faithfulness. Addressing the nations to whom he has been sent, the Servant confesses that he was wrong, and that Israel's "justice" is with Yahweh. In other words, God has not neglected Israel-Jacob after all. This is accentuated by "My recompense was in the hands of my God" (v. 4d), echoing 40.10: "Behold, the Lord GOD comes in might... His recompense before Him." The recompense in 40.10 is the restoration of Jerusalem and Judea, and the emphasis is on it being Yahweh's recompense, rather than one Israel has been able to earn for itself. Here in 49.4 the Servant proclaims that he is prepared to wait for the recompense that comes from Yahweh, rather than the wage for which he has laboured in vain.

The double-voicing of Yahweh's discourse is a major characteristic of the Servant's response and it continues in vv. 5-6. The point to emphasise is that the Servant's response demonstrates he has embraced the discourse by which Yahweh has sought to constitute him. In double-voicing it to the nations the Servant makes it his own; his response to it *witnesses* to its integrity. But in the mouth of the Servant, Yahweh's discourse also has the function of authorisation. It adds weight and purpose to the Servant's utterances to the coastlands.

The Servant begins by acknowledging his kinship bond with Yahweh: "He who formed me in the womb to be His servant" (v. 5b). Yahweh has told the Servant repeatedly that he (Yahweh) formed him, but it was never stated explicitly that Israel-Jacob was formed *to be* the Servant, as it is here (although it is alluded to in 41.9cd). That the Servant expands upon what Yahweh has said to him is consistent with the function of double-voicing in a polyphonic work. The Servant continues to exhibit individuality and the freedom to advance another's discourse for his own purposes. In claiming that he was formed as the Servant from the womb, the Servant effectively commits himself to the role—more than this, he sees "Servant" as his very nature, formed as such before birth and before consciousness. There's no clearer indication of the Servant's acceptance of Yahweh's discourse addressed to him than this.

The purpose of the Servant's call—to bring Jacob back to Yahweh and to gather Israel to him—typically causes monologic reading strategies to overheat at this point, because they are unable to fathom how it is that the Servant Israel has a mission *to* Israel. The typical responses are that "Israel" in v. 3 is a gloss, or that the Servant is the prophet and not the nation, or that the subject of the infinitive in v. 5c is Yahweh. The difficulty arises because this verse is often interpreted in isolation from the previous discourses, in which we've already observed a fluidity between those of Israel who know themselves to be the Servant, and those who do not. But the problem—and the solution—is particular to the Servant's dialogical constitution: the one who is called to restore Israel-Jacob back to Yahweh is the one who has heard Yahweh's call and knows himself to be the Servant. in actuality, this might be the prophet or it might be a section of the exilic community—but when this Servant responds he does so *as* the Servant Israel-Jacob.

The discourse in v. 6 places the Servant on the threshold of his new mission. The thing that is "too little" concerning the Servant's mission is the raising up of the tribes of Jacob and the restoration of the survivors of Israel. What's envisaged here is the bringing back of the scattered of Israel, referencing the Servant's mission of proclaiming forgiveness to those of Israel-Jacob who are in exile beyond the borders of Babylon. Among the first of the exiles to respond to the call to servanthood have been those in Babylon, who were then called to take that word of salvation to the tribes scattered abroad. This is referred to explicitly in Isa. 48.20-22, where the Servant is commanded to flee Babylon proclaiming the redemption of Yahweh. The role of restoring is an active one—one of leadership—on behalf of passive Israel, here in v. 6d described as the "survivors" or the preserved (נצר). The word signifies those who have been watched over— an interesting acknowledgement by the Servant in light of Isa. 40.27-31, where the accusation was that Yahweh had disregarded Israel. Here the Servant admits that Israel has been watched over the whole time. It also evokes the Servant discourse of Isa. 42.1-9, in which Yahweh promised to "keep" (נצר) the Servant (v. 6c). Notably, the Servant also heard that Yahweh would make him a light to the nations, a phrase the Servant double-voices in 49.6e. It appears almost certain the double-voicing is intentional—yet again, it demonstrates the Servant's faithful dialogic response to Yahweh's call. It confirms not only that the Servant has heard it, but that he has defined himself by it. As already pointed out, this brings Yahweh's discourse within the Servant's self-consciousness and makes it his own. This produces a particular effect in a polyphonic text. It elevates the character in terms of his self-awareness, demonstrates that he is a thinking self; someone to contend with, to dialogue with. The Servant is constituted as much by his own discourse as by that of others. This has implications when we come to discussing what the Servant signifies in the final form of the text. For now we can say that the Servant has a purpose and a perspective that no one else has. Bakhtin's way of saying this is that the polyphonic hero occupies a unique semantic space in the discourse.

The purpose behind the Servant being a light for the nations is so that Yahweh's "salvation" (Heb.) will reach to the "ends of the earth" (v. 6f). The phrase refers to the nations, since the "ends of the earth" is set over against the tribes of Jacob and the survivors of Israel. However, the Servant's mission to the nations is an extension of his calling to Israel, not a substitute for it. The point is that the Servant's knowledge of the extension of his mission has been unveiled by Yahweh. The Servant, in turn, reveals this to the very nations to whom he is being sent. In a profoundly dialogic way, the Servant pivots between Yahweh's words addressed to him, and his own words addressed to the nations. We, the readers, stand with him, at the point at which he double-voices a dialogue with Yahweh in order to redirect it outward. We discover him both on the threshold of the mission and at the point at which he accepts it. In other words, when we hear the Servant speak he has already decided to act upon Yahweh's prior direction. We discover him in the process of acting upon it. His self-consciousness is revealed to us as he thinks and puts words to his thoughts. There's no record of this dialogue outside of what we hear the participants say, which means this, in terms of the aesthetics: the Servant exists beyond the normal finishing practices by which we assess a character's "meaning" and function in a text. He remains a character with which we must engage, rather than one about whom we can form a fixed opinion.

And engage is what precisely Yahweh does, in vv. 7-12, where the Servant initially hears that though he is despised by the nations, he will nevertheless provoke a stunning reversal in them; and that Yahweh continues to uphold him.

The new knowledge—new, at least, in the discourses that have constituted the Servant to this point—is that he is "deeply despised" (v. 7c) and "abhorred by the nation" (v. 7d). The Servant hears this uttered, however, in the context of information that he is more familiar with—that he has been redeemed and chosen by Yahweh, the Holy One of Israel. It shouldn't surprise us to hear new discourse about the Servant introduced by Yahweh at this point. Such is the nature of a dialogic text—the dialogue continues to advance and the participants continue to learn new information. If the discourse followed a predictable path it would not be polyphonic. While the Hebrew is problematic (and I have chosen to veer from the JPS at this point), the overall sense is clear: the Servant is deeply despised. This sets up the final song, Isaiah 53, where this description will be echoed. There's a question mark over whether "nation" refers to Israel or is a collective noun representing the "nations" to whom the Servant is being sent as a light. The key is how the Servant understands the reference, and the phrase "the slave of rulers" in v. 7e clarifies it. The Servant hasn't been referred to like this anywhere else—indeed, he knows himself only as the Servant of Yahweh. The imagery contrasts how the Servant is seen by the nations with how he is viewed by Yahweh. The Targum's translation is informative: "to those despised among the Gentiles, to those cast out among the kingdoms, to those who are servants to rulers." The phrase "slave of rulers" depicts Israel-Jacob in its exilic state, scattered among the nations and serving foreign kings. The lowly state of the Servant "of rulers" is contrasted with the stunning reversal that is depicted as kings "seeing" the Servant and falling prostrate because of him. The Targum is more specific about what the kings will see—they will see "them," the servants, the exiles.

The description of Yahweh as faithful in v. 7h is a reminder to the Servant that the nations' reversal will not depend upon his performance but upon Yahweh himself. As if to press the point, Yahweh reminds the Servant of his status as "chosen" (v. 7i). Then, as Yahweh's response to the Servant begins in earnest in v. 8, we're struck by the dominant dialogic style, couched in I-Thou language: "I answer you"; "I help you"; "I created you"; "I appoint you…." My reading is that the moment of liberation from exile is in view—that from the progression in the Servant discourse, and particularly the imperatives of Isa. 48.20-22, Cyrus has already come. It's not the only reason for the tone of fulfilment, however. The Servant has now spoken, actualising Yahweh's promises by coming to know himself in light of Yahweh's speech.

When the Servant is described as "a covenant" in 49.8d the echo of 42.6d is unmistakeable, and also draws in 49.6. The description evokes the promise, because the Servant embodies the promise of Yahweh's redemption to the nations. His witness—namely, his faithful response to Yahweh—is a sign of that redemption to those who remain in darkness (see Isa. 49.9ab and its links with Isa. 42.7 and 42.22). Three infinitive clauses qualify the nature of the Servant's covenantal role: (1) to restore the land; (2) to allot the desolate holdings; (3) to say to the prisoners, "Go free." The roles clearly belong to the first group of exiles to leave Babylon—and they are representative of the Servant who has responded obediently to the call of Yahweh. The "people" attached to the word "covenant" could be understood either to refer to Israel in exile (as in JPS) or to the nations—or, indeed, to both. But in Isa. 42.6 the reference is to the nations, and my reading is that the nations should be understood by "nations" here (as in ESV). If so, then the Servant's re-establishing of the land in Judea is intended to be a sign of promise to the nations.

To "allot anew the desolate holdings," in light of earlier allusions to the patriarchal traditions, refers to the land of promise that was made desolate during the events leading to exile. In Isaiah, the heritages sometimes refer to the people themselves (Isa. 19.25; 47.6), but here the reference is to the land. The land is pictured as a birthright, and the allotting refers to the redistributing of it among those who are its rightful heirs.

The Servant will also say to the prisoners, "Go free," and to those in darkness, "Show yourselves." The identity of the prisoners is questionable, but it's not to be taken literally anyway. The term is a figure of speech, like prison, darkness and blindness in 42.7, to describe anyone who does not know Yahweh. But its use in the context of the imagery of the returning exiles in 49.8-12 suggests that here it is being applied to the exiles scattered abroad.

That the vision of redemption extends beyond the exiles in Babylon is confirmed by the imagery in v. 12. It's also another indication that the Servant does not know himself as *all* Israel. The Servant is a "you" in this discourse, while the remaining exiles are a "they." The effect is to impress upon the Servant that despite his words in the discourse of 49.1-6, particularly in v. 6, and its focus upon the nations, his mission still very much includes the exiles at the "ends of the earth." My reading is that this is the reason the kings and princes of the nations will rise and then bow down in worship—they cannot fail to see the redemptive work of Yahweh on behalf of the exiles because they have been dwelling throughout their own lands.

What the Servant Says about Suffering

Vindication at Hand

The second discourse in which we hear the Servant speak is comprised of two units: vv. 4-9, in which an anonymous voice is heard, and vv. 10-11, in which the voice of the first unit is identified as the Servant's, by a separate though equally anonymous voice that is usually taken to be that of Yahweh. Only Isa. 50.4-9 is recognised as the so-called third Servant song. It isn't immediately apparent that this is the Servant Israel-Jacob speaking, which is one reason why the Servant of the song is presumed to be someone other than the exiles. The song seems to set an individual over against the nation. When the Servant speaks in 50.4-9 he does so in contrast to the nation that is addressed by Yahweh in 50.1-3 but which remains silent (v. 2b). The image of a nation that continues to walk in darkness and doesn't speak is in stark contrast to the figure who self-consciously acknowledges the dialogic nature of his relationship with Yahweh: "The Lord GOD gave me a skilled tongue, to know how to speak timely words to the weary. Morning by morning, He rouses, He rouses my ear..." (v. 4a-d). While the bulk of the Servant's discourse in this song concerns his suffering and his confidence in Yahweh's vindication, this is how he chooses to begin—by acknowledging that Yahweh is the one who stirs his utterance. This is something new that we discover about the Servant, who's also sharing this knowledge for the first time; he is more than Yahweh's Servant, he's Yahweh's pupil (disciple).

The target of the Servant's informed tongue is the "weary" (v. 4b), a term that revives the Servant's connection with those who complain to the prophet in 40.27. The Servant's task is to sustain them with speech (ESV). But who are "they"? The term "weary" has only referred to Israel in Second Isaiah, particularly in the all-important disputation in 40.27-31. This suggests again that, in the Servant's self-conscious, he is someone other than empirical Israel. Does that mean, as some scholars suggest, that in this poem an individual Servant is in view? I've maintained all along that the Servant Israel-Jacob does not occupy the same semantic space as empirical Israel. I've also suggested there's a distinction between the

Servant that has responded to Yahweh's call and the nation that remains in darkness. The Servant's declaration that he sustains the weary is consistent with this, but it doesn't necessarily mean the Servant *is* the prophet. Even though the prophet has crafted this discourse, it is spoken *as* the Servant who has responded to the formative utterance of Yahweh. Even here there is only one Servant, Israel-Jacob.

Israel's inability to hear has been a major theme of Second Isaiah, even outside the Servant discourses (see Isa. 40.21, 28; in the discourses see Isa. 42.18, 20, 23, 24). In spite of, and perhaps because of this, the Servant is commanded to hear (Isa. 44.1), and then to proclaim (the complement of hearing) (Isa. 48.20). The Servant's statement here that Yahweh awakens him to hear (v. 4cd) is a reinforcement of the theme—his hearing and subsequent proclamation are two sides of the one act of servanthood. The opening of the Servant's ear has enabled him to act in a way that defines him as obedient Israel, Yahweh's faithful partner in dialogue, his friend and beloved. "I did not disobey," says the Servant (v. 5b). "I did not run away" (v. 5c). I want to emphasise that the speaker in the song makes no distinction between himself and Israel—the distinction is between a response that is obedient and one that is rebellious. But he does emphasise that he has not responded in a way that is analogous with the response of Israel in the past.

The Servant remains consistent with the polyphonic design of Second Isaiah. In echoing themes that have reverberated through Second Isaiah, the Servant yet again maintains for himself the final word about himself. In responding to discourse about and to him, he demonstrates that he constituted not by arbitrary words, but by a specific word, and by his own specific dialogic response. As Bakhtin says:

> The author does indeed leave the final word to his hero. And precisely that final word—or, more accurately, the tendency toward it—is necessary to the author's design. The author constructs the hero not out of words foreign to the hero, not out of neutral definitions; he constructs not a character, nor a type, nor a temperament, in fact he constructs no objectified image of the hero at all, but rather the hero's discourse about himself and his world. (Bakhtin 1984: 53)

This is precisely what we have here—not an objective image of a hero, as if we could say this is the prophet or this is the nation. We are not afforded that privilege, since this is not a typically monologic text. We have the hero's discourse and through that discourse we have an impression of who it is that speaks. But at the end of the utterances in vv. 4-5 all we can say is that the hero is conscious of being obedient to the awakening word of Yahweh, an utterance that summons all previous accusations against Servant Israel and dispels them—someone has responded to the call, demonstrating both its efficacy and the trustworthiness of Yahweh in uttering it.

In vv. 6-7 an entirely new scenario is introduced, one that is so confronting it has remained through the history of interpretation the dominant paradigm through which to understand this enigmatic figure. To this point in the Servant discourses any "suffering" has been alluded to in a general way, such as in 42.25 and 43.28, both of which are spoken by Yahweh *to* the Servant and allude to the destruction of Jerusalem. Nowhere has the Servant been told or said that his ministry to the nations will involve suffering. But it has been hinted at—in 42.4 it was said of the Servant that he would not grow faint or be discouraged, perhaps in the face of persecution. Those who are incensed at the Servant in 41.11 are perhaps those who will persecute him. And in 49.7 the Servant hears that he is deeply despised and abhorred by the nations. So, while the imagery of persecution used by the Servant in 50.6-7 has no direct precedent, it comes as no complete surprise either.

As a polyphonic hero, it's fitting that the Servant himself introduces this new knowledge—demonstrating that his horizon is broader than our own. Previous discourse centred on knowledge introduced by Yahweh, but now, from his own mouth, we discover something else. "I offered my back to the floggers, and my cheeks to those who tore out my hair" (v. 6ab). The sense is clear—the hero has been beaten, but yet, in v. 6c, he has endured it willingly. The imagery evokes Lam. 3.30, in which the speaker urges those who wait on Yahweh to "give his cheek to the one who strikes" and "be filled with insults." When in Isa. 50.6ab the Servant claims to have willingly taken the suffering that Lam. 3.30 describes, it's difficult to avoid the implication that the Servant sees himself as fulfilling that original exhortation. In other words, the Servant echoes the past experiences of the community, and in the process reconstitutes those memories in a transformative stance before Yahweh. The Servant embodies that new posture. The following observations by Tull are important:

> First, by taking most of its material from the middle portion of the lament, Isaiah places more emphasis on the speaker's hopeful words than on his laments and complaints, which were originally far more numerous. Second, the speaker in Second Isaiah describes himself as displaying the qualities that the Lamentations figure does not claim, but merely envisions and prescribes. Third, all complaint language is removed from the sufferer's mouth and attributed to another speaker... (Tull Willey 1997: 219)

There is one figure who complains to Yahweh in Isaiah 49–55, as distinct from the Servant who utters his devotion. That is the figure of the Daughter of Zion (Isa. 49.14). As Tull points out, Second Isaiah appears to have "reemployed" the figure of Daughter Zion from Lamentations 1–2 in order to voice the community's ongoing complaint to Yahweh, while reimagining the figure of Lamentations 3, who "exemplifies those who contend with confusion and opposition" (Tull Willey 1997: 219), as the faithful, yet suffering, Servant. The Servant has suffered what the community has suffered, and also knows that he has suffered it in a way that fulfils the prescribed act of faithfulness to Yahweh envisioned by the righteous speaker of Lamentations 3.[1] The Servant's acceptance of the harsh realities of exile flies in the face of the prevailing view among the exilic community that Yahweh's punishment went too far (reflected in the community's complaint to the prophet, 40.27, and echoed in the voice of Zion, 49.14).

The Servant also appears to embody a reversal of the prophet Jeremiah's experiences as a Servant of Yahweh. In the discussion of 49.1-6 I noted that the Servant's discourse imitates aspects of Jeremiah's call, re-emphasising his awareness that he has been called to a prophetic office. In the present discourse the association between the Servant and Jeremiah undergoes some development, with one outcome being that we are in no doubt the Servant in 50.4-9 is *not* Jeremiah. Jeremiah's oracles undergo some dialogic revision in the hands of the Servant, much as he has done with Israel's exilic laments. The Servant brings Jeremiah's experiences within his own horizon in order to reconstitute them as a faithful respondent to Yahweh would. For example, we see Jeremiah deeply resenting the ridicule put on him (Jer. 20.7-9), but the Servant accepting it (50.5); Jeremiah wanting to avoid his abuse (Jer. 20.10), but the Servant giving his back (50.6); Jeremiah's statement of trust regarding the shame and humiliation his persecutors will suffer (Jer. 20.11), but the Servant not hiding from humiliation and therefore suffering neither it nor shame (50.6-7). While Jeremiah provides a paradigm by which the Servant's faithfulness can be understood, the Servant acts as a foil, another "voice," that casts a critical hue over the career of the famed prophet.

---

1. Krašovec's description of how the people of Lamentations come to a realisation of God's righteousness, reflects the righteousness of the Servant in Second Isaiah: "The suffering people come gradually to terms with the fact that they are being punished, terribly but rightly. Accepting God's justice by recognising their guilt is seen by the poet as essential to the change of heart needed by Israel for her deliverance" (Krašovec 1992: 225).

The Servant's capacity to face and accept his suffering is enabled by his hearing of Yahweh's word and being stirred by it morning by morning. There's an implicit suggestion that the opposite course of action would be rebellion; that turning away or not accepting suffering would be a lack of faithfulness. This is troubling. How this is to be understood needs to be explored, because it raises questions about the nature of suffering and obedience to God—which is at the heart of damaging religious ideology on suffering. But does it raise those questions? In other words, can we extract from the third Servant song a general theological principle about suffering? My answer is no. The song says nothing about the possibility or otherwise of links between suffering and obedience. The truth of this imagery is dialogical. That is, it's embodied in the Servant, not a general principle, and it makes sense only if the suffering described refers to the situation of exile. To turn away from suffering in the context of the song means to not accept that the suffering of exile was brought about by Yahweh. Turning away means believing that capricious historical forces were at play or that the gods of Babylon were the cause of Israel's exilic misery or even that Yahweh no longer cared about his people. A generalised suffering is not an aspect of the Servant's call, as if his suffering would be redemptive in and of itself. Rather, the Servant accepts what he has heard Yahweh say about Israel's exilic suffering, namely that it was Yahweh who "gave Jacob over to despoilment and Israel to plunderers." It was Yahweh who gave Jacob to utter destruction and Israel to reviling (Isa. 43.28, ESV). Such knowledge and acceptance has become an integral aspect of who the Servant knows himself to be. He cannot be the Servant, Israel-Jacob, if he does not also acknowledge that he *is* the Israel-Jacob upon whom Yahweh brought his judgment. This is why he does not hide his face from disgrace and spitting (v. 6cd).

The Servant acknowledges not only the suffering and shame that have been directed at him, but that the intervention of Yahweh counteracts the effects of his treatment. The Lord Yahweh "helps" the Servant (v. 7a). The assertion is repeated (in v. 9a), emphasising its importance to the Servant's self-knowledge, and his knowledge of Yahweh. It doesn't matter whether the Servant's suffering is literal or figurative—what matters is that the Servant has embraced Yahweh's words and sublimated them to make sense of events that are happening to him beyond the horizon of the text, reinforcing his independence from the discourse that we have access to. We have no description of the suffering that the Servant is recounting, other than his words. But we do have those words, the Servant's own discourse, and what the Servant through that discourse chooses to emphasise is that he has been helped by Yahweh. The suffering itself has been relativised to say something about the Lord to whom Israel-Jacob is a Servant. And it's because Yahweh helps that the Servant hasn't been disgraced (v. 7b). Yahweh's help cancels out the impact of the insults on the Servant. It also enables the Servant to withstand the physical assault upon his own face, which he is able to set like flint—the implication being that when his floggers tore out his beard he was able to stand the pain.

Yahweh's words to the Servant continue to resonate in the Servant's claim (in vv. 8-9) that his "vindicator is at hand" (v. 8a). The nearness, or otherwise, of Yahweh has been a prominent theme in the opening Servant discourses. This imagery not only echoes the content of those poems—the voice of confidence that challenges its audience echoes the form of disputation that is prominent in Isaiah 40–48. The Targum highlights the Servant's surety in his own vindication: "My innocence is near. Who will go to judgment with me? Let us stand up together." This is the voice of someone absolutely certain of their own justification, and it's entirely appropriate considering how much Yahweh's formative words in the earlier discourses has sought to convince the Servant of his forgiveness. So, from his lowly and disheartened state, here the Servant is, ready to stand against anyone who will come against him, secure in the knowledge that Yahweh himself has vindicated him, and not because he is strong in himself. The Servant's challenge, "Let us stand up together!" (v. 8c) suggests the nations and their rulers of Isa. 49.7 are in view, since these have emerged as the Servant's only adversaries in Second Isaiah. When he qualifies that with "Who would be my opponent?" the issue isn't one of his opponent's identity but of their capacity. There is no adversary (literally, "master of my justice") who can challenge the Servant. Having bemoaned Yahweh's neglect of his justice in Isa. 40.27, Israel-Jacob, as the Servant, now challenges anyone to dispute it. And in this, the Servant embodies a complete reversal of Israel's prior attitude towards Yahweh; his confidence is that of a people who have fully moved beyond their doubt. Even accusations of guilt are inconsequential ("Who can get a verdict against me?" v. 9b). The Servant has accepted the guarantee Yahweh has given him. In short, the Servant knows himself as one who has been utterly forgiven, and therefore cannot be accused.

What the Nations Say about the Servant

The Man of Sorrows

The final Servant discourse, in which an anonymous group confesses how their view of the Servant has been radically changed, plays a special role in the Servant's polyphonic design. The "we" who speak in 53.1-10 occupy a unique semantic space in relation to the Servant. Their voice contributes to the Servant's constitution like no one else's has, so what they say with reference to the Servant is of vital importance. Where Yahweh has, in a very real sense, called the Servant into being, and the Servant has been the willing respondent of that call, the "we" testify to the significance of that response upon them. Their discourse gives the Servant a picture of how his faithfulness has and will impact others. It expands the Servant character beyond the I-Thou relationship he has with Yahweh; it opens the dialogue by which the Servant knows himself, ensuring it doesn't become closed but becomes an open invitation for anyone to voice a similar confession.

From an objective viewpoint the speaking "we" are anonymous, but we do get a sense of who they know *themselves* to be. The clue is in v. 3d, where they say of the Servant, "he was despised, we held him of no account," echoing Isa. 49.7 and revealing themselves to be the very nations the Servant addresses in Isa. 49.1. They are also the kings who will "see and arise" (Isa. 49.7). However, since the poem is ambiguous concerning their identity, it's very possible their openness to reinterpretation (by many occurrences of "we") is as much a feature of their aesthetic constitution as it is with the Servant himself.

Goldingay has drawn attention to the chiastic shape of the entire poem (2005: 47) and his suggested outline is helpful in discerning its overall purpose.[1] I'll be guided by its shape in the following discussion, which

---

1. Verses 13-15: My servant will triumph despite his suffering; v. 1: Who could have recognised Yahweh's arm?; vv. 2-3: He was treated with contempt; vv. 4-6: The reason was his suffering for us; vv. 7-9: He did not deserve his treatment; vv. 10-11a: By his hand Yahweh's purpose will succeed; vv. 11b-12: My servant will triumph because of his suffering.

follows three key utterances: Yahweh speaks concerning the Servant; the nations speak concerning the Servant; Yahweh concludes concerning the Servant.

Yahweh Speaks concerning the Servant

Yahweh's discourse frames the poem structurally, thematically and dialogically. His voice of assurance and exaltation sets the tone. It presents the Servant as one whose depth of lowliness is dramatically reversed by his lofty exaltation. This drama is played out in full view of the kings of the nations, whose reversal concerning their perception of the Servant and his suffering is equally dramatic.

As Yahweh begins with "Indeed" (or "Behold," ESV) in 52.13 the sense is that the Servant is a witness to an exchange between Yahweh and the nations. It signifies to the Servant in a refracted manner, by allowing the Servant to observe how his servanthood has impacted others—much like how Scrooge witnesses the impact of his past behaviour upon others in Dickens' *A Christmas Carol*. Except here the opposite occurs—the Servant witnesses his triumph, a triumph based on his faithful response to Yahweh. In 52.14 Yahweh contrasts the Servant's exaltation with the more down-to-earth and imminent reality of the Servant's lowly state. Yahweh's description of the Servant is as close to an objective and finishing image of the Servant as we come. However, the inclusion of the apparently misplaced second person prepositional address in v. 14a ("As many were astonished at *you*," ESV) maintains the polyphonic and dialogic design, perhaps by accident. As it stands in the text, its impact is to make Yahweh appear to turn to address the Servant, before turning back to the kings of the kings to press his point.

The Servant's appearance is emphasised in v. 14bc as "marred…unlike that of man, form, beyond human semblance." This is what the nations see. The Servant's exaltation will force them to see him in a different light, but here Yahweh confirms that the one they will see high and lifted up is the same one whose appearance was disfigured. The Servant has heard himself described like this before (Isa. 49.7). In Isa. 43.28 Yahweh described Jacob-Israel as the one delivered to utter destruction and reviling. So Yahweh's description of the Servant here is nothing new. He already knows himself to be this disfigured victim of judgment and destruction. Those of exiled Israel who have heard Yahweh's discourse and who know themselves by it understand this to be the case—as a nation they have been pummelled by the nations to the point of unrecognisability. Their suffering has left them isolated.

The reaction of the nations to what happens with the Servant is described as the kings being silenced (lit. shutting their mouths). It's another reference to speech, or, rather, the lack of it. The mouth represents discourse throughout Second Isaiah (45.23; 48.3; 49.2; 51.16), and here it's disrupted because the kings "see" (v. 15c) and "understand" (v. 15d) that which they have not been told/heard. In other words, the kings have witnessed with their own eyes and not needed to rely upon the witness of others.

The Nations Speak concerning the Servant

Despite having been silenced by the Servant, the nations do actually speak—in Isa. 53.1-10. Significantly, what we discover about them is not their identity, or their role in the world, or their belief in Yahweh, or how they appear—we discover their thoughts on the Servant's significance to them. The speaking "we" enter the discourse of Second Isaiah in order to relay what the Servant *means* to them. Scholars who hope to find clues about the Servant's "identity" in this poem inevitably leave frustrated, because it's not what the confession is about—it's a highly subjectivised account of how the nations have come to realise the Servant's significance, a powerful corollary to Yahweh's call for the Servant to step out of the darkness, and an equally powerful response to the Servant's faithfulness in the face of suffering.

In both 53.1 and 10, the nations claim that what they have witnessed has been according to the purpose of Yahweh. Their realisation seems to be the cause of the astonishment with which v. 1 begins. This note of incredulity sets the tone for the entire poem—the nations can scarcely believe what they themselves are confessing. This much is indicated by the opening rhetorical question: "Who can believe what we have heard?" (JPS), or "Who has believed what he has heard from us?" (ESV).[2] As Muilenburg has pointed out, the question anticipates the answer "No one!" (1956a: 618). What the nations have witnessed, and the significance they have come to attribute to it, was something they never thought possible. Part of what they have come to realise is that the Servant's "sickness" that is depicted graphically in the main body of the poem is not a random occurrence but is caused by Yahweh. Their purpose, however, is

---

2. לשמעתנו is variously translated with "we" as the messenger, so "our report/message" (KJV/NIV) or with "we" as the recipient of the message, "what we have heard" (RSV; cf. JPS). Since the speaker is in the act of speaking about the Servant my preference is to recognise him/them as the messenger in 53.1a.

not to make a general statement on theodicy, but to demonstrate that the nations are aware of Yahweh's involvement in the Servant's plight—and the explicit idea that Israel's exile represented the payment of a debt for sin, which is first introduced in Isa. 40.2.

In all of Yahweh's discourses addressed to the Servant, he never suggests the Servant is a guilt offering, as occurs in 53.10b, evoking the use in Leviticus of the word אשם.[3] The Servant doesn't refer to the imagery either, in his responses. But what the nations suggest in Isaiah 53 is that the Servant has compensated Yahweh not only for his own sin, but for the nations' sins as well. Yet again, I stress how this signifies dialogically— that is, the nations are describing what has happened to the Servant in the language of offering for the *Servant's* sake, that by this discourse he will come to see himself in light of the significance his suffering has had upon the nations of the world. The signification is not that the Servant is an actual sin offering, but that the offering metaphor has meaning for both the nations and for Israel. The latter's narrative of exile takes on an entirely new significance if the Servant interprets his suffering as compensation to Yahweh for the sake of the nations. And according to the nations in Isaiah 53, this was Yahweh's will all along.

Add to this the belief among the nations that the Servant not only suffers as part of Yahweh's plans but that, as a result of his offering, the Servant's life will be extended. He will see offspring and have long life (v. 10c) and through him Yahweh's purpose will prosper (v. 10d). It is difficult to see how the Servant will have prolonged life if he is an historical figure (other than the nation); but if the Servant is a paradigmatic figure by which Israel is invited to recognise itself, then it is possible to see how such a figure cannot be finished off. Unfinalisability is a key feature of a character who is constituted dialogically, so life after "death" is consistent with the Servant's dialogic constitution. The Servant paradigm will live on even after the prophet has gone, or indeed after the exilic generation has been forgotten. This is consistent with the promise of offspring that has been a vital element of the Servant's self-knowledge (see Isa. 44.3). From the unique perspective of the nations in Isa. 53.10, the possibility of offspring is linked to the giving of the Servant's life as a guilt offering. This reflects Israel's situation historically—in exile, there is a very real possibility of the extinction of a nation. If the Servant had not responded to Yahweh's call—that is, if at least someone of Israel had not responded to the prophet's message—Israel-Jacob would have faced the prospect of languishing in Babylon until the remnant's presence had been wiped

---

3. See Lev. 5.6-25; 6.10; 7.1, 2, 5, 7, 37; 14.12-28; 19.21; cf. Num. 6.12; 18.9.

from the geo-political map. Only the Servant's acknowledgement of Yahweh's righteous action against Israel-Jacob, the flip-side of which was redemption at the hands of his chosen agent Cyrus, opened the way for the possibility of offspring. The prolonging of the Servant's days echoes Isa. 44.5. I have already argued with reference to that text that descendants of the Servant would continue to know themselves in light of the Servant's call, and it's in this way that the Servant survives "death." In other words, there will always be people who frame their response to God in light of the paradigmatic call and response of the Servant to Yahweh, as will be demonstrated in the story of a real life Servant of God in the second half of this book.

Contempt for the Servant and his Unjust Treatment

The Servant's "life story of suffering" (Muilenburg 1956a: 619) is told in vv. 2-3, 7-9 of the nations' confessional poem. The imagery used to describe the Servant's lowliness and suffering in vv. 2-9 has a narrative arc, beginning with his youth in v. 2, to his death in vv. 8-9. So the poem's purpose is not to document a particular period of persecution in the life of an individual; the poem utilises the literary genre of biography to depict an entire life of humility and suffering. The hero of this biography is the Servant, acting as a metaphor for a nation that has been formed in open view of the mighty nations of the world, which have witnessed not only the Servant's formative years, in which it stumbled like a toddler into nationhood, but also its troubled mid-life and then, more recently, its "death" at the hands of the Assyrians and the Babylonians. What we have in Isaiah 53 is an account of Israel from Exodus to Exile and beyond—or, to reflect the language of Yahweh's discourse to the Servant, from formation to redemption. The images of intense suffering describe the nation's exilic years, using language that intentionally evokes the nation's bondage in Egypt.[4]

As a discourse that outlines how one group of people has come to see someone else in a different light, this section of Isaiah 53 contributes a particular type of knowledge to the Servant's understanding of himself. In life, the realisation that we have impacted others shapes what we say to ourselves *about* ourselves, as well as what we say to ourselves about *them*.

---

4. Says Muilenburg: "If the servant is understood collectively as corporate personality, as the Israelite indeed who is the true Israel from beginning to end, then the description can be taken in part, at least, as her historical existence as the nations observed it, and indeed as Israel herself experienced it" (Muilenburg 1956a: 620).

So it is in aesthetics, at least here; the Servant, in the nations' discourse, discovers how his story has impacted them. That impact is unique—no one shares the nations' perspective. How could they? As Bakhtin reminds us, each one of us occupies the centre of our own space and views the horizon in a unique way. It's no less the case in an aesthetic work, such as here, in which the nations occupy a unique semantic space in the world of the Servant.

My reading of this section of the poem is influenced by this awareness of the nations' unique perspective. For one thing, it acts as a caution that we are not reading a list of theological propositions but the uniquely dialogic perspective of a group of people that has been changed by the Servant in a particular way (aesthetically if not historically speaking). For example, the description of the Servant as a "young plant" (ESV) and like a "root out of dry ground" (v. 2ab) says as much about the nations as it does the Servant. The imagery encapsulates the Servant's insignificance to those observing from outside; to the kings of the nations he was nothing more than a fragile shrub struggling for nutrition. He had no majesty to look at, and no beauty to desire (v. 2cd). The first image echoes the words of Yahweh concerning the *seeing* of the kings (Isa. 49.7; 52.15c). The nations' statement that there was nothing to look at highlights the before-and-after aspect of Yahweh's original claim: it is the one who is despised who will make the kings see (cf. 49.7). In echoing Yahweh so explicitly, the speakers associate themselves with the "many" who were appalled at the Servant. The significance of this to the Servant is that he no longer has only Yahweh's words to evaluate how others have perceived him; he hears it from the many themselves.

The explanation, or justification, for why the nations didn't esteem the Servant, continues into v. 3: the Servant was "despised, shunned by men." In 49.7cd the Servant is said to be both despised and abhorred by the nation. Here he is despised and "shunned," or given up on. The description emphasises the Servant's lowly state, yet again, but not in an objective sense—these are relative terms and here they serve a dialogic purpose. The point being made is that the nations viewed the Servant Israel-Jacob as being unworthy of retaining.

The translation "man of sorrows" (KJV, ASV, RSV, NASB, NIV, NJB, ESV; JPS reads "man of suffering") in v. 3b, skews the reading of this section of the discourse. It results in an individualistic interpretation of the Servant figure and pictures his suffering as more psychological than physical. The Servant is also "familiar with disease" (v. 3b), variously translated as "grief," "suffering," "disease" and "infirmity." My reading is that "sickness" or even "disease" more accurately connotes the physical, emotional and psychological weakness that comes with sickness. It's a holistic breaking down, a complete collapse.

Some external references may shed light on how the Servant is being perceived by this imagery. In Isaiah 1, which some commentators see as having been crafted to read as introduction to the final form of Isaiah,[5] Yahweh tells Israel the "whole head is sick" (ESV, v. 5c). In Isa. 17.11 the day of judgment upon Jacob is described as a "day of grief and incurable pain" (ESV), combining both terms that occur in 53.3b. In Isa. 33.24 a day of restoration and forgiveness is described as a time when no inhabitant of Zion will say "I am sick." And Hezekiah, too, suffers a sickness (Isa. 38.9) that parallels the sickness of the city. In this paradigmatic tale, both Hezekiah and the city only find relief from "sickness" when they turn back to Yahweh. The point is that "sickness" and "pain" appropriately describe the suffering of the nation as much as that of any individual within it. Overwhelmingly, the Isaianic imagery relates to the judgment of Israel. Outside of Isaiah these terms are consonant also with the nation's suffering under Egyptian rule.[6] The description of the Servant as "sick" or "full of pain" is hardly new to the Servant. He's already accepted that his condition is as a result of Yahweh's actions (Isa. 43.28).

The Hebrew in Isa. 53.3c—translated "as one from whom men hide their faces"—is obscure, but the major translations, like the ESV, view the subject of the clause as those hiding their faces (from the Servant). However, JPS is the more natural, "As one who hid his face from us."[7] The complication is the Servant discourse in Isa. 50.6, where the Servant proclaims that he did not hide his face from disgrace and spitting. But my argument is that the apparent contradiction is precisely the point. The nations, before their revelation, have misunderstood the Servant, Israel-Jacob. He proclaims that he didn't hide his face but they say that he did. By contradicting the Servant, the nations actively associate with those who have beaten the Servant in Isa. 50.6, since in 53.3c they claim he turned his face from "us."

The repetition of "despised" in v. 3d creates an inclusio with v. 3a. More importantly, it introduces the confession that the ones who rejected and despised the Servant in v. 3a are actually the "we" of the confession: "we

---

5. See, e.g., Dumbrell (1985); see also Clements (1982: 117–18).

6. The word מכאב is consonant with Israel's suffering under Egypt, which is paradigmatic of the Servant's suffering in Babylon. In Exod. 3.7 Yahweh says to Moses that he knows his people's מכאבי.

7. The masc. sing. noun מסתר suggests that the Servant and not "others" are the subject of the clause.

held him of no account" (v. 3d). The confessional aspect of the discourse gathers force from this point, as the speaker brings his fellow confessors into view. This is the real purpose of the discourse, to confess how their regard for the Servant was reversed; from being of no significance at all, the Servant became highly significant.

The imagery of the Servant's suffering is intensified in the second half of the poem, where the biographical device narrows in on the Servant's later years, including those of his apparent death. The Servant's silence in the face of his persecution has clearly impressed itself upon the speakers since the parallel images of the Servant not opening his mouth, in other words remaining silent, in v. 7b, e, frame the description of his suffering. The Servant's silent acceptance of his persecution is consistent with the Servant song of 50.4-9, particularly the idea that Yahweh's vindication has enabled the Servant to face his persecution. It also loosely alludes to the discourse of 42.1-9, in particular Yahweh's observation that the Servant would no cry aloud or lift up his voice. That the Servant's silence has been alluded to in three separate discourses suggests itself as an important ingredient of his dialogic constitution. If the Servant is a paradigm by which Israel is called to know itself, then the Servant's silence becomes a pro forma for how the nation should respond. Either that, or it's how Israel did respond to the exile—in silent acceptance—and the nations' testimony concerning the Servant draws for Israel a picture of how the Servant's response has been viewed among the nations.

The language of persecution is more explicit in v. 8, particularly in 8a: "By oppressive judgment he was taken away." That the Servant was oppressed (Isa. 42.22-25; 43.28; 50.6) is nowhere disputed. The use of "judgment" (משפט) meanwhile recalls one of the most loaded words in Second Isaiah, at least where the Servant is concerned. The prophet echoed Israel's complaint regarding Yahweh's neglect of its justice in Isa. 40.27, and this provided the basis for Yahweh's disputational discourses to the Servant in chs. 40–48. In the Servant discourse of Isa. 42.1-9 the Servant discovered that not only had Yahweh not neglected his justice but he was preparing the Servant to bring his justice to the nations. We know the Servant took this to heart because in the first discourse in which the Servant speaks he acknowledges that his justice is with Yahweh (49.4c), signifying a major shift with Israel's attitude in 40.27. That the Servant was taken away by oppressive judgment is something Israel-Jacob may have refuted. But the Servant acknowledges this—that his being taken away from the land of the living was not a sign that Israel was being neglected, but was indeed at the heart of Yahweh's intended "justice" for the nation, as well as for the nations.

I have argued that the Servant discourses have challenged a perceived belief among the exiles that the people of Yahweh have come to an end. The Servant poems have sought to re-establish that the line from Abraham to the present remains unbroken, and the Servant is an heir to the patriarchal promises. This came to the fore in the great salvation discourses, Isa. 42.18–43.7 and 43.8–44.8, in which the destruction of Israel-Jacob at the hands of Yahweh's instruments of wrath was set in the larger context of Yahweh's assurances of salvation. These assurances were couched in creation imagery that emphasised Yahweh's creative redemption, bridging a chasm in Israel's history—a chasm that the nations now witness to in Isa. 53.8: "For he was cut off from the land of the living through the sin of my people, who deserved the punishment." Note the sudden introduction of the first person address with "my people." It's consistent with a number of oddities that we find in the Servant discourses.[8] The emergence of a singular voice at this point in the discourse heightens the tone of personal repentance that dominates the second half of the poem. It also reflects the similar emergence of a singular voice in the Servant discourses of Isaiah 49 and 50. It draws attention to the confessional theme, switching from the more generalised "we" to a specific "I."

The Servant was meant to dwell in the land of his fathers, the land of Abraham, Isaac and Jacob. Instead, "his grave was set among the wicked" (v. 9a), meaning a foreign land, with not only the wicked but also with the rich. The nations then proclaim the Servant's innocence, which is at odds with the general thrust of Second Isaiah which constantly argues the people have fully deserved their judgment (e.g., 42.24; 43.27-28). This is one of the principal reasons for identifying the Servant of Isaiah 53 as someone other than Israel. And granted, if we read the poem cut off from the developing dialogue that has brought us so far it is difficult to see how the Servant could be both the guilty nation and an innocent victim of oppression. But voices in a dialogue are not always in harmony. Sometimes they quarrel. It's still a dialogue. And because a polyphonic hero is constituted by several lines of intersecting discourse he is able to embody a number of apparently contradictory points of view simultaneously. Dialogic truth is comprised of unrepeatable utterances that contribute to a dialogic whole. In the Servant's case, the utterances of several speakers—Yahweh, the prophet, the Servant himself and, in Isaiah 53, the nations. Each speaker views the Servant differently,

---

8. Note Yahweh's sudden address to the second person singular "you" in 52.14, and the reference to the singular "nation" in 49.7.

from their own perspective and for their own purposes. The Servant's self-consciousness comprises and reconstitutes them all, even if (or especially if) they contradict one another. The more diverse the voices (heteroglossia), the more sculpted the Servant's character. For example, the Servant is blind and deaf yet he is a witness who sees and then speaks. He is a thresher that will raze mountains but at the same time he won't extinguish a faintly burning wick. He has wearied Yahweh and yet is loved and honoured by him. In other words, competing voices are not the problem they are often perceived to be. Each voice contributes in a unique way to the grand assemblage by which we come to know the Servant, Israel-Jacob.

On the issue of the nation's guilt or innocence the Servant embodies no fewer than three competing points of view simultaneously: he is culpable for his punishment (42.24; 43.27-28); his sins have been blotted out like a cloud (44.22); he suffered even though he had done no violence and had not lied (53.9). I could also add the position that the people's strife is payment for their sin and, having paid it, they are now pardoned (Isa. 40.2). My question of the polyphonic hero in the aesthetic world of the Servant is, How does he hear these utterances and what does he make of them? Only then might we ask what the corresponding "Servant," Israel-Jacob, makes of this paradigm. In the case of the Servant of Second Isaiah, the figure who knows himself to be both culpable *and* forgiven is afforded the opportunity to see his judgment a third way—through the eyes of the nations for whom the Servant was punished for *their* sin, not his own. This is not a general "truth." The Servant is not innocent—he knows that. But in the eyes of the nations he *was* innocent, because through some astonishing reversal in their realisation of their own culpability, he was punished for *their* wrongdoing. In their astonishing confession, they have eyes only for their own culpability, and in view of their own guilt they see the Servant as having suffered unjustly (v. 9cd) and, even more astonishingly, for their sake (v. 8d). But none of this is written for the nations—not immediately. It is written for the Servant. History bears out that the nations will, indeed, pick up this text and evaluate their culpability before God by it—which is astonishing enough. But in the first instance it's written for the Servant so that he might be afforded a glimpse of how Yahweh has used the Servant's suffering in a creatively redemptive way to reach the nations and convict them of their own sin. And by this, Israel-Jacob is invited to see its exilic sufferings in a redemptive way. The exile was not merely the punishment for the sins of a previous generation, but the means of taking Yahweh's salvation to the ends of the earth (49.1-6).

The Significance of the Servant's Suffering

The heart of the poem also contains its most staggeringly confessional language. The central section, vv. 4-6, forms the core of the poem structurally, emotionally and dialogically, the latter because this is where the purpose of the discourse, as a confession of the nations concerning the Servant's significance to *them*, is expounded. All the themes of the poem pivot on this section. We see the Servant's suffering through someone else's eyes. The nations, for their part, don't objectivise the Servant or his experiences—they engage with them, reflect upon what the Servant and his suffering means to them. They interpret the Servant's suffering in light of their own internal discourse, which leads them to the threshold of a new discovery.

How the nations got to this point we aren't told. But it's no treatise on suffering. They have begun a dialogue with the Servant himself and what we "see" and "hear" is not a system of thought or a theological principle, but the interior processing of the nations. It isn't representative of Isaianic theology and it certainly isn't a new doctrine on salvation. We overhear a confession.

In v. 4, the nations say that the Servant's affliction was punishment by God. There's no ambiguity about this. "We accounted him plagued, smitten and afflicted by God" (v. 4d). The reversal comes in v. 5 when the nations confess that it was not for the Servant's own sake that he suffered, but for theirs. Their astonishing realisation is conveyed in four clauses, two parallel couplets, each emphasising two separate but related dimensions of the Servant's significance to the nations. The first couplet emphasises that the Servant suffered for "our" sins, the second that his punishment was for "our" peace (shalom).

The wounds (ESV; "bruises," JPS) that the Servant has suffered (v. 5d) and by which the nations are healed evoke imagery associated with Israel under judgment in Isaiah 1, where the nation suffers a number of complaints that are also suffered by the Servant in Isaiah 53 (see Isa. 1.6c). At the same time, a distinction is drawn between the Servant who suffers and the nations who do not. The Servant suffers and the nations experience healing. In Isa. 19.22, in an oracle against Egypt, Yahweh's judgment will result in the Egyptians turning to Yahweh, who will heal them—so the confession of the nations in Isa. 53.5d is consistent with Isaiah's vision for the nations.

The discourse of the nations in v. 5 raises a number of questions, such as how best to understand the transference of guilt and the apparent vicarious suffering of the Servant, and how the healing of the nations is effected in actuality. The imagery of vicarious sin-taking possibly echoes Lam. 5.7 and Ezek. 18.2 and the belief among the exilic generation that they were paying for the sins of their fathers.[9] But in the mouth of the nations this imagery undergoes a radical revision. In Isaiah 53 the nations turn on its head the belief that the exilic generation has borne the sins of a previous generation, by confessing that the Servant has actually borne the nations' sins. This also calls into question a prevailing sentiment that is reflected in the Psalms, that Yahweh turn his wrath towards the nations that have ridiculed Israel in its time of suffering, for example in Ps. 79.7-8, where the psalmist pleads for retribution against the nations, and for the sins of the fathers to not be held against them (cf. Lam. 3.58-66). The effect is similar to the revision that occurs in the stylistic narrative of Jonah, in which the heathen characters are quick to repent, to the surprise of not only the eponymous prophet, but to his nationalistic readers. The language of sacrifice on behalf of another is a counter-balance to the ideology of vindication that is clearly evident during the exilic period.

In the nations' confession the Servant hears that his witness (43.10, 12; 44.8) has not been in vain. Indeed, the nations now see. Yahweh's call for the Servant to be a covenant for the people and a light to the Gentiles (Isa. 42.6; see also 49.6, 8; 50.10) has produced fruit. In reinterpreting the Servant's experiences, the nations broaden Israel-Jacob's self-awareness; they make the Servant reflect upon the possibility that Yahweh's work of redemption, embodied in the Servant and enacted in his liberation from exile, continues on, unfinished, in the coming to knowledge of the nations. In their testimony, the Servant's suffering has brought *peace* and *healing*. How are these terms to be understood in actuality, distinct from what they mean in the aesthetics of the Servant's development in the text? I don't believe their significance is in what they literally depict but that it is the nations who claim that peace and healing have come via the Servant Israel-Jacob's hardship. It's an astonishing paradigm shift that confronts Israel in this poem. It calls Israel to believe that because it has suffered, the nations have and will be blessed. It doesn't validate the suffering, but it does offer a way for the Servant to see beyond Israel-Jacob's despondency and step up to a new call. Effectively the nations' discourse becomes a doorway to new possibilities beyond the age of suffering. It calls Israel to a wholly different future. The Servant is invited by the nations to consider the purpose that his exile now serves: the redemption of the nations who perceive his suffering to be for their sake.

9. See Clifford 1984: 179.

Yahweh Concludes the Servant Discourse

The conclusion to the poem, 53.11-12, is more obscure than Yahweh's introduction, and the major translations rarely agree on how it should be interpreted. But while the opening words are fairly opaque, their echoing of major tropes from the Servant discourses throughout Second Isaiah is unmistakable. One of those motifs is the Servant's blindness. As the Servant came to consciousness of his calling and his mission to the nations, the success of his witness was described in ways that double-voiced his own deficiency, specially that kings would see (Isa. 49.7; 52.14-15). And the confession of the nations in 53.1-10 seems to fulfil this, as discussed above. But now Yahweh lends his voice to the chorus of those singing the Servant's praises, saying that from the Servant's anguish (v. 11a) the Servant shall *see*. Many translations follow the key Qumran texts and slot a direct object in here, but in the MT there is none. So the reward for the Servant is not that he will see something, it's that he will see at all, reversing the judgment upon Israel in Isa. 6.10, where the prophet's mission was to close the eyes of the disobedient nation.

The righteousness of the Servant referred to in v. 11c is bound up with his sight and signifies his obedience to the call of Yahweh. It reflects the Servant's response, as in 49.1-6 and 50.4-11—the willingness of the Servant to say, "I am Yahweh's" (44.5). It's through this righteous acceptance of Yahweh's call that many others are made righteous—that is, they will come to a realisation of the significance of the Servant, and come to know themselves in light of it. This is what we see in the confession of 53.1-10—the nations being made righteous through their confession of the Servant's impact upon them. Yahweh's response in 53.11-12 is a divine imprimatur on what the nations have confessed, binding together dialogically the themes of the introduction, the body of the poem and the conclusion. Indeed, much of the conclusion serves to bring Yahweh's voice in line with that of the nations, as if to demonstrate that the nations are not alone in their understanding of the Servant's mission. For example, Yahweh echoes the nations' words in 53.8-9 when in v. 12c he says the Servant exposed himself to death, and that he was numbered among the sinners (v. 12d). What the nations have confessed is now on Yahweh's horizon, being reworked for his own purposes—which seems to be to affirm what the nations have testified concerning his beloved Servant. Yahweh also underscores what is said in v. 11 when he reiterates that the Servant bore the guilt of the many (v. 12e). It returns to the theme of the introduction and how the "many" once viewed the Servant. The parallel statement, "And made intercession for sinners," echoes 53.6d and the acknowledgement of the nations that Yahweh allowed the punishment of everyone to hurt the Servant. The Servant continues to embody this representational activity. His role as one who intercedes for the nations and those languishing in darkness continues. The witness of the Servant who suffered at the hands of the Babylonian captors, died in exile but was re-born in the call of Yahweh to be his Servant, continues to signify to the "many" in a way that provokes their confession.

The Servant as Polyphonic Hero

We have seen from the discussion of Isaiah 53 alone that the dialogically constituted polyphonic hero is able to represent several competing points of view simultaneously without requiring them to be harmonised. The advantage is that a single character in an aesthetic work like Second Isaiah can appeal to an entire people group, among whom there are bound to be deeply held and diverse ideologies and theological positions. The polyphonic hero can embody several fundamental but apparently contradictory "truths" concurrently, while a monologic reading seeks to harmonise these discrete perspectives and risks missing what a character like the Servant potentially signifies and to whom. Bakhtin calls this phenomenon the hero's "voice idea," and more will be said about this with reference to the Servant in the next chapter.

In the case of the Suffering Servant, his dialogic constitution allows him to represent and actually embody a process of critical reevaluation of those deeply held and diverse ideas and theological positions, when otherwise their revision might be resisted. It is one thing to challenge a prevailing idea with an alternate view—it is quite another to have a character in an aesthetic work (and religious text) *embody* that idea and undergo a transformation in the process of which the ideology is deconstructed and repurposed. We see this happening in Isaiah 53 with reference to the idea of Israel's suffering in exile. A cause for complaint to Yahweh, which is then viewed as a sign of the Servant's faithful response to God's call, ultimately becomes a sign to the nations that someone has suffered on their behalf, resulting in their repentance. We also see it in Isa. 50.4-9 with reference to the prevailing view of a prophet's role, particularly that of Jeremiah.

A dialogic approach to a collection of texts such as we find in Second Isaiah gives us the opportunity to imagine how the Servant has heard the speeches that constitute him as a character, in order to interpret those speeches outside of a typical monological approach which seeks to finalise the character and harmonise the competing voices. In doing so we can revisit what it means that the Servant is called (41.9; 42.6; 43.1,

7; 49.1), that he is an offspring of Abraham (41.8), that he is a worm and a threshing board (41.14-15), that he is blind and deaf (42.18-19; 43.8), that he is a witness (43.10, 12; 44.8), that he is called to bring justice to the nations (42.1, 3, 4), that he is despised (49.7; 53.3), that he is a light to the world and a covenant to the nations (42.6; 49.6). I have argued that when we hear the discourses from the Servant's perspective then we realise that there are not multiple Servants—for example, Israel-Jacob in chs. 40–48 and the prophet from ch. 49. When we hear the discourse as an "I" to whom that discourse is addressed and who it concerns, there is only one Servant, Israel-Jacob, who comes to know himself by that discourse, and responds to it in a way that demonstrates that Yahweh has found an obedient dialogic partner. However, I have also argued that the Servant, Israel-Jacob, does not necessarily occupy the same semantic space as empirical Israel. There is some distance—a certain amount of fluidity—between the Servant Israel-Jacob as he is constituted by the intersecting discourse, and the nation that is called to know itself *as* the Servant. This semantic fluidity gives us licence to describe the Servant as a paradigmatic figure by which Israel is invited to understand itself, its relationship to its God, its purpose and role in history, and its standing as a covenant promise to the nations, in a new way. Empirical Israel is implored to situate itself in the dialogue and to reimagine itself as one freshly called by the same God who brought the nation out of nothing; to speak the words of response that the Servant speaks, a faithful response to Yahweh that it sees and hears modelled in Isa. 49.1-6 and 50.4-9; and to reimagine its exilic suffering not as a nation abandoned by its God, but as one who has died and is risen again as a witness to the very nations who now proclaim that the Servant's suffering was because he was bearing the punishment for their sin and not his own.

THE VOICE-IDEA OF THE SUFFERING SERVANT

The Uniqueness of the Servant

As we see in the case of the Suffering Servant of Second Isaiah, the polyphonic hero who is constituted dialogically in the aesthetic world of the text occupies a unique semantic space. Because the hero is constituted at the point where various lines of discourse intersect, no one is positioned relative to the world around them quite like they are. No one sees the world as they see it. It's the same in life. As Bakhtin observes in *Author and Hero*:

> When I contemplate a whole human being who is situated outside and over against me, our concrete, actually experienced horizons do not coincide. For at each given moment, regardless of the position and the proximity to me of this other human being whom I am contemplating, I shall always see and know something that he, from his place outside and over against me, cannot see himself: parts of his body that are inaccessible to his own gaze (his head, his face and its expression), the world behind his back, and a whole series of objects and relations, which in any of our mutual relations are accessible to me but not to him. As we gaze at each other, two different worlds are reflected in the pupils of our eyes. It is possible, upon assuming an appropriate position, to reduce this difference of horizons to a minimum, but in order to annihilate this difference completely, it would be necessary to merge into one, to become one and the same person. (Bakhtin 1990: 22–3)

In the creation of a polyphonic hero, an author represents this fundamental aspect of human reality aesthetically, creating a character whose view of the world is not shared by anyone else, not even the author. That is what is achieved with the Suffering Servant, and which is one reason he has remained mysteriously elusive for more than two millennia. No other character signifies in the same way either. Their point of view on the world—their ideology or voice-idea—can't be shared or represented by another consciousness, since each is constituted at different places on the matrix of discourse that comprises the final text. It makes sense then that what the polyphonic hero utters concerning their world represents a unique point of view. Someone else may repeat what the hero says but it can never signify in the same way, because that "consciousness" does not see the world from the hero's place in it. But more than this, *who* the hero *is* is as significant as what they say. Since they are constituted dialogically what they *say* is who they *are*, and who they *are* is what they *say*.

The Suffering Servant of Second Isaiah is constituted at the point of convergence of ten discourses that are uttered by four discrete voices: Yahweh's, the prophet's, the Servant's, and the nations'. The Servant's response to the discourse of others contributes as much to his voice-idea as what the Servant himself volunteers. Bakhtin says that the polyphonic hero's discourse about the world "merges with confessional discourse about oneself" (Bakhtin 1984: 78), and we see this with the Servant. When he speaks in Isa. 49.1-6 and 50.4-9, he not only does so about himself, but about his environment, his God, his persecutors, his understanding of prophecy and about his own calling. His discourse concerning the world can't be unravelled from his discourse about himself. This means that the Servant's "truth" is not easily stated in propositional terms. The Servant has not been constructed to utter "truths" that we can simply extract from his words. His truth is about where he is positioned in the text in relation to others who speak and how he engages with what is said to and about him.

It is easier to grasp Bakhtin's concept of the voice-idea in a polyphonic work once we have a clear view of the more familiar idea in a monologic work. The major difference is that while the voice-idea in a polyphonic work is inextricably bound to the hero who is dialogically constituted, the monologic idea is not bound to a character at all. Indeed, for a monologic idea to retain its ability to signify it must remain distinct from the characteristics of any one character. For example, a character in an aesthetic work might be described as overweight, likes to wear baseball caps, and engages in the propagation of white supremacist material. In this example, the *idea* of white supremacy does not signify directly—it is one characteristic among many. For the idea of white supremacy to signify directly it must remain a propositional statement that can be uttered by one character or another, in which case its "truth" isn't compromised because it remains within the monologic system of meaning constructed by the author. Who utters the idea, or in what context, is, for the author, a matter of composition, or "convenience," or stylistic consideration. Says Bakhtin:

> Such an idea, in itself, belongs to no one. The hero is merely the carrier of an independently valid idea; as a true signifying idea it gravitates toward some impersonal, systemically monologic context; in other words, it gravitates toward the systemically monologic worldview of the author himself. (Bakhtin 1984: 79)

An example from the Hebrew Bible should help clarify this: the books of Samuel and Kings raise certain ideas concerning the monarchy and its function and purpose in ancient Israel, even its culpability for the disasters that befell the nation, such as the destruction of the northern and southern kingdoms and the exile to Babylon. Scholars are able to discern what author/redactor "the Deuteronomist" believes concerning the role of the monarchy in relation to its demise and the disintegration of the separated kingdoms. These ideas exist apart from the aesthetic crafting of the characters who populate those books; they belong to the author's worldview. That's not to say the worldview of the author doesn't have implications for the characters, or that the world of the characters does not contribute to or shape the author's worldview. A character such as the prophet Samuel may make certain utterances that echo the ideology of the author, but the idea itself is not inextricably bound to his character; if it was, it would cease to signify directly since the character exits the narrative (in 1 Sam. 25, though his ghost makes an appearance in ch. 28). The idea would exit the story with him. But as it is, the ideology of the monarchy's culpability continues to signify, since it exists on a plane not impacted by that of the characters; the "systemically monological worldview" of the author/ redactor. In a monologic work, ideas are not represented or embodied; they are "expressed directly" (Bakhtin 1984: 84).

In contrast to the directly signifying idea in a monologic work, the idea in a dialogic work signifies as a voice-idea, which is Bakhtin's term to describe an idea that is bound to the character who not only utters (voices) the idea, but who also embodies it, lives it out, and knows him or herself according to it. In order to be extended beyond the character who embodies it, the voice-idea must enter into dialogue with other voice-ideas, demonstrating its open-endedness and anticipatory nature. It has no ability to directly signify and continue on beyond the character, but carries on in open dialogue that continues to engage with it, as in the case of the Suffering Servant. In a monologic work, other ideas are not represented as valid voices in a dialogue; they can only be assimilated or repudiated, because it is the author's ideology that dominates. "Other truths do not have the right to demand an answer from the reader; that right is allotted only to the author's truth" (Morson and Emerson 1990: 238). In a polyphonic work, this dialogue of voice-ideas isn't made up from scratch; it engages ideas heard in the epoch of the work, even with epochs of the past. It also anticipates ideas of the future since the dialogue generates new possibilities or "linkages of ideas" in the worldwide dialogue (Bakhtin 1984: 91). We have seen such "idea-prototypes" scattered through Second Isaiah, and they have made vital contributions to the dialogical constitution of the Servant. Of the ideas of the past that dialogue with the voice-idea of the Servant's, those of Abraham and the covenantal promises, David and the messianic hope, Moses and the deliverance of the exodus, are among the most prominent.

The Significance of the Servant

It should be clear by now that whatever "truth" the Servant signifies, it cannot be grasped without an engagement with the Servant himself. And when dialoguing with the Servant, we have to resist assuming that the prophet constructed his character according to predetermined ideas. The idea that a polyphonic hero could express their truth propositionally is a contradiction of the hero's very nature. A good example of this is the idea of vicarious atonement that is sometimes transferred from systematic theology to the Servant poem of Isaiah 53. But the idea is alien to the dialogical make-up of the Servant figure, as we've discussed already. It is a directly signifying idea that does not emerge from a dialogue with the Servant, but is usually imposed upon him as if he was a typical character in a monologic work. When we engage with a polyphonic hero like the Suffering Servant we also need to resist the temptation to summarise their voice-idea propositionally, since this was not the intention of the text. We can't even say that the character *is* this or that idea. He is "born of the idea" (Bakhtin 1984: 85), he is not the idea itself.

The constitution of the polyphonic hero and the emergence of his voice-idea occur simultaneously. We've observed this with the Suffering Servant. Nowhere in Second Isaiah does the prophet seek to outline what the Servant represents apart from the discourse that constitutes him. There is presented no monologic idea of what "servanthood" signifies other than in the discourse directed to the Servant, or said about him, or spoken by him, or in the confession of the nations. We come to know the Servant as we come to know what he embodies. We actually participate in the event of his unfolding voice-idea, since as he responds to Yahweh's discourse in Isa. 49.1-6 and makes himself known to the nations, we also discover how he has made Yahweh's discourse a feature of his own internal discourse. What the Servant says, particularly his double-voicing of Yahweh's discourse and other "ideas," is new to us, as it is new to Yahweh and the nations. In other words, the prophet allows the Servant to signify directly. Although the prophet is present in the text as a speaking "I," he doesn't interfere in how the Servant *means*. The "idea" that the Servant embodies is unique to the discourse that converges upon him and which enters the dialogic "field of battle" (Bakhtin 1984: 88) with him.

Some clarification would help at this point.

Before we hear the Servant speak in Isaiah 49 our knowledge of him comes predominantly from the discourse that is directed to him by Yahweh. If Yahweh's discourse was all we had, we would, with some justification, suggest that what Yahweh utters concerning Israel-Jacob represents the ideology of the prophet—that the prophet is using the utterance of Yahweh to give voice to his own ideas, which is what Bakhtin calls refracted discourse. What that is would be reflected in the things Yahweh says to the Servant. For example, there is imagery in Yahweh's discourse that is drawn from the nation's Davidic hope and the transference of that hope to the people themselves. If this was a monologic text we might suggest that the prophet's ideology embraced the reassertion of Israel's national identity in the face of the destruction of the monarchy. However, when the Servant speaks in 49.1-6 he double-voices Yahweh, thereby bringing Yahweh's discourse within his own "dialogic field of vision" (Bakhtin 1984: 73). The Servant's discourse then goes beyond that of Yahweh and demonstrates that as a consciousness he is not confined by Yahweh's utterance, or by the idea that has been suggested by his discourse. The author, Second Isaiah, achieves this by having the Servant speak not to Yahweh in his response but to the coastlands. This is vitally important; the first time we hear the Servant speak he is responding to Yahweh's discourse by acting upon it. In acting upon it the Servant demonstrates that he has been impacted by it. The allusions to Yahweh's discourse are for the sake of the nations, not to demonstrate that the Servant can parrot Yahweh's words. The Servant shows that Yahweh's words haven't closed him down—they have provoked a self-conscious response, a decision to act, a brand new utterance. The Servant is a consciousness in his own right, albeit one who exists within the aesthetic world of the text. And that consciousness knows himself to be the one to whom Yahweh has spoken.[1]

This is emphasised by the Servant's double-voicing of Yahweh's designation of him as the Servant, in Isa. 49.3. By echoing this most important of Yahweh's utterances the Servant embraces it as an element of his own self-consciousness. In proclaiming it to the nations, he announces that he accepts the designation. From this moment on, the knowledge we, the readers, have of the Servant regarding his purpose is no longer limited to knowledge we have obtained from Yahweh's potentially objectifying discourse, but knowledge we obtain from the Servant himself.

---

1. Bakhtin outlines this aspect of the polyphonic hero in his discussion of Dostoevsky's "Notes from Underground," particularly with reference to the Underground Man who eavesdrops on those above ground and anticipates their discourse about him in order to retain the final word concerning himself (Bakhtin 1984: 53).

It is also emphasised in Isa. 49.4 when the Servant recounts a dialogue with Yahweh that we have no other record of. He situates himself outside the discourse by which we have come to know him, in chs. 40–48. It is even more suggestive that in this double-voiced dialogue the Servant resists Yahweh's call by claiming to have laboured in vain—indeed, he begins the account by emphasising the personal ("But I!"), thereby enforcing his individuality over against the speaking "I" of Yahweh's discourse.

When the Servant alludes to his physical sufferings in Isa. 50.6, he further reinforces his independence as a thinking "I," by discoursing on imagery that originates outside Second Isaiah. If the imagery of striking the back and pulling out the beard refers to a literal historical event, it is an event we have no access to apart from the Servant's discourse. This in itself would be significant. But the discourse uses these referents to reveal something new to the Servant; indeed, their significance *to* the Servant is all we are permitted to know of them. We would like to know more, of course—such as who is inflicting the beatings, and why are they doing it—because we are wired by literary convention to expect an objective record of the event; an account that would elevate us over against the Servant, rather than settle for his own retelling. But the text's polyphonic design doesn't allow us this.

The Servant's Dialogic Field of Battle

Bakhtin observed that the voice-idea of an individual character could not remain the sole possession of that character without, ultimately, ceasing to signify; ceasing to have meaning. The idea, if it is to live and expand, must enter into dialogue with other voice-ideas—in other words, the consciousness of the hero must encounter other consciousnesses who occupy equally valid semantic spaces. A particular viewpoint on the world discovers more about itself when it encounters other points of view and then dialogues, or even (especially) quarrels, with them. Says Bakhtin:

> The idea lives not in one person's isolated individual consciousness—if it remains there only, it degenerates and dies. The idea begins to live, that is, to take shape, to develop, to find and renew its verbal expression, to give birth to new ideas, only when it enters into genuine dialogic relationships with other ideas, with the ideas of others. (Bakhtin 1984: 87–8, emphases original)

It is no surprise that of all the Servant poems the one that creates most intrigue is Isa. 52.13–53.12. This is partly due to its importance to the Christian interpretation of the death of Jesus Christ and its ongoing inter-pretation in the early church fathers and throughout church history. But it is also due to the artillery the discourse brings to the Servant's dialogue field of battle. The poem's value to the doctrines of the Church may have been weighted by the type of discourse that it is. Of all the Servant discourses, it is this final one that gives the dialogue that converges on the Servant its unfinished, open and anticipatory dimensions. It's nature as a confession by an unnamed group concerning the significance of the Servant's *idea* breaks open the closed circle of dialogue between Yahweh and the Servant. It invites participation by *others*. The semantic position occupied by the Servant primarily invites participation from Israel-Jacob. This has the potential of isolating anyone who is not of Israel, restricting the Servant's signifying power to the nation of Israel alone—which is also a way of finishing off a hero so that he ceases to mean beyond the immediate context. That hasn't happened with the Servant, however, as we have seen in the brief survey of religious and scholarly interpretation. That is because of the advent of another voice in the text that provides a way into the discourse from beyond the borders of Israel. The voice of the nations invites anyone who has overheard the Servant's dialogue with Yahweh into direct engagement (dialogically) with the Servant himself. The confession of the nations, though brief, is such a profound voice-idea concerning the significance of the Servant that it cannot easily be dismissed. Centuries of scholarship on the identity and purpose of the Servant is testimony to this, as is the ongoing debate surround what it is that the Servant has achieved. The Ethiopian's question to the evangelist Philip in Acts 8.34 is precisely the response the discourse of the nations foreshadows. The Ethiopian, by asking who it is that is being spoken about in Isa. 53.7-8, takes a dialogic position in relation to the Servant that approximates that of the nations. The question is notoriously difficult to answer, since the discourse of the nations does not represent an objec-tifying monological description of the Servant, but a point of view—a voice-idea—and a signifying position in the Servant discourse as a whole. It is a confession of signification that seeks a dialogue partner. Prior to the confession of the nations in Isaiah 53, a dialogue between voice-ideas has been well-established, but it has been limited mainly to two conscious-nesses, those of Yahweh and the Servant. The dialogue proper does not begin until Isa. 49.1-6, when the Servant finally responds to Yahweh's oracles from the preceding eight chapters. When the Servant responds in a way that affirms he is awake and listening to Yahweh, the latter's discourse is given new significance. When Yahweh then responds to the Servant in 49.7-12, echoing aspects of his own and the Servant's discourse while also introducing a new idea—that of the nations' despising of the Servant—the Servant's voice-idea is broadened, given new scope. New opportunities for fresh dialogue are opened up. But it's the confession of the nations in Isaiah 53 that gives the Servant idea its unfinished quality. The Servant's idea finds new fertile ground in the discourse of the nations, and the confession demonstrates the germination of new thought that would not be possible without either Yahweh's discourse, or the Servant's response.

A brief review of one aspect of the Servant's voice-idea—that of suffering—should demonstrate how the dialogic field of battle extends an idea's complexity and opens it up to the "great dialogue" of its immediate epoch, as well as those of past and future generations. The association between the idea of suffering and the figure of the Servant is first made by Yahweh, in Isa. 42.22, 24-25 and 43.27-28. In 42.22 the suffering is described as a situation of being plundered and looted, trapped in holes and "hidden" in prisons. In 43.28 the suffering is described in more dynamic terms. It is a profaning, and a giving over to utter destruction and abuse. In both instances, Yahweh says the Servant's suffering is a just reward for his sin: the Servant, Israel-Jacob, would not walk in Yahweh's paths or obey his law (42.24de); his first father sinned and his "mediators" transgressed (43.27). As an utterance of Yahweh, the idea of suffering that is bound to the Servant is a simple one. Even so, the idea is enlarged by the redactional juxtaposing of salvation oracles immediately following each discourse on suffering, in 43.1-7 and 44.1-5. The oracles, like the disputations, are uttered by Yahweh, but the generic voice of assurance in both casts a new dialogic hue over the words of judgment. Meaning this: in the discourse of Yahweh in Second Isaiah, the idea of suffering that is bound to the Servant always stands at the threshold of forgiveness. So it is not enough to say of the Servant that he embodies the idea of righteous judgment, for example. The Servant's suffering is anticipatory. In the discourse that constitutes the Servant from Yahweh's own point of view, judgment and mercy are two consecutive episodes in the course of the Servant's history.

I stress again that I'm not proposing abstract (monologic) theology here. One cannot say that judgment is always followed by mercy on the basis of the Servant discourse, since the "truth" of Yahweh's utterance is dialogic—that is, bound to the Servant and his experiences. However, I also stress that for as long as the idea exists purely as an expression of Yahweh's words to the Servant, its monologic character remains intact. It is discourse seeking a response, but if such a response is not forthcoming then it takes on the character of an objectifying and finishing definition—a powerfully monologic and very limiting view of the Servant, Israel-Jacob. But the Servant does respond to Yahweh, in both Isa. 49.1-6 and 50.4-9. His response to the "idea" of suffering comes in 50.6; when the Servant speaks to it he does so not in the language of Yahweh's discourse but in language that evokes Lam. 3.30. When the Servant speaks of his suffering by echoing discourse that is not Yahweh's, he steps around the words that have sought to define him thus far. But in echoing Lam. 3.30, a text that describes one who waits for Yahweh as volunteering his cheek and willingly accepting insults, the Servant brings the imagery to bear upon his own suffering and claims for himself the role of the willing sufferer of the laments. In doing so he authenticates what Yahweh has said of his suffering; he accepts that his suffering is the result of righteous judgment, since the contemplative sufferer in Lamentations 3 has accepted his situation and is now waiting for Yahweh's compassion. Another way of looking at this is that the Servant has brought within the semantic range of his voice-idea the historical experiences of ravaged Judah, and in his response to Yahweh has submitted those experiences to the idea of suffering generated by Yahweh's discourse. In the process those experiences have been subjected to a transformation. As embodied by the Servant, they are no longer a cause for lament and complaint (as they are in Lamentations, as well as in 40.27-31), but an opportunity to acknowledge guilt and to return to Yahweh. The voice-idea of the Servant's suffering embraces a new dimension that was not possible without his response. When we consider that the exilic community is being invited to identify as the faithful Servant, the power of the voice-idea to signify where the propositional statement could not, takes on extra significance. The Servant's discourse compels the community to "feel" and experience the truth of the idea of the suffering Servant, rather than just hear it and assent to it. The Servant offers the community a point of view on its suffering that does not come naturally to it, one that has been made possible only by the dialogic constitution of the Servant, and by the expression of his unique perspective.

The monologism of the idea of suffering introduced by Yahweh's discourse breaks down even further as a third voice is introduced. This voice is brought into direct dialogic engagement with both the Servant and, albeit in a more indirect way, Yahweh. The "they" of Yahweh's introductory discourse in 52.13-15 merges with the "we" who speak in 53.1-10, meaning the voice represents the point of view of the nations in response to what Yahweh has just said. The discourse of the nations is taken up completely with the Servant's suffering, which in itself gives the idea of suffering an added dimension, since in the discourse between Yahweh and the Servant, suffering played a relatively small part. The nations make a unique contribution to the Servant's voice-idea—for them, his suffering takes on a significance it did not have for either Yahweh or the Servant. For Yahweh, the suffering of the Servant was a symbol and a consequence of Israel-Jacob's sin, but it also anticipated Yahweh's compassion. For the Servant, his suffering became an opportunity to endure in the belief that Yahweh's compassion (or his vindication) was assured. It became a living symbol of the Servant's faithfulness, an embodiment of the community's hope in the face of its laments as expressed in Lam. 3.30. But in Isaiah 53, in the voice of the nations, the Servant's suffering takes on the character of witness. It becomes a symbol to the nations of their own guilt before Yahweh. Here again the suffering is seen as anticipatory—the nations recognise that the Servant's suffering is a prelude to new life and offspring (53.10). In other words, the Servant embodies a narrative of redemption that testifies not only to the Servant's faithfulness in the face of suffering and shame, but also to Yahweh's restorative power. The nations do not just proclaim this idea in a monological way, as a general principle. They testify to its impact. They make it personal, embodied and lived through. They bear witness. The content of their discourse is the significance of the Servant's voice-idea to them. Their discourse isn't pedagogic, since they aren't theologians or academics. It is the recounting of an experience that has transformed them. The nations, like the Servant, embody the truth of what they are saying. Neither do the nations claim that the Servant's suffering is objectively and perpetually vicarious. But they do claim to have been transformed by what they have witnessed in a way that makes his suffering vicarious for them. For the nations, the Servant's suffering is covenantal, in that by it they see the promise of redemption, where previously they were not even aware they needed it.

The emergence of this "multi-faced" idea of suffering that encompasses judgment and forgiveness, confession and repentance, witness and redemption, voiced by multiple consciousnesses, each one illuminating the others in their world of "yoked-together semantic human orientations" (Bakhtin 1984: 97), has a clear advantage over a monological declaration. By it, the prophet's target audience, the exiles themselves, are drawn into a dialogue that compels them to participate. It is one thing for the prophet to tell the exiles that one day the nations will repent when they witness how Yahweh has enabled the exiling community to return to Judaea. It is quite another for them to "experience" this truth dialogically; to be caught up in an unfolding idea that is being "played out at the point of dialogic meeting" (Bakhtin 1984: 88) between consciousnesses. It is a dialogue in which they are urged to discover themselves in light of the blind but redeemed Servant. In the dialogic field of battle that rages through the poems of Second Isaiah, the exiles hear themselves being called as Yahweh's Servant; they hear themselves responding faithfully and hopefully, even willingly; and ultimately they see themselves reflected in the consciousness of the nations, as they (the nations) repent because of what Yahweh has achieved in and on behalf of the Servant, Israel-Jacob. This is the future orientation of the Servant's voice-idea. It anticipates that the exiles will leave Babylon and return home, and in doing so worship Yahweh as redeemer (see 44.26; 48.20-21). It also anticipates a chain reaction in which exiles scattered further abroad will return home (43.6). The existence of Third Isaiah, chs. 56–66, suggests that there were at least some among the returning exiles who recognised that future orientation of the Servant voice-idea, particularly as the "heroes" of this third collection of oracles are the "servants," who are understood by some to be the offspring of the Servant. In other words, some did experience the truth of the prophet's message as *event*—and by it they not only understood the idea of redemptive suffering, they *experienced* it. In the embodied voice-idea of the Servant, the community's voice, for so long couched in the form of lament for what had occurred in the past, found a form more characteristic of the enduring prophet who faithfully hopes for deliverance.

The Voice-Idea of the Servant

The polyphonic hero dialogues with ideas that have been generated in Israel's remote past as well as ideas that are of more recent origin. In some ways those ideas are more precious to the exilic people than those associated with Moses, Abraham and David, since they have enabled the people to find an identity in the face of the destruction of monarchy, temple, city and nation. I'm referring to ideas like the suffering of the righteous. In encounter with the Servant's voice-idea, the axiom that the people are suffering unjustly for the sin of previous generations undergoes a radical transformation. The suffering of the present generation becomes the catalyst for the redemption of the nations, a "truth" that is not a generalised theological idea but an embodied point of view expressed exclusively by the nations themselves in Isaiah 53. If the Servant's voice-idea is a *live event*, to use Bakhtin's words, then it is a critically transformative one, a process in which some of the ideas the people hold as truth are exposed to the abrasive dynamic of the Servant's dialogic encounter with Yahweh and are radically subverted.

Another axiomatic truth that is transformed in the same way is that of Yahweh's wrath against the nations, which Israel expects as just recompense for the destruction of its temple, city and identity. Nowhere is this idea more clearly expressed than in the lament of Psalm 79, which powerfully voices a nationalistic ideology that was sure to have engendered popular backing during the exilic period. Yahweh is invoked against the nations who have "entered your domain, defiled Your holy temple, and turned Jerusalem into ruins" (Ps. 79.1). The poem echoes language we have encountered in the Servant discourses: the inhabitants of Jerusalem are called "Your servants" (vv. 2a, 10c); there is a plea for God to not remember the nation's former iniquities (v. 8a; cf. Isa. 43.22-28); there is an appeal for the "prisoners" (v. 11a; cf. Isa. 42.7); the exilic people are described as "sheep" (v. 13b; cf. Isa. 53.6). But the lament's call for judgment against the nations is radically at odds with the vision of Yahweh's concern for the nations in Second Isaiah. Yahweh is involved to pour his anger on the nations who do not know him (v. 6a); his judgment upon them will be seen as vengeance for the outpoured blood of the "servants" (v. 10c); and the taunts of the nations against Yahweh will be returned sevenfold (v. 12). The people justify their anger on the basis that the devastation was brought upon them not because of their sins but because of those of former generations (v. 8a). All aspects of the ideas voiced in the lament are transformed by the Servant's voice-idea. The idea that the exilic people are suffering unjustly meets the Servant who has burdened Yahweh with his sins (43.24); who has been given up by Yahweh (42.24-25); who is blind and deaf (42.7, 18, 19; 43.8), but nevertheless has had his sins blotted out like a mist (44.22; cf. 43.25). The Servant, Israel-Jacob, who responds to Yahweh, does not complain about unjust suffering but acknowledges that he has laboured in vain (49.4a); and he has not turned away from those who strike his back and rip the beard from his cheeks (50.6), imagery whose source in Lam. 3.30 casts the Servant as the one who accepts his judgment. Additionally, the idea that the nations will be struck with the wrath of Yahweh for their taunts against Israel meets the Servant who will bring justice to the nations (42.1d, 4b); who will be a light to the nations (42.6d); whose liberator will come from the nations (Isa. 45.1-7); and who ultimately will send a proclamation of Yahweh's redemption out to the nations (48.20). When the Servant responds he has no thought for vengeance. He acknowledges his role to the nations (49.6). Indeed, the nations themselves acknowledge that the Servant has suffered for their sake, that they might have peace and healing (53.5).

These competing voices aren't nullified in the Servant's response, however. They keep their validity and their power. A voice-idea retains the semantic validity of the voices whose dialogue comprises it, as is the case with the Servant. The ideas of Psalm 79 retain their signifying, unmerged quality: those who strive against the Servant *will* perish (41.11cd, 12cd); Egypt *will* be traded for the Servant's redemption (43.3-4); the Babylonians *will* be brought down as fugitives (43.14); Cyrus *is* given licence to subdue the nations before him (45.1). And in Isaiah 53 the testimony of the nations echoes the lament concerning the servants' unjust suffering—the Servant has indeed suffered unjustly, not for his own sins but for those of the nations.

Second Isaiah discerns the mood and thoughts of his age—he hears the voices of the exiles and crafts a polyphonic hero, the Servant, who speaks to those ideas, dialogues with them, quarrels with them, subverts and upholds them. There are no simple resolutions to the quarrels, and no straightforward outcomes from the dialogue. Rather, they cause the people to "feel" the diverse points of view at play. The prophet draws the people in a dialogic tussle in which they are invited to see themselves in a new light—*as* the Servant. Whoever is willing to understand himself or herself *as* the Servant will discover a new orientation. They have not been convinced to hold to a new idea, because Second Isaiah does not present these ideas as finalised, as if they could merely replace old ideas that are no longer relevant. Psalm 79 remains scripture, and the ideologies attached to the Moses paradigm or the Abrahamic promises or the Davidic hope are still vital. The exiles are invited to consider the dialogue from a new perspective—the one generated by the converging discourse of Yahweh, the Servant and the nations—and to hear each voice and see their world differently.

Bakhtin says that Dostoevsky thought not in thoughts but in "points of view, consciousnesses, voices" (1984: 93). I suggest that Second Isaiah is similarly composed not of ideas but of voices, each one spoken from a unique place in relation to their world.

PART II

DIALOGUE WITH JARED, A SUFFERING SERVANT

Meeting Jared

A Chance Encounter

I hope that it's obvious by now that in including the story of Dr Jared
Noel in a biblical studies book about the Suffering Servant, I have no
intention of harmonising those two discourses or interpreting one via
the other. My hope is that they truly dialogue around the themes of the
Servant's voice-idea outlined in the previous chapter—not to justify each
other's existence, but merely to play and to explore in a more dialogic
way themes of suffering, or faithfulness, or fear of abandonment, of
redemption, and of witness.

I had completed my doctoral studies and was already back in journalism
when I came across Jared, publishing a news magazine in the suburbs
where Jared lived and also co-owned a cafe with the members of his faith
community. I came to his story late in the piece—he was already almost
five years into his terminal diagnosis and was more well known for his
blog than he was as a newly trained aspiring surgeon or Christian speaker.
A writer for my magazine wrote an article on the incredible fundraising
effort that had enabled Jared to finance powerful drugs that would slow
the growth of his cancer long enough for him to meet his unborn (at that
stage) daughter, and from then on I followed his story from a distance.
But it was almost a year later that I got a phone call from a friend of his
to ask if I would write his book in the time he had left.

It's fair to say the thinking I had done around suffering, which in
turn was sparked by my doctoral work on the Servant, gave me a solid
framework within which to hear Jared's story and start to piece together
his narrative. Despite my years in journalism, it was not easy to interview
someone in the final weeks of their life, and it was my work in Second
Isaiah rather than my interview techniques which framed our conversations. I'd also experienced the recent breast cancer diagnosis of my wife,
so knew from painful personal experience something of what Jared and
his wife Hannah and the family were going through. And his resonance
with the story of the Suffering Servant certainly helped. Here was a young

man of faith who had confronted serious questions about the role of God in his life; had experienced the apparent "broken promises" of God's own call on his life; was eager to respond faithfully to God but had to constantly revise what that looked like against the backdrop of suffering's capricious nature; against that backdrop he nevertheless remained hopeful and faithful, using his circumstances to spread his message even further than he might have had he never been sick; and in the process he had discovered that there was no redemptive value in suffering—none whatsoever—and yet suffering was a context in which real love could be experienced in new ways.

The following conversations, Part II of this book, document something of that journey of mutual discovery, via snapshots from our dialogues around life, death, suffering and hope.

My initial meeting with Jared was in a West Auckland hospice on Tuesday, August 26, 2014. The following day, he returned home to spend his final weeks in his own house, surrounded by his family, including Hannah and their eight-month-old daughter Elise. Our interviews began the day after, on August 28.

The last time I spoke with Jared was on September 24. He texted me before we met to say that it would be our last conversation. It was our 21st interview; most of which had lasted an hour or more—typically beginning around noon each time, once the doctor or the hospice nurse had left for the day.

I never saw Jared again after the 24th. I did receive a text message though. I was hospitalised with pancreatitis on September 29 and was told there was a high chance I wouldn't last the week. Jared sent a message during the week to check on my status. The irony that I might die before him didn't escape either of us. I survived to tell the tale, however.

Jared, meanwhile, died on Wednesday, October 8. He was 33.

SACRED SPACES

Jared Alone

There is no graceful way to enter the bedroom of a man who is dying, with a great, cumbersome camera bag slung over your shoulder and your mind racing over the many conventions that probably exist to govern such encounters, but which, in the moment, you can't seem to bring to mind because suddenly here you are, walking across the bedroom towards him, your shoes off, ostensibly to protect the carpet but really, as everyone knows, because this is sacred ground. And although the bedroom is small—not tiny, by any means, because this is a great house—it takes an age to reach him, because you feel clumsy, awkward, a little like you don't know where to look, since the marriage bed is just here after all, and everyone who enters to say their goodbyes must be thinking the same thing. Except that Jared Noel isn't in the marriage bed—he's propped upright on a hospice bed in the far corner of the bedroom, with the brightest backlight behind him (the sun) so that you can't clearly define his features, which must work for a dying man who doesn't want people to notice how rapidly he's deteriorating, but doesn't really work for you, because on top of not really knowing what to say you're also now squinting, trying to make out whether he's looking at you or not. So, it takes even longer to reach him than it should, not only because he's on the far side of the marriage bed but also because there's a great chasm between him and you—a chasm opened up by the fact he is looking at the world from a point of view we only get to experience once, which is the sure-fire knowledge that very soon—probably within between five to eight weeks in his own, informed opinion—he will die. And anyone who enters this sacred place in order to dialogue with Jared about this very thing knows full well that no matter how close you sit to him, how many questions you ask him, or how many times you peer against the backlight to get a good look at his eyes, you will never, ever know, until you're in the very place that Jared now occupies, what it feels like to be staring down the barrel as he is. As I enter that room for the very first time, Jared is—quite literally, figuratively, spiritually and symbolically—alone.

Encounter

Almost every day for a whole month, from August 28 until September 24, 2014, Dr Jared Noel and I sit together in his room—Jared propped up in bed, while I sit facing him from an armchair positioned at the side of the bed. The conventions that we follow, each and every day, are established here at our very first meeting. It occurs to me several times over the course of the month that each day we follow a pattern we have established for no particular reason. I wonder if all relationships proceed this way? Do we all follow a blueprint we draw up at the first encounter? Or is this peculiar to Jared and me because we know we will have only a month, roughly, to get to know one another well enough to plumb thoughts and feelings that people typically avoid? Mainly around suffering, death, isolation, and the silence of God when we need him to make his presence felt more than ever.

The pattern goes pretty much like this: as I enter Jared's room, I try not to speak until my iPad is set up and recording, in case he says something profound that will be lost forever. This results in an awkward period of silence almost every day. I place the iPad on his bed, near his feet, and arrange a small microphone close to his hands, which causes him some irritation from time to time as he tries to avoid interfering with the device, and becomes ever more unnaturally aware of what his hands are doing. We are interrupted early in the conversation every day by someone bringing coffee—Hannah, his wife, or Ruth, his mum, or even Frances, his mother-in-law. The first time this happens I find myself surprised, for no apparent reason, that people dying of cancer still drink hot coffee—a macchiato, in Jared's case.

Our conversation begins awkwardly, since we are aware from the start that we are discussing matters of life and death, sickness, suffering, sadness, doubt, grief, regret—all the key elements of the human drama that everyone experiences but which our many conventions help us avoid in typical conversation. This is particularly so between men, and even more particularly between men who barely know one another. Yet here we are, brought together by strange and compelling circumstances to talk specifically about such things. It is intimate, to be sure. But the intimacy, at least at the beginning, feels fabricated—by necessity, no doubt, but nevertheless contrived.

We become acutely aware on this first day that no matter how much we talk, or how daring we are in the matters we discuss, I will never alleviate Jared's isolation, let alone his suffering. His path was set well before I entered this room. The most I can hope to achieve is a small understanding of what it is like to feel the shadows encroaching—this man of suffering, familiar with disease (Isa. 53.3).

First Time in Jared's Home

As Jared and I talk for a full hour of fairly awkward intimacy, life in the household buzzes serenely along. The Noel home is clean and bright, not sterile by any means, but the things of the house are in their right place. The breeze is allowed to blow through and the bright walls and open-plan living create a generous sense of space, and air, and life, and growth. It is very much the type of house you would expect two young doctors to make their home. There is a baby in the house too, Elise, the daughter of Jared and Hannah, the little girl neither of them thought Jared would see as her birth approached. But, due mainly to the generosity of complete strangers, Jared has been able to not only see Elise but also to spend seven months with her—as if it was granted that he "might see offspring" and thereby "have long life" (Isa. 53.10). This juxtaposition is a hefty piece of the backdrop as Jared and I talk—in an upstairs bedroom a life is coming to an end, while elsewhere in the house another one is very much beginning. Some days, Elise is asleep in her room close by. On other days she's out on a walk with her maternal grandmother, or she's downstairs having lunch. On this first day she's sitting upright in her chair beside the dining table, with chubby, flushed cheeks and sparkling, intelligent eyes that hold your gaze. Present, animated, and so expectant. And also ignorant of the reason behind all the activity that comes and goes on such a regular basis.

So, despite my expectations before entering the home, this does not feel like a young man's final resting place. There are no hospital odours, no tears, no gloomy shadows caused by drawn curtains. There are plenty of medicines on top of the dresser, and there's a drip bag hanging from a stand beside Jared's bed, but the light seems to burn these elements from the picture. This feels like a young couple's marital home. It's a home that expects a future. There are rooms for more kids, there is space for more activity, there are vacancies on the bookshelf. There are over-sized Scrabble tiles on the fridge door linking the names of the three people who occupy the home: Jared, Hannah, Elise. There are framed family portraits on the walls showing no sign of sickness. There are items of wedding memorabilia placed carefully in the bedroom, the family room, the upstairs lounge. And there are several pairs of shoes in the hallway beside the stairs, which immediately tell you this is a home that guards its cleanliness, that requires you to leave things of the outside at the door.

I stand undone at these shoes the very first time I see them, not quite able to process whether to follow their convention or not. Mostly though I am undone by the fact Jared is not there at the front door to greet me. I have forgotten already that he is bedridden, that the muscles in his legs have wasted away enough in a short space of time to render them largely ineffective. I notice that none of these shoes are his—that they probably belong to Hannah, or her mother, or Jared's parents—all of whom greet me in the doorway with bare or stockinged feet. Jared will never wear shoes again, it occurs to me; will never greet visitors at the door again, nor walk down these stairs. None of this is in my mind in the moments before I step through into this extraordinary situation, with all these contradictory realities, and these people who are tag-teaming admirably in an effort to keep this space as normal, as hopeful, as peaceful as they can.

Decision to Come Home

Jared knew he would die at home. In fact, he requested it. He didn't know when but he knew that he would. Six months before our conversations begin, Jared prepared an Advanced Care Pathway with his GP in which he stipulated his preferences once the need arose for palliative care: dying at home was his first priority, hospice was second, hospital third. The pathway was prepared well before death seemed imminent. It was done as a matter of duty more than anything. Jared knew it would be required at some point but at the time he prepared it he felt so well. Now here he is. Home. As planned. Almost ready to die.

But he still looks so well on this first day. Sure, his face is much thinner than it was the last time I saw him up and about—though only ever from a distance—and with his full beard and glasses and pyjama top he looks very different from the Jared who is framed up on the bedroom wall with his family—the "public" Jared, the face familiar to anyone who paid attention to his story on the front page of the national newspaper, or on various television programs, or in the pages of parenting magazines, or speaking from the stage. The face that greets me, and the "Jared" that I carry in my memory, is the one who has "no form or beauty, that we should look at him, no charm, that we should find him pleasing" (Isa. 53.2). And yet, despite the weight loss and the dry throat, which is due to laryngitis and not something more insidious—and yes, even the terminally ill get sick in more innocent ways—Jared is, well, upright—in posture, certainly, but also in spirit, in presence. He is all there, engaged, ready to talk, determined. Indeed, this is Dr Noel more than it is Jared. All self-assurance, rationality, clipped and precise syntax, a general let's-get-down-to-business demeanour.

There is never a discussion between us about any limits on our conversations. It is assumed by both of us that we will talk about anything. And why not? If Jared's estimates on how long he has left to live are accurate, there is, quite literally, no time to waste—and also nothing to lose.

My opening question is straightforward enough: how did you make the decision to come home to die? Jared answers by talking about the Advanced Care Pathway. Being home for Jared is about control, dictating, as much as he can, how these final days will play out. And this is consistent with how he looks, and speaks, and acts—a man who is gently steering the course of his life towards its end.

"We decided that if I could get home during these last days that it would be the best of outcomes," Jared says, his voice hoarse and weak. There's something in his manner that suggests he knows all about working the outcomes. "It means I'm among friends and family. Family don't become visitors all of a sudden—they are just there. And I can spend more time with them. And hopefully more memorable time as well, for Hannah, particularly. Rather than memories of having to get up and come visit me every day, she wakes up and I'm there."

Not Being Tied Down to a Place

When you listen to Jared's story—I mean, really listen, as in take note of the bigger themes, the recurring motifs, the places where his memory puts most emphasis—some key ideas emerge. This is partly due to the fact that Jared has told his story often. Shortly after hearing his terminal diagnosis, Jared quite literally accepted the Servant's call to be "a light of nations, that my salvation may reach to the ends of the earth" (Isa. 40.6)—determined to accept any speaking engagement that was offered him, as well as writing a daily blog that was read by thousands around the world. So, his story is a little shop-worn. It becomes a bit like laying railway tracks—subsequent tellings tend to follow a pre-established formula in order to reinforce themes that Jared has become aware of in the repeated telling, over time, to different types of audiences and on different occasions. One of these themes is the absence of a fixed place to call "home" during his childhood. "I've moved around a lot," is how he says it. Born in Raetihi in the central North Island of New Zealand, Jared had lived in two different towns by the time he was five. He would move back and forward to

Auckland throughout his childhood and he would link this lack of a fixed family home to his love of travel as an adult, and perhaps even his desire to work overseas.

But at the end of his life, home was very much the goal. These people, this building, this room. Propped up against his pillows, Jared is every bit the master of his house. It's his castle. He speaks about his happiness at rejoining the family, having been absent for eight weeks. He wakes up and he's home, he says, a familiar environment and familiar surroundings. As he speaks he's forced to swallow, suddenly and without warning. It takes him by surprise but this will become a regular feature of our conversations in coming days.

"I guess on a practical level what I bring to the home is more work for my wife," Jared admits, "because she is caring for me. But at the same time, it's a reunification of the family—whilst we can have it, for as long as we can have it."

Jared's Parents

Jared's parents Royston and Ruth are downstairs as we speak. I can hear them preparing to leave as Jared recounts his early family life, and while he says nothing negative about his childhood I'm feeling cautious on their behalf. I hadn't expected to meet mum and dad, but they were there at the foot of the stairs when I arrived. It was like being presented with the principal actors before the start of the play—the wife, the mother-in-law, the child, the parents. Before Jared had uttered a word about the main players in his life drama I had faces for them all. In the case of his parents, those faces were smiling, hopeful, even appreciative. I was caught out by this, then realised what it meant—I was the scribe who would keep their son's story alive. I was Second Isaiah, in some respects, ensuring the transition from life and ministry to death would not be glossed over; that its significance would be recorded. My very presence assured them of something—that their son's special life would not be forgotten. Royston and Ruth are sprightly people, youthful and deep-rooted, people of quality. I tried to imagine how it might feel for them, visiting their young adult son in the place of his dying. I was at once both pleased and daunted by their expectations, but couldn't begrudge them the comfort they took from this, Jared's final project. Their pride in him is in my mind as Jared talks about being taken around the North Island because of his dad's studies and his various professional appointments—but never with bitterness, or accusation. For Jared, each move is a piece of fabric that when stitched together displays the whole of who he is.

Where Jared Grew Up

Jared's early childhood was spent here, there and everywhere. He was born in the central North Island in the days of three-digit phone numbers and a staffed telephone exchange. The "middle of nowhere" is how Jared describes Ohakune, his first home.

Jared tells friends later that recalling so much of his story to me is difficult, and certainly he is constantly battling the effects of whatever painkillers he is on. He has a reputation for being incisive with his brain functioning, with an eloquence and vocabulary to match, but to me Jared speaks in constricted sentences, and where distant memories are concerned, he lists events as you might present them in a curriculum vitae. But every so often his retelling is punctuated with flashes of colour, as memories illuminated by moments of emotion burst through the drowsiness, like one particular memory from Rotorua.

"It was round about the time Halley's Comet was whipping through, I remember that. We went over to a friend's house who had a telescope. And I didn't really know what I was looking at but I said I could see Halley's Comet. Apparently, everyone else could, but I had no idea. I do wish I was older now because I would have quite liked to have seen it."

Jared takes time with his speech, avoids lazy contractions, and seems to derive pleasure from taking the long way around to say something. His medication raises hurdles for him, particularly around articulation, conceptual formation and diction. His laryngitis makes speaking painful—it requires extra effort to be heard. And dipping into relatively mundane memories is not particularly stimulating. However, Jared never complains—"like a ewe, dumb before those who shear her" (Isa. 53.7). Every now and again he will show some irritation—the merest glimpse of an eye roll or an extra heavy sigh. But even in those moments he drives himself onward.

What Jared Wanted to Be

I ask Jared whether he knew what he wanted to be in the early stages of his life, moving frequently around the North Island. His dad was a teacher, a former mechanic, and the family were Baptists—elements that probably shaped his chosen path later on. Certainly, they influenced Jared in such things as faith, and pragmatism, and social awareness. But already a different path was presenting itself.

"I think if you had asked me at that stage I might have said things like fireman or policeman, what a typical eight or nine-year-old might say,"

Jared says. "But for me I didn't have any particular ambition of what I might be or do with my life.

"I think I was always scientific. I was never really arty. Music came a little bit later, when I was older. But I would never have described myself as arty. My sister was. And I guess I was scientific because I always had the inquisitive mind. I wanted to know why things worked the way that they did. I do remember my parents buying me presents like electronic build sets…and that you could build a radio."

A Clinical Description

As Jared sits upright in bed, the only signs of his illness some weight loss and the occasional bout of burping, his vision for life is as bright now as when it first formed. It was years in the making, at least in how Jared constructs the arc of his story. And when you've told your story so many times you risk retouching certain elements to help them fit more naturally into an overarching narrative like Jared's, where there was a defined trajectory and a profound vision of what he would become. He uses the word "greatness" at key moments in the narrative, as if greatness is an obligation. Others use the word of Jared too—destined for greatness, they'll say, his wife among them. And there's a nobility to Jared even in these circumstances that permits you to believe that he was destined for greatness, and perhaps even still is. It's not "greatness" that you might associate with ego, but a real sense of being chosen for something truly significant, like the Servant in Isa. 42.1, the "chosen one" in whom Yahweh "delights."

But our talk of vision, and trajectory, and grand narrative, is set against a much more pressing reality—Jared is dying, and his story will soon come to an end, whether he experiences "greatness" or not. Before our conversation advances much further, we address this, the most obvious discussion point.

"Why are you dying?" I ask.

"It's complex," Jared answers.

Put simply, it began with bowel cancer, the symptoms of which didn't surface until the disease had advanced beyond what current treatments, including surgery and chemotherapy, could successfully address. Jared believes he was genetically predisposed to bowel cancer, though not in straightforward ways, since there was no record of any family member having suffered it.

"It's only recently described in the literature and so not well under-stood," Jared says, in a manner that is characteristic of the way Jared the aspiring surgeon, Jared the scientist, likes to speak. "It's not simple genetic in that I have it therefore my daughter will have it. It's quite complex genetically. I have it so therefore there's an increased chance my daughter will have it. I have no family history of people who have had it. So that's an example of why it's complex. Whereas the simple more Mendelian genetic component is, if your father has it, you are more likely to have it. And being such a young person it's also highly unusual.

"Those changes that happened, probably from my early 20s, happened under the radar. Then I was diagnosed at 27, because at that point it had grown enough that it had caused symptoms elsewhere in the body for it to be recognised. But it had also grown enough that modern day treatment was unable to address it sufficiently for me to survive from it."

"So, you knew on initial diagnosis that it was terminal?"

"The very, very initial diagnosis—if you were to use population data as your evidence for citing survival sources—was that I had a 40 per cent chance of surviving it five years. Which I've done, to be honest. But for different reasons."

"Where is the cancer now?"

"When I was first diagnosed, I presented with a bowel obstruction, and so they operated. They did a right hemicolectomy, where they removed the righthand portion of my large bowel. And they thought they removed it all, including some surrounding tissue areas—that's why they thought I was in the clear. But it recurred in the lymph nodes, basically. And it has since recurred in the mesentery, which is the tissue that supplies the blood, the lymph supply, to all the intestines. And it has now recurred in the liver. So my liver is completely rampant with it. And it will slowly occur through the abdomen, through the liver, and infiltrate all of that in these final days."

"And what will cause you to die?"

"Eventually, it has a mass effect, i.e., your body can't survive with that mass blocking what it is trying to do. It will shut down your organs by just getting in the way. It's a mechanical effect rather than a physiological effect."

I ask Jared about his current symptoms—what is the cancer doing to him at this moment?

"The main thing is that I have partial bowel obstructions—more areas of the bowel which have begun to obstruct but not completely. The symptoms with that are nausea and vomiting, when I eat. And they have been able to stent some of those obstructions to hold open the bowel so that food can pass through. But also there seems to be obstructive jaundice, where parts of the liver that drain bile into the gut are also blocked. It means your bile can't drain, your bilirubin goes up, and that can be toxic to the liver."

And all of this was diagnosed when?

"I had surgery on November 14, 2008. And I got the histology that confirmed that I had cancer on November 20."

Being Home

I ask Jared a clumsy question about home, and what his impact will be on the household in these his final days. Except that it doesn't come out quite so clearly, and he responds with one of those disarming looks that he has when you haven't been able to express yourself with the precision he expects. So, I ask it again. And fluff the question a second time. But Jared obliges, and also addresses an earlier question about what he expects, as a person of faith, to happen after death—his "portion," to draw a clumsy connection with Isaiah 53.

"I think for me, personally, it is coming back to the family that I've created and helped create with my wife, and that's an important part of it," he says, to answer the first question. Then this:

"The transition period that you talk about, interestingly, I've not found myself pondering what that is yet. A lot of people talk about what's going to happen in the next phase, but I've not yet found myself being in that place. I sometimes wonder whether I should wonder. But I think I know enough of theology and I have enough in my faith to know that mankind's attempts to truly understand what the next life is like have often been met with lots of speculation and crazy ideas. At the bottom of it, it boils down to the fact that we don't really know."

I mention the U2 song, *One Step Closer*, about the death of Bono's father, and Bob Geldof's observation that the old man is at least one step closer to knowing whether there is any life beyond death.

"And so I'm just one step closer to knowing," Jared agrees, quietly.

Sense of Time

If the limitations of space are a major defining element of our daily conversations—Jared in his place, me in mine—then time is another. We are aware that our timelines have crossed in a fortuitous way for these conversations to happen. We are also aware that each daily dialogue can last no longer than sixty minutes—Jared is too weary to talk for much more. There is also the bigger timeline to consider, namely Jared's estimation on how long he has left. But even he cannot say with any certainty for how much of that time he will be well enough to talk.

Jared's documenting of his illness over the previous five and a half years has created its own narrative framework, a sense of time constructed around his major hurdles, his small and large victories, his disappointments and achievements. His life in the spotlight has become a plot sequence, a drama in which he, the protagonist, has been moving purposefully and inexorably towards a tragic end, but which for so long has seemed so far away. He has a knack of pushing the deadline back and circumventing what seemed inevitable. Jared seems to have his own *Deus ex machina* of Greek theatre, dropping in when all seems lost to create another way forward. But the story over recent months, from the birth of Elise in January, has been told at a different pace—it has been slower, more reflective, more private. The blog entries have become more scarce, and when they have appeared they have been written in a melancholic tone.

I put all this to Jared and say that I find it difficult, impossible even, to imagine what it is like to experience time as he is, knowing that time was approaching its end. Is he packing more into the minutes and hours and days, or are they slipping away like water through the fingers?

"I find time blurs," he answers. "The days of the week don't have a lot of meaning to me. Monday and Saturday, if it's the weekend or not the weekend—it's all very much blurred. Time in some ways slows down, but also I'm not doing a lot with myself because of energy levels and because I'm just not capable. So, in that sense you don't pass time the same way or quite the same way. You can get bored but at the same time you don't have the energy levels to do anything about that boredom, in any way that you might have done previously. Once upon a time I might have read a book but now because of the drugs that I'm on I don't have the concentration ability to read that book and maintain it."

"How do you ascertain how much time you have left?"

"Any doctor will give you a very convoluted answer. And me being a doctor, I would also give a convoluted answer. It's a combination of factors: looking at the condition of the body, the condition of the organ systems based on blood tests, and then just the nature of the disease itself. How fast is it growing, how aggressive is it, where is it, what is it doing? The answer in my case is that probably it's measured in weeks—it could be eight weeks, but it could be two weeks or one week. If it was at the one week end of the spectrum you'd probably suggest something would happen between now and a week's time that would cause me suddenly to deteriorate. But at the five, six, seven, eight-week mark, it would probably be a slow deterioration until I get to a point where my organs basically give up—I go into organ failure. Whether that's kicked off by my liver, where the disease is quite strongly advancing, or systemic organ failure, where they all give up together. They've been fighting together and they give up together."

I give Jared my own, uninformed, opinion. Based on how he is looking, I say he will still be with us in eight weeks. I realise even as I say it that I am hoping already—hoping that his time, our time, will be extended. Perhaps I am hoping also that something miraculous will occur that will alter his course, some act of divine healing in line with the miracle stories of the Bible he quotes from time to time.

"It could be," is how he responds, not really considering my opinion. "I think that my suspicions, both as a doctor and as a patient, are that around the five to six to seven-week mark is probably round about where it would be accurately placed. We can't see into the future, but that is my suspicion."

What It's Like to Face Death

Jared faces the ensuite bathroom from where he is propped up in bed, and can see a sideboard and mirror, and the door to the outside lounge area, all of which are behind me, out of my view unless I turn around. Sometimes he puts his hands behind his head and looks beyond me, as if there's a tableau forming behind me that is playing out the scenes from his childhood. At other times he looks me full in the eye, locking on to the ideas that I am prompting him to engage with. His gaze is made all the more intense by his illness, which has caused his eyes to be deep set and heavily shadowed, a fact obscured to some degree by his glasses. But there's no mistaking the heaviness of his fatigue.

I look beyond Jared most days to the outside world. The curtains are pulled away from the corner window behind his head, and there's a view from the upper room to the suburb outside, the first hints of the warmer New Zealand months already evident—some warmth on the breeze, the faintest heat haze off the houses. Jared cannot see what I see, and I wonder whether he still has any interest in the outside world or the summer days that he will never see again.

Something else Jared sees that I cannot is the onset of the long sleep… the end of his days.

"I think it's different for everybody," he says, describing how it feels to be here, now, experiencing this. "I've had this conversation with a number of different people. A friend of mine who visited last night had a mum die of breast cancer in the last six months. For her, the reality of facing death was a scary reality and she wanted to avoid that at all costs. And so she fought to try and fight the cancer for as long as possible. But for me, because I've accepted the outcome, the idea of facing death isn't a scary one. The decision to go palliative was a big mindset change more than anything else. It required me to move from one phase of thinking, which is the treatment phase, and still trying to stay alive for as long as I can, whilst knowing that death was always going to be on the cards, through to the next phase—which is about being comfortable.

"Knowing that I have advancing disease, the goal of the medical treatment now is to keep me comfortable rather than to keep me alive."

Frustrations

In the earliest days of his blog, while he lay bored in Auckland Hospital receiving treatment, Jared made a random post titled "Tips for parenthood," which contained a humorous graphic on the dos and don'ts of raising a baby. Jared made the point that he wouldn't really need the tips for another five (or ten) years. That was February 2, 2009, and as it turned out his prediction was true almost to the day. Elise Alexandra Grace was born on January 17, 2014.

I ask Jared how difficult the time had been following the birth. My suspicion is that along with the elation of having a baby in the home there must have been frustration too, knowing that his time with her was so limited.

"Only over the last two months," he says. "Up until two months ago I was pretty well. And basically she was a kid who had two stay-at-home parents with her for the first four to six months of her life. And you could tell—she was a bit spoilt because of that, I think.

"But it's been frustrating since I've been in hospital. I've seen changes in her that I'm missing out on. I come home now and sometimes I look at her and she's a different baby because of the development that's happened while I've been away. And the skills she has developed. You do feel like you've missed out. Little things like fine motor control, watching her develop what she can do. As doctors, Hannah and I are aware of all of that, the developmental milestones that babies and kids go through. We are watching for them and can probably pick out some of the more subtle stuff most parents wouldn't."

Elise

It's to Elise that our conversation naturally gravitates as it draws to a close on this first encounter. This will be the pattern of things each time we meet. I will ask Jared in the coming days what his purpose was in deciding to commit his thoughts and memories to writing, filtered as it is through our dialogues. One reason is so that his daughter might know her dad, and through these conversations to get a sense of how it was to encounter him, to join him on the journey if only for a short distance, and through the experience to see life as he saw it. I've been called in as a witness, it occurs to me—a chronicler of the short life of a chosen one.

I ask Jared to imagine Elise's first school day. The thrill of the new uniform, the hair bouncing in a ponytail, the backpack with its little lunchbox and freezer pack inside. My own memories provide the source for the image, and the differences between us are never more stark. I have those memories, of daughters readying themselves for school. Jared will not.

I ask Jared what he would communicate to Elise on that day, and how he would prepare her for the rough and tumble of the schoolyard.

"I think we want to instil a sense that things happen like this," he says, "that it's not the end of the world when it does happen. You do see some parents swarm in around the kid when the most minor of bumps and scrapes happen, and they turn it into a big deal. And we wouldn't be those parents. We'd be the parents who say, Look it's only a bump and it's ok, you can keep doing what you're doing and you don't have to keep crying. We would try and instil that kind of thing in her."

"And play? How important will play be in Elise's formational years?"

"I want to get down and I want to play with her as much as possible. And teach her lots of different things. And Hannah's been very specific from a very early age about reading her books. So she has lots of children's books that are being read to her already. And she loves them. She'll sit and listen already and look at the pictures. It's part of her go-to-bed routine as well. They actually had to go and buy some more books the other day because she got sick of reading the same ones. We've already got like thirty or forty.

"One of the things is that if I was well I would actually be working as a general surgeon—I would be at work for up to ninety hours a week. And that does restrict my ability to be involved in her playtime quite significantly. Unfortunately, that just comes with the job. It comes with the territory. In an ideal world I'd be down there on my hands and knees and playing with her all the time. But in the actual situation it probably would have turned out to be weekends that she would get to have that time with me.

"Daddy time would have been a bit more rare and a bit more special because of that."

Hannah

Elise is downstairs as I leave, being fed by her grandmother. I see her as that five-year-old child, hungry to learn, her mind already opened to possibilities by parents who daily breathe in the vastness of the world and see only opportunity for new experience.

Hannah is there too, standing, pivoting as if to move. I begin to give her a summary of my first conversation with Jared, but before I have finished she rushes past me from the room and heads upstairs to be with her husband.

The Boredom Blog

Our suffering often seems so great to ourselves, a giant tree that is only so large because we stand right in front of it, blinding us from the even larger trees in the forest that stand before others. When we take a step back from our tree and see the context in which we live, it makes it so much harder to complain. Our tree is never as big as it seems when seen in context. And when we begin to focus on other people's trees, their suffering instead of our own, all of a sudden the tree that seemed to loom so large begins to appear smaller than we thought.

If there is one thing my life's turn of events have taught me, it's that focusing on others instead of me removes myself from the picture. I realise my life is only one of many lived on this planet, and whilst I will die young, I will die blessed with the life I have been given. Hopefully, in return, I can bless others with that same life rather than focussing on my own. It is ironic that through having an "others" focussed approach, I find the peace required to deal with my own circumstance.

Life was never meant to be lived with us at the centre, that only brings misery, self-ambition, and loneliness. When life is lived with others at the centre, that is when we find community, friendship and love…it sounds really soppy, but it works…

Jared Noel, The Boredom Blog
"Chemo 54.0"
January 22, 2013

WRESTLING WITH GOD

No Tears

There are no tears in the Noel house. I expected tears. They must happen in the evening, when no one is looking, in closed rooms and quiet moments, in reflective conversations or times of prayer, begging God to pull out his finger and do something amazing. Perhaps they come at unbidden times around mementoes, and photos, or favourite mugs, or notes tucked away in books. Perhaps they happen around the streets, with Elise in the pram, walking and walking for ages with the excuse that Elise needs to sleep, when really it's because Hannah, or Ruth, or Frances…need to weep. The tears are probably happening everywhere. Just not for me. Or not around me, at least. The closest I come to tears is when Hannah, as we sit down for an "official" conversation at the end of my second chat with Jared, warns me that tears might come. But they don't, and I'm disappointed. I expected a house of dying to be a house of tears. A house with no tears feels unnatural, like everyone is holding them in. But what's the point of tears anyway? What do they achieve, apart from sore faces and puffy eyes, running noses and awkward sniffles? There is plenty of time for tears. What the house needs—what the house has—is laughter. And conversation. And baby noises. And stories. Lots of stories. Not just for Elise, but for Hannah, and for mum and dad Noel, and for everyone else who comes here to say goodbye. Tears are exhausting. Jared himself tells me so. He's had enough of tears. Which is why I never see them. But moments of love. Moments of life. We can't get enough of them.

There will always be time for tears. Later.

Breeze through the Window

Tiny moments are often the ones that have most significance when you're dying. They can appear so innocuous when measured against the bigger events that make up our lives, but for peculiar reasons, and at the meeting of particular times and places, they take on what seems like eternal weight. C. S. Lewis tells a powerful story about one such moment. It's when he first glimpses a little garden his brother has made from bits of flora and fauna from the back yard of their home, all assembled in a small box. The young Lewis is overcome by a feeling he can't immediately name, but which he comes to describe as "joy." It's life-altering because, for him, its significance stretches beyond the moment, beyond the garden and even beyond the feeling, to a sudden and overwhelming awareness of beauty itself, and of moments so full of life that they seem to signal the possibility of more transcendent realities, of a great lake of joy from which such glimpses are drawn like glasses of fresh water.

I experience such a moment with Jared. It's our second day, a Friday, in many ways an encounter that could not be more different to that of the day before. Except that the sun is still bright, and summer is on the air and in the noises of the birds and the flying insects. The window behind Jared is open again and the breeze is blowing through into the bedroom. It catches Jared's hair as it blows past his head. I watch as the hair wafts outwards from behind his ear, flapping gently as if we're chatting beside a river over lunch on a late spring afternoon. I'm transfixed by this—the movement, the life, the calm and the beauty. Jared's hair, made wispy by almost six years of chemotherapy, has life in it yet. Yes, there is fragility, but there is also grace. Something about it echoes the flowing river of life that continually sweeps through the house no matter how close to the end Jared is. It's the briefest moment, the tiniest sign that life continues despite the onset of death, that it blows through this room even now, and graces Jared's scalp and the pale skin of his cheek.

I wonder whether Jared has noticed—I also wonder how significant such a moment might be for him. Is every such moment like a final meal, a final kiss, a final prayer, a final touch? Or is it obscured by the gathering momentum of the greater struggle, the unremitting deterioration of Jared's body, mind and spirit?

Ultimately, it's not a moment shared between us. It's my observation and remains my observation. It's an example of the suffering of the other viewed from outside. I can't know what Jared is experiencing. I can only observe. And after every such moment of projecting myself into his situation, I discover myself back in my privileged position and everything about Jared joins the rest of the picture that I have in front of me, like a character from a movie climbing back up into a cinema screen. There is a gulf between us that in most ways we can never bridge.

A Dialogue on Faith

Like C. S. Lewis, Jared is a man of faith. Like Lewis, he's also a philosophical rationalist, which means despite his faith (or because of it) he engages life and truth and meaning—and death—with his eyes wide open. Even now, approaching the biggest step on anyone's faith journey, he is content with what he doesn't know. His awareness of the limitations of his knowledge only reinforces for Jared that some things will always remain outside his knowing. And he's okay with that. Or so he says. I remind Jared of Lewis's own doubt in the face of death, particularly as expressed in *A Grief Observed*: "Not that I am (I think) in much danger of ceasing to believe in God. The real danger is of coming to believe such dreadful things about Him. The conclusion I dread is not 'So there's no God after all,' but 'So this is what God's really like. Deceive yourself no longer.'" Jared appreciates Lewis's view, but says that it's not one he shares.

Jared's faith is an obvious though infrequent component of his blog and anyone who follows along recognises that it's a key element in the way he has faced his illness and the kind of life that illness produces. His uncompromising honesty about the physical suffering and emotional turmoil that he has experienced is authentic and compelling. Jared is able to hold in tension a belief in God with an unqualified sense of disappointment that life has not turned out the way he thinks God has said it would.

"I guess, fundamentally, the way that I think is very analytical and very process-driven," he explains to me, as our conversation settles into a discussion about faith and doubt, hope and disappointment. "But at the heart of that I know there is something spiritual, something bigger that can't always be quantified the way science can quantify things. And there's a reassurance that if my scientific foundations were to fall down there are faith foundations that won't fall down.

"From the beginning, there's been that reassurance that there's something bigger going on. I don't necessarily understand it, but I'm a part of it."

Faith was always going to be part of Jared's story. His was a family of faith that belonged to various communities of faith throughout his childhood, no matter where the Noels lived. Even so, there were particular times along the way when the need for faith, or for the accoutrements of faith, became more pressing.

"Life didn't exist outside of the faith component because that was such an integral part of the home environment. But I do remember when we moved to Hawkes Bay, it resulted in me turning to my Bible more. The Bible was a place of some kind of refuge; some kind of place where I might find hope or find what it was that I wasn't getting in the new school environment. I remember in fourth form at some stage deciding that I was going to try and read my Bible in a year. It didn't happen. But I developed some good Bible reading habits."

I ask Jared what it was about the Bible that gave him comfort.

"I think it was a little bit what I was reading. I've always been a New Testament kind of person. I always found the Old Testament a little bit hard to relate to. The New Testament for me was where I would find the story and life of Christ, and his teaching—it's where I got a lot of my food."

Jared recalls a pivotal moment in his faith journey during his Hawkes Bay years, one of those rare moments—one of only two or three in Jared's life—when he believed God had spoken to him. Subjective impressions of divine messages are problematic as sources of knowledge, something Jared knows only too well. He has this in common with the Suffering Servant, as we will see. The Servant is addressed by God too, and must work out its significance for himself. Whatever the source of Jared's particular impression, what it communicated would alter Jared's life at the time, and ultimately played a more significant role when that voice was echoed later in life.

The occasion was a youth camp, a combined church event to which Jared's much smaller youth group had been invited. Jared had a sudden conviction that he needed to be baptised—that he needed to step up and own for himself the faith that he had grown up with. It was from that moment that Jared gave the faith component much more prominence in how he came to envision the future and his part in the human drama.

"Faith" is sometimes viewed by skeptics as the fairy tales people believe in, the fantasies they rely on to shape their lives even when there is no evidence that they have any truth to them. But "faith," in the sense that Jared uses the word, is best understood as story, or the story in which he has chosen to locate his self-understanding, as well as his understanding of time and space, the world about him, and his sense of purpose in it. According to the story of Jared's faith, there was an historical moment in which God—the God Jared believes in—intervened in human history. This intervention was beyond scientific verification, but not beyond the historical witness of a small group of people who were convinced that they had seen the impossible—a man who had come back from the dead. It's this "impossible possibility" that Jared holds as a fundamental truth of history, and which shapes his belief in possibilities beyond death. It seems incredulous as we sit and talk about these things that a man of science, a medical doctor no less, would also ground his broader worldview in something not able to be repeated. Yet here, at the end of his days, his faith in such things seems to be gathering momentum.

"What it meant in my faith actively," he says, of that moment of conviction, "was that all of a sudden it took on a much higher priority, in terms of my life. It just had a much more personal component to it, rather than just what my family had brought me up with. And a hunger for it, definitely."

Vulnerability

It's ironic that as we talk about faith and certainty, there's a vulnerability to Jared that hasn't been there before—at least not that I've witnessed. In our first conversation, Jared seemed to be looking forward to these weeks at home. He had a clear idea of what this time might look like, even if he didn't know for sure how long it would last. He was confident, back in his favourite place, bunkering down for the most challenging season yet. Today, though, he's been shaken. I see his fragility up close, and the contrast is a surprise.

Meanwhile, the sun is bright behind his head and the movement of the breeze on the curtain and the sound of machinery somewhere in the middle distance, rising from the suburban streets, are reminders of life going on all around us—and of our place in it.

Jared fell overnight, he tells me feebly, as if he's done something wrong.

He was repositioning himself, he says, and leaning towards the small round table upon which he puts his coffee and water. He discovered too late that he had lost more core strength than he realised, and because of the weight of his upper body he was suddenly overbalanced, and toppled headfirst from the bed, crashing into the table.

"I just couldn't pull myself back," he says. There's a real sadness about him as he says it. But I understand now the fragility—that it's not so much about sickness, as shame. Something new has occurred to him about his situation. In this moment, he's the little boy who's tried so hard to show his parents and friends how capably he can perform a physical feat, but who has hit the wall of his own limitations in full view of everyone.

I'm struck by two things: my own response, which is suddenly very protective (of Jared), and Jared's own willingness to talk about how the incident has made him feel. If ever there was an example of Bakhtin's "I-for-myself" and the "I-for-the other"/"the-other-for-me," it's this moment, as Jared goes outside himself to see and hear in my response the more fixed image of what the incident signifies—to himself, about himself.

"I've lost what would normally have been in my thighs and hips and stuff," he says, about his lost core strength. "It's balance you take for granted, and I had taken it for granted until I didn't have it. I toppled off and smashed into the table. That was an interesting thing, because that was a bit of a..." Here Jared pauses, and I wonder what he is weighing up. He pushes on, without explanation: "...a realisation about your deterioration. You go, okay, what can I do to try and rehab that? But I can't really do anything to rehab that. And so that was a hitting home of the deterioration."

There's a pause as we sit in silence for a moment, pondering his last words.

"And also," he continues, "to be honest, it was just embarrassing. As an adult male you like to think you can do basic things like balance—things like that—and I just totally lost my balance and fell over and smashed into that," he gestures to the table, "and the bed. To the point where I had to have people pull me back up. That was about an hour after you left."

Jared's voice trembles a little. I ask him whether the fall has affected him emotionally and his voice is thin when he answers, and not only because of the laryngitis.

"Yeah, it did actually—it made me cry. Because, one, it was embarrassing. And, two, it was that realisation that I'm going downhill—and I'm not going back uphill—I'm not climbing back up that hill again."

I ask Jared whether he can professionally detach himself at these times. I'm wondering where the boundary is, between Dr Noel and Jared, between the aspiring surgeon who's a philosophical rationalist and the distressed patient.

"Well, that's an example of when it affects the things you take for granted in life. You realise that you really have deteriorated. That's when you feel like the patient all of a sudden. And the detachment just allows you to analyse it a bit more. But when it physically affects you, and emotionally affects you, that's when you're being the patient."

I ask him whether that impacts the family.

"I think so," he answers. "I think for Hannah, it was all part of the process of watching me slowly deteriorate. She knows it's going to happen anyway—so do I. But Hannah is very open to me talking about this, because I've been open about the journey from the very beginning. So, in that sense, this is just another part of that—of that openness."

Mission to the Nations

Vulnerability is a key motif in Jared's life story, at least in how he articulates it now. He may have articulated things differently before diagnosis day, but on this day, feeling the way he does, Jared highlights moments of fragility as if they were the foundation stones for how he now tackles his sickness. Such moments steered him towards new communities and friendships, or helped give him a more defined sense of his own values. These seasons of weakness, such as his school years or a period of depression in his twenties, have more meaning, perhaps, in his current season of vulnerability. They are certainly more pronounced today.

"I actually didn't necessarily know what I wanted to do," Jared says of leaving school. "I had ideas. When I left school I applied for med school. And that was because I was smart enough to do it, really. In retrospect, that was the only reason why I did it—and I had friends who were doing it as well. But I really didn't know what to do career-wise. And a Bachelor of Science was the obvious area of study because science was what I enjoyed."

Jared suddenly excuses himself as he tries to reposition: "I seem to be quite burpy," he says, in some discomfort, leaning forward to force the wind from his abdomen, before sitting upright to clear his throat.

"One of the key things was that at the end of 2000 we did a three-week trip to the Philippines," he says, the "we" being a church youth group, his main community at the time. The trip was a short-term mission trip. "That was the second realisation in my life of where God was calling me," he says. "And that was where this calling for overseas work began."

Jared remembers hearing people coming to church to speak about their experiences of working in the developing world, and being compelled by the idea of living with such purpose, and of making that sort of difference. It was the convergence of a number of things for Jared—his faith, his rationalism, his awareness of economic disparity that he had seen in his childhood, and his compassion for humanity. Something was brewing in him that he knew was about more than a job. It was actually about identity and where he fit. It also resonates with a Servant who in Isa. 49.6 is called in this way: "I will also make you a light of nations, that My salvation may reach the ends of the earth."

"After going to the Philippines, there was this massive eye-opening as to how most of the rest of the world lives, in so much abject poverty," Jared says. "I found myself thinking, how can I live like this in the first world and justify it—live in it guilt free when all of this stuff is going on? I couldn't sit idly by."

Jared's response—and for Jared, determined action always seems to follow these existential moments—was to apply for med school again. But this time it was with a greater purpose. Not that it made any difference.

"As it turned out, I didn't get into med school the second time around either."

Deterioration

I show Jared the back of my camera. I've displayed a photo that I took of him the day before. It's the first time for a while that he's seen himself—his deteriorating self. The "other-for-me" giving Jared a finalised image of his self.

"Boy, aren't I a skinny person?" he says, genuinely shocked. "There's photos of me two months ago and I look completely different to that."

I say that I'm surprised by the change in his condition from one day to the next, and wonder what that indicates about the rate of his decline. I suspect by the way his face responds to this that he isn't fully prepared for what might happen in the weeks ahead. I ask him where he is feeling the deterioration the most.

"Definitely the cognition," he says. "But that's something I've had to deal with over a long time because the chemo has affected my cognition as well. That's something I've just got used to and coped with. But coming home, it's the fact that I can't just automatically walk into the next room. I'm stuck in this one room. What's affecting me now is that lack of mobility really, more than anything else."

"It's your third day at home," I say, "and you were looking forward to being here. But it seems to me like it's both a blessing and a curse."

He agrees, to a point.

"I can't mow the lawns, I can't get outside, I can't enjoy…in that sense you come to your home and you realise just how limited your movement is. But I think that's outweighed by the advantages of just being home."

"What do you fear about the next few weeks, in terms of your deterioration?"

"I very much just cross each bridge when I get to it. So, I don't know, is the short answer. I know that in a week's time things could be very different. But I don't know what will be different and what might have changed.

Wrestling with God

From around the time Jared went on a short-term mission trip to the Philippines, his vision of what he would do with "the rest of his life" began to take form. That vision became more contoured during his mid-twenties. Even with the disruption of his illness, and subsequent operation and cancer diagnosis, his sense of "the rest of his life" was undiminished.

The rest of his life now, though, looks very different. And very brief. I wonder about his faith, in particular his confidence in a God who can apparently perform miracles at will, and who is said to be love itself—a God who, Jared is sure, gave him a vision that went beyond his thirties, beyond New Zealand, beyond his work at Auckland Hospital. C. S. Lewis comes to mind again, and the book he wrote following the death of his wife to cancer, *A Grief Observed*. In it, Lewis says this: "Meanwhile, where is God?… Go to him when your need is desperate, when all other help is vain, and what do you find? A door slammed in your face, and a sound of bolting and double bolting on the inside. After that, silence."

It's out of my own questions around this, not Jared's, that I ask whether he has wrestled or pleaded or argued with God.

"Yep," he admits, "there have been times." I see those times become suddenly present for him. Jared clarifies whether I'm talking about the recent or the more distant past, then he goes inside himself. It seems that his wrestle with God has a bit of a history.

"Well, I think when I was first diagnosed, this was just another step in the journey. Or, at least, it felt like that. It was a very big step, and I was going to need some help jumping it. But as time progressed there were definitely issues that were raised that had less obvious answers and required quite a bit of wrestling. And that was around my calling to do medicine and my calling to work in the third world. So, it was difficult to reconcile that with the reality of the fact that that was looking increasingly like it wasn't going to happen. And I'm not sure that I've actually…" And here Jared pauses, and in this briefest of moments it's as if there is encapsulated a whole history of humanity's wrestle with suffering and grief… "It's one wrestle I don't think I've come to a conclusion on," Jared finally says. "I don't know why God called me so strongly and so fairly clearly down a certain path of life, only to have it ripped out from underneath me."

I say to Jared, "You have no doubt about that calling, do you?"

"No doubt about it, yeah. Even now, if I was suddenly healed tomorrow, back up and full strength, I'd be working towards how I could take my job overseas and work in an overseas environment."

In the hospice, Jared and I had discussed how people of faith often give suffering validity and value by saying it's God's will, or pointing to the "benefits" and changes and maturation the suffering has triggered. I remind Jared of this, and say that I can't imagine anything more meaningless than a disease that prevents a person pursuing his dream—even his calling—of taking medicine to the underprivileged. Can there be anything so absurd as a God who calls someone to live a life of service to others, and yet cannot prevent his untimely death? I'm aware even as I say it that the question could apply to the Suffering Servant of Isaiah as much as to Jared.

"That's almost like the active meaninglessness of suffering," Jared says, agreeing. "It's the active destruction of a hope or a calling. That's where the meaninglessness of suffering isn't just a passive thing but an active thing. It is actually destroying something."

"So, how would you pray during times of doubt?" I ask Jared. I realise after I've said it that I have posed the question as a challenge.

"I've never genuinely been angry with God," he says. "I've been tearful. I think in some ways the experience of what we're talking about fell to the side because it got replaced with this new struggle. The new struggle was, not so much how to survive, but how to battle the new current issue, of cancer, of what it was doing to me, and the hope that maybe there's healing—there's physical healing—so that it can still come to fruition, the other hope."

"Are you saying the hope of your calling was still driving you?"

"To a certain extent, yes."

Hope

"What do you hope in right now?" I ask Jared.

"What I hope in right now is probably—in this moment—is probably kind of hard to answer," he says. He sounds even more vulnerable than he did earlier, when talking about his fall. "What I hope in right now is a loving God who is journeying with me in this process and who…to be honest, what I pray for is to know his presence in this process. Because I feel a little bit distant. I feel as though I don't know his presence right this instant. And I would like to know it a bit more because you only go through this process once in a lifetime, and I just…I'm hoping and wanting in that reassurance, that God is here with me. And then I guess I don't fear death because I have a hope that supersedes death—and death itself isn't really the thing that scares me because of that."

"I'm surprised to hear you say you don't feel God's presence," I say. "I would have assumed you would feel more of God's presence. Would you not expect that?"

"If I was to take the last two years—or the last five years—and look at it retrospectively, his presence has been there quite clearly as a divine thread through everything that's happened. But it doesn't mean I've felt it at the time. And I suspect his divine thread is weaving its way through everything that's happening now. That doesn't necessarily mean that I feel it right now."

"You're talking about the absence of a feeling you would like to have?"

"Yeah, I'm actually talking about an emotion or a feeling type thing. But the flip-side is, have I given him the time to have that feeling? And probably not, to be honest. My disciplines have fallen by the wayside a little bit, and I haven't really been allowing him that time to really just be there and for me to be part of it and listen to what he has to say. So, it's not an outright broad accusation to God, saying where are you? It's probably, in part, an indictment on my own disciplines."

I struggle with the idea of a God, whether in reality or in someone's imagination, who requires a dying man to work harder at his devotional practices in order to be more present. But I keep this to myself. I ask this instead: "Don't you consider all the acts of love around you at the moment as the presence of God?"

"I'm smart enough to know that God's here in a bigger context," Jared says, defensively. "I've come home to a loving family and I have a wife who is doing all these things to take care of me. And God's present in all of that. I'm almost regressing a little bit, and perhaps with what I'm saying what I'm really looking for is that emotion."

"What you're wanting is more a folk religion experience, because you've felt that in the past?"

"Exactly. And I think there is a place for him in all contexts. I think there's a place where you just want to feel him. So to call it regression is probably a bit harsh. But I think, as your faith progresses, you do tend to move away from that emotional-based faith stuff because it can be quite fickle. But sometimes it's what you want."

As I leave the house I wonder whether I will witness the turning up of God to comfort Jared before he dies. But then all I can think about as I head to the car are those haunting Good Friday words, "My god, my god, why have you forsaken me?"

Significance

I strive for a life of significance.

Significance reaches out beyond our normality—it reaches beyond our suffering, and it makes a difference in the world. Significance is embracing the fact that each of us have the capability to change the world, regardless of our brokenness. Changing the world doesn't have to be on the scale of Gandhi or Nelson Mandela…but it might be.

I want normality in my life, because it is scarce. But I know normality is a pipe dream.

What I crave more than normality is significance, something that reaches beyond normalness and into the lives and hearts of those around me. I want the world to be a better place because I was here…even if it is fleeting.

Jared Noel, The Boredom Blog
"I just want normality"
February 9, 2010

GOD'S CALL

Best Laid Plans

There are so many plans at stake in dying. The best laid plans made with the best intentions. A plan for this, for that, for now, for after, for then, for whenever. Plans to follow, plans to guide, plans to break, plans to believe in and plans to make us safe. Plans to help us control what can't be controlled. There's a plan for dying—a plan for pain, for sleep, for anxiety, for nausea. There's a plan for death—for goodbyes, for grieving, for speeches, for flowers, for music, slide shows, memories, stories. There's a plan for life without Jared. A plan for life with Jared. A plan for that life in between, when Jared is here but not here, fading in memories but very much alive—on birthdays, and anniversaries, and special days like Christmas. There are plans for the here and now, for conversations, interviews, messages to the living, biographical stories, theological reflections, philosophical discussions. There are plans for visitations, staggered schedules of friendly goodbyes and final chats, each one exhausting and emotional and as final as the one before. And long before all this, there were plans and more plans. Plans for advanced care, for chemo, plans for rest and recovery, plans for work, for after work, plans for travel, plans for a family, for surgery, for study, for a home, for a cure. And further back still, plans for the future, plans for a career, for vision, for mission, for a purpose, for a way to create a life of significance and meaning and "greatness." Plans to make a difference.

None of these plans seem to matter much anymore. In the hospice we planned eighteen conversations, around eighteen stages of life and eighteen topics of reflection. But what are plans when death can do its worst at any moment, on any day, and at any time? We like plans, Jared and I. Mind-maps, lists, sketches, schedules, words, words, words. But do they really matter?

Jared had big, big plans. The best laid plans made with the best—the very best—intentions. He lays those plans before me, like blueprints on a draftsman's table. Glorious plans. Plans to change the world. Not for money, or for fame, or for monuments to success. But plans to serve others. Plans drawn up in faith and in hope and in love. As fans of Apple and of Steve Jobs, we are both familiar with Jobs's Stanford commencement address from June 2005. His perspective resonates with Jared's own: "Remembering that I'll be dead soon is the most important tool I've ever encountered to help me make the big choices in life. Because almost everything—all external expectations, all pride, all fear of embarrassment or failure—these things just fall away in the face of death, leaving only what is truly important."

Jared's plans, so carefully drawn, seemed to have divine endorsement. But it just goes to show, old Robbie Burns was right. Even the best laid plans of mice and men go awry.

Med School

The vision that propelled Jared through the final, difficult season of his life hung on a moment, a flash of revelation that came out of the blue, unbidden, one morning before work. Of course, when it came Jared had no idea what direction his life would soon take. For all he knew, it was confirmation of a dream he'd had for years, the hope that one day he could work in the developing world where he could make a fundamental difference to people's lives and achieve a level of "greatness" that he was sure was his destiny. Lofty dreams that some might call arrogant—but Jared was convinced of his calling, and this moment seemed to confirm it. It was the missing link, in some ways, between the passion developing since his trip to the Philippines, and the practicalities of taking that passion overseas.

I am eager to hear about it, when we met again. Why was this moment so profound for Jared that he would forever think of it as the "voice of God"? And why would this voice also fail to mention that Jared was dying of cancer, as it raised his hopes for a magnificent life?

We are pushing onto fertile ground for Jared, with the whole idea of purpose and calling. This is no small thing. This calling was more than Jared's vocation, it was his identity—an identity he wants to keep intact, even in these final weeks. As Steve Jobs well knew, death brings with it a sharper focus for those things that matter, and as each day passes I get a sense that Jared's achievements in the area of his passion and calling are taking on greater significance. It isn't my intention to take the sheen away from those achievements, but I am keen to get to the bottom of this voice from out of the blue, and its partial disclosure.

"I was working full time as a forensic scientist," Jared says, setting the scene. "I was flatting. I was finally free of my university years. I had an income, which was nice. I still held very strongly onto this commitment that God was leading me over into the third world but I couldn't figure out why on earth he would use forensics to do so—I didn't know how that was going to be reconciled with this clear calling. But that was who I was. I had this identity."

This is always the crux of it for Jared, which is why he had such drive, even through months of chemotherapy. There's a scene in the movie *Inception*, where Leonardo DiCaprio's character is discussing how to influence a person's mind so they accept a truth to which they are thoroughly opposed. The secret, he argues, is to plant a positive emotion in there, and the required behaviours will just follow—because positive emotion trumps negative emotion every time. I think of it in connection with Jared's final years. A fire was ignited in Jared that burned deeper than the rational. It burned in the emotional, as deep as his own self-understanding.

"I had given up on med school at this stage," Jared says. "I had done five years of university and the idea of going back to med school seemed ludicrous."

But then one morning during a time of reflection before work—Jared remembers it being the middle of winter—a compulsion came over him that he hadn't experienced so forcefully since his teens, when he'd felt the urge to be baptised. God may as well have spoken to him audibly, Jared says, it was that clear. It wasn't audible though, he adds, for clarification. It was another subjective impression, this time directing him to apply, yet again, for med school.

"I was just like, really?" Jared says. "I thought about it a bit more—contemplated it. I was like, this is interesting. It was a dream I had held passionately but had actually given up on at this stage."

When Jared checked the closing dates for applications he discovered he was a week out. But he made the deadline and to his surprise got an interview, which was further than he had been before. And then the interview led to an admission.

"All of a sudden it was going to be a complete transformation of my life," is how Jared remembers it. "I was going back to university, going back to being a student again."

This was June 2004, and Jared would begin the second year of med school the following February.

I ask Jared what he feels was different about this application—why was this one successful? He lists several reasons: he was postgrad, so was applying under a slightly different category; and, he had attained his master's degree with a first-class honours, which "bumped up" his grade point average.

But then there was the divine factor: "A real feeling about it," Jared says. "A pretty strong sense that it was now time."

I say to Jared that his vision of working overseas was with him for so long, this must have been a moment of thinking, "Of course—this is how I'm going to get there!"

"In some ways, yeah," he agrees. "I mean, I remember when I got the admission letter telling me I had got an interview. I came home for lunch, from work, and opened the mail and it brought me to tears. It was almost this realisation of a dream I'd forgotten about. And as I started to relive the dream—or re-dream the dream—it was actually quite emotional."

Rain

The sunshine of the past two days has gone. It is raining outside as we talk today and instead of listening to the sounds of spring through the open window I'm watching the rain hit the glass. More moments. I'm thinking of the contrast, between Jared's mood and the gloominess of the weather. Walking down the long driveway to the house from the street, the rain was icy on my head, and two things occurred to me: I was probably going to have to take off my shoes; and this was more like cancer weather than the previous two days. As I headed upstairs—with my shoes still on—I expected Jared's room to reflect the dreariness of the skies and the cold of the rain, as if the dying man's quarters were like the set of a movie and ought to correspond to the weather.

But the contrast was immediately apparent. The room is warm and bright, as usual, and Jared is nothing like a terminal patient. He is in story-teller mode and has energy for today's talk.

It causes me to realise that the coming weeks will be unpredictable. Jared's condition is not likely to follow a pattern, any more than the weather will. I know that there will be some aspects to his journey that are typical of people in palliative care. But Jared's experience of dying will be as uniquely individual as the life that preceded it.

Jared

Another observation about Jared today: he is far more present, his spirits are brighter, and there's a punch in his voice. The whole topic of purpose fires him up, as it has for some years. It's the place in which he is most resolved. But he is thinking and speaking without hindrance, too. And this creates a different dynamic between us. I feel more fired up by the conversation as well. Argumentative, even. Certainly more daring to push the parameters of our dialogue and explore those troublesome areas of Jared's testimony. And I suspect he is more willing to go there too.

I don't admit this to Jared, but I am unsettled by the stoic nature of his faith. I am far more comfortable with doubt, even anger, when it comes to the question of God. When C. S. Lewis says that God slams the door in your face and double bolts it from the inside, he echoes humanity's long wrestle with the divine absence in moments of suffering. It's an authentic voice, and one that I know Jared has spoken with in the past. But now, just weeks away from the end, and with fundamental questions about his life as yet unanswered, I wonder whether he has fallen back on stoicism to void unnecessary anxiety in these last weeks.

God's Call

I push Jared some more on the moment itself. If it was like a voice, what did it sound like? Was it a vision, perhaps? A line of poetry? I'm interested by moments of inspiration that give an entire life its purpose—and why it only happens to certain people. People like Steve Jobs. I see Jared as one of those people. But Steve Jobs, as far as I know, never heard a voice from heaven.

"I don't remember how and what it was," Jared says. "My recollection is more that it occurred to me—thoughts that came to me that morning, somehow, through whatever it was. Through whatever means."

I argue a little with him on this.

"You're a man of science—intelligent—and yet you're talking in terms that are inconsistent with science. What would you say to patients or non-believing colleagues about hearing the call of God, and allowing it to shape your whole life?"

"Certainly, most colleagues would probably be atheist," he says, blaming the med school system for that. "But I think most people can relate to the fact there is some faith component in their life anyway. They won't have too much of a hard time trying to reconcile it to their life, just based on their own life experiences. As a scientist, yes, it's almost a mutually exclusive thing to say I'm a scientist, a physician, on one hand, then to have this faith side of me on the other hand—which is not a science, not evidence-based at all, but is, in some ways, airy fairy. It appears like a crutch sometimes, and relies on this entity that can't be tested."

"Not to mention there are scientific reasons—neurophysiological explanations—for why we rely on belief," I add.

"There can be, yep. So I guess…what was the question? Oh yes. I think you'd be hard pressed to find anyone, apart from maybe Richard Dawkins or someone like that, who is so hard core atheist, that they cannot allow for this other component in life. And I think you'd be hard pressed to find most scientists and colleagues that I work with who also cannot allow for that other component in their lives. They often acknowledge it exists but they just don't know how to describe it. They don't know how it works out in their own life, because it's this other thing that's not fostered or nurtured. Most people, though, have this thing. It may for them be the Christian faith, but for other people it might be different variations of faith. It might be a belief in the universe itself. But there is that component to their life, that they do understand."

God's Presence

There's a question hanging over from our conversation the day before, but I've been holding back with it. It's a question about Jared's faith in God, and his almost childlike desire for God to be more present. Like the experience of Lewis, Jared's experience is that God seems to be staying away.

My question, though, isn't whether there is a God or not, or if there is why God would be so distant, but why Jared would believe the onus was on him, a dying man, to do more in order to feel the divine presence. I ask him this, and in asking it I'm aware of the bigger question that still hasn't been answered—why God would call Jared to train to be a doctor with a view to serving in the developing world, when Jared had cancer all along?

"What sort of God would require you to put the work in right now?" I ask him. "Why would God not just grant you his presence?"

"My experience of God is that he's always required me to put in the effort in order for me to get returns," Jared says, without being defensive. "And that's probably the faith component of it, I think. You have to step out in faith, put certain things on the line in order to get returns off it. It's almost like how you invest—you take a risk with your investment and then get returns."

"The conventional church doctrine about suffering is that it's meaningful because it makes us turn to God," I suggest. "Do you feel that?"

"There's a component of truth to that answer. I think in suffering we do often turn to God. There's so many stories written in the last two thousand years, in hymns and all sorts—you know, like Amazing Grace of people who do turn to God in the middle of their suffering. So, there is a component of truth to that. But it's not the whole truth. I don't think it explains it all. Because then you would have to fall back on believing all suffering happens in order for us to know God, and I'm not sure about that. I don't think a loving God requires us to suffer. I think we can know God lots of different ways—suffering is just one of those ways."

"So, how are you experiencing God's presence right now? Do you still feel that absence? Do you still feel maybe you haven't done enough—or suffered enough?"

"I don't think they are the reasons why," Jared says, pushing back. "I think it's just sort of a juvenile response, to want the emotional comfort of God's love. But, if I take a step back and look, I am receiving God's love. I mean, through my family. I've got a massively supportive family. That includes my wife and extended family. So, parents on both sides. And through community. They are the indirect ways of receiving God's love. The fact that I can be home going through this process is humbling—I have to humble myself to come here, to have my wife wait on me—because this is not what I envisaged when I said the vows. But it's also me receiving God's love through that, through my wife and through my family.

"So, I do see God's love in a different perspective, in a different light. It's just the juvenile side of me that wants that emotional part of his love."

Excitement about the Future

Jared chats easily about his clinical training and his expanding awareness of the different specialties that he has the option of pursuing. He discovered early that the surgical discipline best fits his personality and seemed to be the most beneficial to take overseas.

"A surgeon overseas is often quantifiably valuable compared to others," he says, in his straight-talking way. "Not saying that other disciplines aren't valuable, but a surgeon is often incredibly valuable in terms of what they can offer."

So, it's to surgery that Jared sets his mind and heart. I point out that always in the re-telling, he anchors the narrative back to that call, relating all aspects of the story to the vision.

"Yeah, there was always the question, how am I going to take this back to that context overseas?"

Jared believes that if you have a calling, then you do what you can to keep fuelling the passion for it. For him, that meant revisiting countries to enhance his sense of what he could do to make that difference he hankered after. So, during med school he spent a couple of months in India and another three months in the Philippines. What he wanted was an idea of whether he could manage to live in those places for lengthy periods of time. He also wanted to know what the practice of medicine was like in the developing world. So, he spent a month of the India trip in a hospital. This was early in his studies, before his clinical experience, so what he gained from the experience was limited. Nevertheless, his passion for the calling was burning brighter, even if precisely where that calling would take him was still an unknown.

"For me, Africa was at the back of my mind," he tells me. "I've never been to Africa."

Observations of Jared

Our conversation dwells on the minutiae and those things that I am observing in Jared as we talk. With no future to speak of, our attention is constantly drawn to things of the past, but also things of the present. We notice things we would ordinarily look beyond, and particularly those things that exist in the between, that are occurring as part of the conversation itself. The way Jared speaks, for example, which has bemused me these past few days. I tell him what I observed on our first day, that his usage of certain words and phrases reminds me of Enid Blyton.

"I think that vocabulary is actually one thing that's developed in my latter years," is his response. "And largely to do with medicine. One of the things they teach you through med school, if not directly then certainly implicitly, is communication. From a practical point of view, when one doctor is handing things over to another, concerning a patient, you need to be able to communicate succinctly and accurately. The other doctor has to know without a doubt what it is that's going on with the patient. And it's got to be done in a way that doesn't waste any time. If you're a person who's being communicated to, there's nothing worse than sitting there listening to somebody trying to explain to you about a patient in a clumsy phraseology. So, I guess it comes from that. And it probably comes from reading as well. Just reading certain books and learning to phrase things in an efficient way. I don't know, that might be what you're referring to."

"But there's a quaintness too," I add. "It's poetic more than it is efficient."

"I'm not entirely sure where that came from. I was terrible at English. What stopped me from getting into med school the first time around was my English mark. I always considered myself useless at the arts. And at English. And it's something that seems to have evolved later on, as I've got older.

"Hannah grew up in a relatively traditional old school in Dunedin," he continues. "She was head girl, dux in the school. She was that person who did well in everything, whatever she applied herself to. She's the one who would have the better phraseology, better grammar and syntax. And would correct me if my English was wrong. Maybe being married to her has actually reinforced it."

Jared's Vulnerability

There's a switch in our conversation as we talk about friendship, and it takes us back to the question of what's most important in life. It's one thing to be a friend to others—it's quite another to let others be a friend to you. Jared says he is good with one but finds the other much harder. And it's a reversal—love's reversal—that mirrors what has taken place in his life. His goal was always to serve others, but—as Cathie has only just demonstrated by bringing his lunch—he is now the one who needs help. It's a whole new experience of love for Jared, a level of vulnerability he had not experienced before he got sick.

"I think instinctively I'm a proud person," he admits to me. "So, it does require me to humble myself in order to receive it. I always envisaged—when you go back to what my whole idea of what my life was going to be—I was going to be the person giving the love. My entire life was meant to be me going out into the world, overseas, giving God's love. So, it's an about turn basically. Where I am now—five and a half years after the fact—it's a complete about turn to where I was, where I envisaged I was going to be. Complete."

"You're actually the patient," I say for him.

"I'm the patient now—who requires almost full care. I have to use a bed pan while I'm sitting here. That requires me to humble myself to the point where I can accept somebody coming in and taking that kind of care of me. And I was never going to be that person in my life plan, obviously."

"You said earlier that your purpose, your calling, was also your identity. So, this is a complete mind shift for you in terms of how you understand yourself."

"It is a complete mind shift. It's been a mind shift that's happened over five and a half years, so I have had time to readjust. But the place where I am now, I'm quite helpless. I am reliant on my wife's service and my family's service. I've become that person."

"Have you reconciled that shift in your thinking?" I ask him.

"I have no choice but to accept it. And sometimes I think that's what God does. He brings you to a place where you don't have a choice any more. You just have to accept it. You have to accept love. Often I think we like to see grace as one door in a corridor of many doors. We like to try the other doors because they are the self-sufficient doors—whether it's in jobs or careers or life decisions or whatever. There are always many doors you can open and try—more often than not, instinctively. I'm that sort of person. You want to open the doors that enable you to do something on your own steam. But you can open those doors, fail, and then end up having only one door left anyway—which is having to accept grace and love. Or, if you have enough insight, and have enough experience, you are able to pick the door straight off the bat that is love and grace, and just go through it. And save yourself the agony of failing anyway."

"Have you come to have a different understanding of love, then, over the last five years?"

"Yes, I think so. I don't think that I could go through it all and not have come to a different understanding. If you were to take the person who didn't go through the last five years, but who went through a different journey—the one I thought I was going to go on—I'm sure we would be in different positions on what our ideas of love are."

Questions over Purpose

What I'm struck with by our conversation today is this clash of realities: a very clear sense of purpose and calling, and then this event that changes everything—surgery and cancer. There is an inherent contradiction in the clarity with which Jared saw his life unfold, with what then transpired. He admitted as much in a blog post on October 31, 2009, titled "Cancer has stolen my future": "It's hard to know what God is planning now..." Jared admitted.

My reaction to this dissonance in the story is to be slightly irritated by it. I want to know how Jared has reconciled the resurrection of his dream with its subsequent crucifixion. The story was not meant to happen as it did, so how did he cope with the disappointment? I put the question to him as a statement.

"You have this dream, then you have this call," I say, "and then you have the unreconciled nature of that dream—if there is one big question over your life, it's this. And it's still unanswered."

There are more unanswered questions around this too—about the existence of "God," and the issue around hearing a divine revelation. And there are more basic questions around humanity's mechanisms for coping with profound disappointment. In the immediate setting, that of Jared and I discussing these major themes of his life, there are also questions around how to reflect well on your life's missed opportunities and unfulfilled purpose as you approach the end of that life.

"Yep, it's still unanswered," Jared says, in response to the first of these questions. "I've come to peace about it not being answered. But it is still unanswered; it's still a big question mark. But I'm in a place where I'm okay with that."

Not satisfied by this, I press again: "Is there a part of you not praying, in the time I have left, could you please give me an answer?"

"Yeah, but I think I'll get an answer in the time I'm going to have as well—in the next life. It would be different if I had a normal lifetime. I know that my life has been cut short so there are obvious reasons why I can't complete the vision. But as to why I was given such a strong calling and can't complete that, I don't know."

I tell Jared about an elderly RAF pilot I once interviewed and wrote about, Harry Carter, who was buried alive following the crash of his bomber during World War II. Hanging upside down in his cockpit, several metres below ground, he was suddenly overcome by an almost spiritual sense of calm and was able to dig his way out to safety. He spent the rest of his life searching for some explanation for the "miracle" that had occurred. When he found it, at the age of 90, it had nothing to do with "god."

The point I want to make is that sometimes it can take an entire lifetime to find answers to life's most profound mysteries. But Jared no longer has an entire lifetime.

"No," is all he says, not nearly so eager to find an answer to those mysteries as I am.

Every Moment

I have learnt to appreciate even the most ordinary things of life: getting in the car to drive somewhere; eating a meal; catching up with friends; enjoying a good coffee; holding my wife in my arms...

Things that might not exist for me in a few years' time...

Things that I will be incapable of experiencing...let alone enjoying.

All of a sudden, every moment counts, be it the ordinary or the extra-ordinary, the mundane or the special. I get frustrated that my cerebellum, doing what it is supposed to do, is stealing my moments from me. I don't want my life to disappear into an abyss of faint memories, I want it to be real, I want it to be present, I want it to be experiential.

I'm training myself to change this...if that is at all possible.

Life is far too valuable to let skip by.

Jared Noel, The Boredom Blog
"Every moment"
November 21, 2009

BEATIFICATION OF SUFFERING

The Camera Never Lies

In the photos Jared smiles his signature smile, all dimples, and innocence, and joy and delight. Photos of Jared with Hannah, photos of Jared and Hannah with Elise, photos of Jared just with his daughter. They are on the walls, in magazines, wedged above the vanity mirror on the sideboard in the bedroom. One that I love has Jared and Hannah holding hands, on a beach, the ocean to their backs, their bare feet on sand, touched by wind, touched by water, touched by one another. Photos of romance and life, of hope and never-ending happiness. So much life. Photos captured on more innocent days than this. Days of plans, and dreams, and vision and purpose.

There are photos captured on other days too. Photos that tell two stories. They say the camera never lies, but here is proof the camera tells half-truths. Or perhaps the camera tells fuller truths. Images of joy and contentment, family life, happiness, celebration, and behind the images something else besides. Something unseen, not captured, and more than a vignette encroaching on the image. A shadow of something far more sinister that evades the shot but is there nevertheless. The shadow of Jared's illness.

And then there are my photos, documenting Jared's daily decline. Jared frowning, Jared compliant, Jared off-colour, Jared bored. Looking at the camera, looking away from the camera. Smiling broadly despite himself. Looking absent in spite of himself. Jared sitting patiently while I shoot random images from here, or from there, against the light, with the light, front on, from the side, let's try the other side. One day I build a mosaic, from shots up close. Jared's temple, his forehead, his ear, his cheek, Jared's nose, and lips, his bearded chin, then his eyes. The closer I get the more life I see. Micro signs of life that the engagement and wedding and family photos don't show. Dandruff. Bits of wax. The stray hairs of his moustache. The flecks of yellow and white in the corners of his eyes. The vein in his temple. The sweat on his brow. The hair pulled behind his ear. A spot of moisture on his beard.

They say the camera never lies. And what the camera sees are the signs of life. Everywhere it looks, every image it captures, every frame he fills…Jared is here, breathing, awake. His spirit is present. Sure, his colour is all wrong. The subject is static. The smile is forced. But the camera never lies. Jared is alive. Jared is Real.

Being Real

Two days have passed, because we've had Sunday to recuperate. It's raining again, as miserable as it was when I saw him last. I convince myself that it must be easier to prepare for dying when the weather is so horrible. The sunshine is cruel. It reminds Jared what he's missing out on. The rain, particularly rain as cold as this, is something we curl up against—close our eyes, enter darkness, wait for the next warm light to come.

But Jared is animated today, in defiance of the outside conditions once again. There's a buzz about him. I realise it's a leftover energy from the weekend activity—a wine and cheese night with family on the Saturday night, and a visit from his faith community friends on the Sunday. It's remarkable how much of a lift the connection with people has given him. His extroversion, and the strength he draws from it, is on full display. He confirms what I have come to understand about genuine human connection—it has healing properties, and generates its own energy at a level deeper even than where Jared is experiencing fatigue. The colour in his face, the dance in his eyes, and the clarity of his conversation, are like a last line of defence against the degeneration.

Jared tells me a story from his clinical training days. It's a story indicative of the theme that's been emerging from our ongoing dialogue, but which comes to the fore today. The theme is life itself, in all its harsh contradictions. Jared himself personifies this. At least, his life story does. Hope set against the bleak reality of suffering. Moments of joy that lift the narrative beyond the ordinary, followed by moments of deep sadness and irreconcilable disappointment. It's not so much a roller coaster, Jared's story, as a length of rope, both realities woven together, distinguishable one from the other, but utterly inseparable. The beauty and the ugliness, the sacred and the profane, the glorious and the broken.

The result is a Jared who is very much Real, Real as the Skin Horse from Marjory Williams' *The Velveteen Rabbit*, which we talk about, particularly this quote: "'It doesn't happen all at once,' said the Skin Horse. 'You become. It takes a long time. That's why it doesn't often happen to people who break easily, or have sharp edges, or who have to be careful kept. Generally, by the time you are Real, most of your hair has been loved off, and your eyes drop out and you get loose in the joints and very shabby. But these things don't matter at all, because once you are Real you can't be ugly, except to people who don't understand.'" There's an authenticity about Jared that feels like it's been forged on an anvil, so that whether he's talking about pain or talking about love, he does so with his eyes fully open.

And on this wet and cold Monday in September 2014, the two of us settle in for a discussion about life—authentic life. The type of life only those who have opened their eyes to both things that are wonderful and to things that are terrible can hope to experience. Things like love and romance, loneliness, work, Christmas, chemotherapy, parenthood, guilt— all thrown together in one life, and in this case, one conversation.

As Freddie Mercury sings in the opening lines of Bohemian Rhapsody, itself a song about contradictions, "Is this the real life?"

The P Addict

The story Jared tells me is about a meth addict who is experiencing acute withdrawals. She has been taken into the emergency department of Auckland Hospital, where Jared is doing a shift. He had nothing to do with the patient from a medical point of view, and yet the image of her, and of her suffering, has stayed with him.

"I remember distinctly the encounter," he says. "She was a young twenty-one or twenty-two-year-old. She was a P addict and was going through acute withdrawals. And, of course, the emergency department is not a place you can go to for acute withdrawals, there are other places for that. So, they couldn't really treat her there. She had been injecting methamphetamine into the spaces underneath her fingernails to try and get it into her system, because she had used up all her veins and everywhere else, every other way of doing it. And because she had gone through rehab more than once it obviously hadn't been successful.

"That one particularly stands out because for some reason, in that moment, I just felt prompted to pray for her. I just took a step back, while the doctor was dealing with her, and took a moment to pray. I don't know what happened to her or whether she's still alive or who knows. But, you know, there weren't too many places like that where it just felt like you had to do that and that's why that one stands out. I guess my heart just went out to her, this young girl who was a victim of some of her own decisions. Methamphetamine is so insidious like that. She was no longer really the product of her own decisions but a product of the drug addiction. She was miserable, she was convulsing on the bed and curling up into the foetal position and sweating, all of which is part of the withdrawals."

I say to Jared that it sounds like a sudden outpouring of love on his part. All he says is, "A form of, yeah."

But it is love, all the same, and it comes out of the same place as Jared's desire to serve overseas. With a profound awareness of the human condition comes an outpouring of compassion, which not all people show.

When I ask Jared to expand on those training years, and what he loved about them in particular, his answer reveals more about his heart for people in that context.

"I guess it was the days where you interacted with patients," he says, "where you feel like you made a difference. You get more of those days as you progress through your career. But as a student you did feel a bit superfluous. You are just there to observe. At other times you got to do stuff but it was the days where you interacted with patients and felt like you were part of the process and made a difference, or at least part of a difference in that patient's life. Those were the satisfying ones. You really do begin to be invited into people's lives in a very privileged situation as a doctor, when they are often dealing with stuff that is emotionally quite dark for them. Medicine allows you to come into that place without having to establish a prior rapport, and hopefully help make a difference."

Mother and Son

Jared's mum interrupts us with coffee. For a few moments we are drawn back into the present again. The mundane. And also, the glorious. I witness the interaction of mother and son for the first time, and the contrasting images are present here too—the unconditional love of a parent for her child, and the sorrow she must be feeling at his deterioration.

There's an extra treat for us both today. Ruth has brought up a citrus slice, which she places on a plate on the corner of the bed to my right. She's brought some for Jared too.

"Do you want a plate?" she asks him.

"Yeah, I will do," he answers. "It's real crumbly."

Clinical Experience

In the two years prior to getting sick, several things were occurring at once for Jared. There was ongoing training and a growing sense of who Dr Jared Noel would be. There was a growing bank of knowledge around the specialties that he could choose to move into. There was a growing sense of his calling. And then there was Hannah.

When I hear Jared speak about this period, I feel excited on his behalf. Jealous, almost, of the opportunities that lay before him. Of course, the awareness that he gets sick and that most of these opportunities shut down tempers that excitement. But to have these things emerging concurrently at such a young age—how fortunate Jared was. And, yes, how tragic his story became.

But, for a season, he could not have been happier.

"Yeah, overall, the clinical years did hone that understanding of what my sense of calling was—because it was me starting to put into practice what I had done all this learning for. There were days I would come home and it was just exhausting, and wouldn't be that fun. But there would be days that you come home and you would be like, yeah, this is what I'm here to do. And this is what I love. And when I did the surgical specialties, that particularly energised me. I wasn't going to write off any specialty—I was going to be fairly open about it. But there were times when I did some of those specialties and came home at the end of the day and felt particularly energised by it. You feel that, yes, this is one of the specialties I could easily do and quite happily spend my lifetime doing."

"And you must have been thinking about the practicalities of taking some of those things overseas?"

"Yes, and one of the appeals of surgery was that a surgeon is quite a valuable person overseas. There's lots of different fields of medicine that are valuable overseas but surgery in particular—a surgeon can be hard to find. Offering just basic services can make a big impact on people's lives."

A Firming Vision

I picture Jared as that trainee doctor, tasting possibilities as his vocation takes form, driven daily by a sense of his greater purpose and where it might take him. The future is a wide-open landscape with multiple roads leading off towards a discernible yet undiscovered destination. And when Hannah enters the frame, it only confirms the direction Jared is headed in.

"What was Hannah's vision in your early conversations with her—was it similar to yours?"

"Yes—she had come off the back of doing an elective in Nepal and had spent some time there. A little bit of that elective had been in Scotland as well. Because of that experience she had really developed an affinity for wanting to do what she could in impoverished countries. Both of us were completely open to the idea of where—neither of us had any particular location in mind."

'Til Death Do Us Part

As if to illustrate the juxtaposition of things amazing with things broken throughout our conversation, Jared's joy at sharing with me how he met Hannah is suddenly offset by its counterpart—a moment of sadness that comes over him unexpectedly, as I bring the discussion back around to the fusion of his calling with his budding relationship.

I say to Jared that I'm struck again by how deep was his sense of calling and, in equal measure, by the sense of injustice that it was all cut short.

"Your calling fuses with marriage," I say to him, "so, it's not just a calling that is cut short, but your marriage as well."

"The sense of marriage being cut short is a whole different can of worms," he says, and he chuckles, but this time it's not through enjoyment. "It is a huge thing—a huge thing. Particularly eleven months into your marriage. We were newlyweds and we only got to experience that newly-wed phase for eleven months, because our lives were shattered after that—not destroyed, but shattered. We were putting the pieces back together—trying to—because they just took on a whole different sort of... and we...it's difficult, for me, personally. It's difficult for Hannah as well, but for different reasons, I guess."

"Did you feel any personal guilt at the time of diagnosis?"

"I feel guilt now. And I know I'm not guilty, but I still feel it."

"What do you feel guilt about?"

"Well, when we got married I wanted a different life for Hannah. And I feel like, even though there is no responsibility I can take on myself, I feel like I have sold her a dummy, so to speak." He says this quite forcefully, to my surprise. "That she has ended up with a dud. And I know it's not my personal fault, but it's me ultimately that's carrying it all. I still feel guilty now."

"I guess, if it had happened five years into marriage when you had journeyed together..."

"We were still idealistic," he says, cutting me off. "Are we still idealistic?" he adds, to himself. "We were still fresh-faced anyway, and experiencing life for the first time."

"It might have occurred to me to say to a new bride, off you go, I don't want to take you through this. Did those thoughts occur to you?"

"Not literally, but certainly there was just this massive sense of, I guess it comes back to feeling guilt. Me wanting to apologise and just go, I'm so sorry—this is not the life that I wanted to give you. Particularly as a guy, because I think a guy carries a certain instinctive persona into a marriage, of what they think they should be doing for their wife, and providing for her."

"You were inviting her into a dream as well, a dream that had also been hers."

"Yeah, yeah—all of that. Not just the fact that it was the absence of that—that the dream got shattered—but also the fact that I've had to drag her down the pathway that we've ended up going down. Which is the one that we have had for the last five and a half years—of chemo, multiple rounds of surgery, all of that kind of stuff. This: me being at home and her looking after me."

"So, not just your vision cut short, but also Hannah's."

"Mm. Yeah. And in some ways, Elise is at least one thing that I have been able to give her. And that was part of the reason why we decided to go ahead and have Elise. This is something I can at least give her—part of that dream, anyway."

Suffering and Dostoevsky

Before I came to see Jared today, I was reading about a scene from Dostoevsky's novel *The Idiot*, and in light of our conversation it reminds me that there is a perverse way to fuse life's beauty with its ugliness. And Christians, in my experience, are particularly good at it. It's the process of beatifying suffering, of minimising its impact by glossing over any or all of suffering with a veneer of spirituality—much the same way that classic iconography beatifies the suffering of Christ, by depicting even the crucified man as blissfully untouched by human pain. I tell Jared about my reading, and he is immediately attentive.

Dostoevsky depicts a scene in which his characters are contemplating a painting by the German artist Hans Holbein. Dostoevsky himself was fascinated by the painting, and by the grotesque depiction of the crucified body. In the novel, the character of Prince Myshkin, the "idiot" himself, refuses to look at it for fear it will cause him to lose his faith, something that has already happened to the character Ippolit. Dostoevsky's point is that even the disciples would struggle to believe resurrection was possible if they truly beheld the full horror of suffering and death.

I ask Jared about this, as someone who has suffered and is staring death in the face—about the reality of suffering versus its beatification, particularly among people of faith.

"It's interesting," he begins. "The beatification often comes from people who haven't suffered. Or they have suffered a little bit, and therefore have some interest but haven't truly suffered. There are varying degrees of suffering, and what is suffering for you is going to be very different from what is suffering for me. I get comments all the time—people leap to the defence of Christ, or the defence of God—not saying necessarily that there's a reason for this, but unable to allow for the fact that God is allowing the suffering to happen; that there is some kind of purpose, some kind of reason.

"I was just commenting to mum earlier—everyone likes to say how I will feel God's grace and peace during this time. Everybody is telling me what I will feel. And I think that is leaping to the defence of Christ, or the Christian experience, by a person who hasn't experienced it.

"Whilst I have suffered during this experience, I don't feel like I have truly, truly suffered. This, again, is another pithy saying that I hate to hear: Christ doesn't give us anything that we can't handle. The problem I have with that is, what about all the people in the world who go through suffering who don't overcome and who die? I flicked on Al Jazeera yesterday, in fact, and it's a depressive state of world affairs at the moment. Usually, there's one thing going on in the world somewhere, but at the moment there are multiple sites around the world of conflict and war and suffering—and atrocities that are almost the worst I have seen committed in a long time: Islamic State in Iraq, the Jordanian war, and what's building up in the Ukraine. And then there was the Jewish and Hamas conflict. The problem is, a lot of these people die. You come across a village and there's a mass grave of one hundred people—well, those hundred people didn't overcome their suffering, did they? They are tortured; horrific atrocities."

"And in many situations that suffering is happening to people because they are Christians," I add.

"Yes, particularly in the Islamic State situation. So, I don't think that you can say that if you encounter suffering that you will always overcome it. And I think you have to have an understanding of suffering that accounts for the many, many people—which would probably count in the millions in the current world—that don't overcome. Famines in Africa, for example. That's suffering that people don't overcome. The beatification of suffering, in some ways, doesn't actually take into account those people, the reality of it. In reality, it doesn't work. My faith has always been a very pragmatic faith. I sort of look at the reality of what goes on versus what's taught—as in, ideology. If the ideology doesn't match the reality well I think something's wrong with the ideology."

"Are you becoming more intolerant with those pithy sayings?"

"Yeah, there's a lot of them that I can be intolerant of. And you switch off to them after a while. They are meant in good heart, the people who say them, but..."

"Do they give you any comfort at all?"

"Erm. No. I just read them and write them off."

Beautiful and Ugly

How do you live today when the future is, at the very most, short, and, at the least, gone altogether? My life, and my world, is both simultaneously beautiful and ugly. I can't help but admire the beauty of the world, and lament the brokenness of it.

I have realised that this simultaneous juxtaposition is required for us to be able to appreciate either of these extremes. We need ugliness in the world in order to appreciate the beauty, and vice versa. It's through my ugliness, my brokenness, that I now appreciate the world in a whole new light. It's my suffering that makes the world that much brighter, that much more colourful, and that much more worth living. It is cancer that has brought a whole new meaning to life, even if that life is much shorter than anticipated.

Conversely, it's the beauty of life that allows me to recognise the ugly—the injustice, the oppression, the suffering, the poverty, the needless loss of life, the insatiable greed for material goods. Recognising this does not empower me to better avoid it, but to better be a part of the solution of it. I think we instinctively use this recognising ability to avoid the ugly, instead of perhaps being the solution to it. Being the solution to the ugly and the brokenness...

That's powerful...

...or, even better...it's beautiful.

Jared Noel, The Boredom Blog
"Beautiful...and ugly"
November 27, 2009

THE RELUCTANT SERVANT

Jared Alone

There is no graceful way to enter the life of a man who is dying, coming alongside right at the end for a crash course on a narrative thirty-odd years in the making, as he scrambles around in the darkness because there's no way out of this situation, just a slow resignation to what has to come, his mind already closed to the future, and turning instead to the past—the distant past, the past carved out in recent years and months, and the newly created past, caused by the passing of every moment. Each one of these moments feels ectopic, like a school project hurriedly thrown together at the last minute, with time so limited there's no chance you're going to enjoy it, or do it well, or have the knowledge and experience to give it what you know it requires, demands and deserves. This is a life that's coming to an end, after all. A life. Not a project, or a campaign, or a calendar week, or a trip down south. It's a life. When this thing's done there's no coming back, no second chance, no revision or correction. It's gone. Yet here you are, marking the passing of these moments with conversation. Listening, talking, questioning, laughing, directing. Recording this life, giving it structure, identifying its themes, emphasising its goals, making sense of the moments in respect of the whole, finding the threads and following them all the way through, from their beginnings to this end. And all the while you're finding that your role is changing as you go. You were the stranger. Then the writer. Then the biographer. And then the counsellor. Then the priest. As Jared nears the end, it feels less like a project, more like a quest. And not the sort of quest where you scale the peak and then make your way back down, but the sort of quest from which you feel there may be no return. A Frodo and Sam-type quest, weighed down by evil the closer you get to its source. Forging on despite the weariness and the threat of danger, taking each and every step in the full knowledge that they take you closer to the end, yet there's no way to turn back now. With each step, Jared changes, and before too long you realise you are here to document these transitions. One day to the next, a new colour, a new feeling, a new way of talking, new things to grieve, new people to bid farewell, more memories to reveal, more emotions to display.

There is no place like this. Except maybe the slopes of a volcano ruled by a Dark Lord, whose soul you bear around your neck. This truly is the point of no return. And whichever way you look at it—physically, mentally, emotionally, spiritually—its proximity is transformative, in a terribly destructive way.

No wonder that in our day-to-day lives we tend to stay away from places, from moments, like this.

A Real Conversation

On the very day, December 22, 1849, that the Russian writer Fyodor Dostoevsky was granted a reprieve from the firing squad, as he stood there with a group of fellow political activists waiting to be executed, he wrote to his brother in a scrambled, passionate outpouring of joy at the unexpected insight he had been given into his own life, and human life more generally, by coming face to face with his own death. He repented of the "futilities" of his past life, declared that "life is a gift," and claimed that in that moment his life had been reborn. It is universally acknowledged that Dostoevsky's work after this event possessed an insight into the human condition, and the grander spiritual reality to which it corresponds, that it hadn't possessed before. In the same letter to his brother, foreshadowing a lengthy sentence in a Siberian prison, Dostoyevsky said: "I am neither downhearted nor discouraged. Life is everywhere, life is in ourselves, not in the exterior. I shall have human beings around me, and to be a man among men and to remain one always, not to lose heart and not to give in no matter what misfortune may occur—that is what life is, that is its task."[1]

Dostoevsky is still on my mind from our weekend conversation, particularly the similarities between his dramatic conversion and many of the insights Jared has become aware of. The immediacy of mortality has given Jared new eyes, as it did the writer, so that in some ways he sees life more clearly, and in more brilliant colour, than he did when death was still some distance away. And, like Dostoevsky, his sentence has given him an almost rabid determination to make his life count—regardless of how much of it he has left. I read Jared Dostoevsky's words from the letter to his brother: "When I look back on my past and think how much time I wasted on nothing, how much time has been lost in futilities, errors, laziness, incapacity to live; how little I appreciated it, how many times I

---

1. Frank 1990: 62–3.

sinned against my heart and soul—then my heart bleeds. Life is a gift, life is happiness, every minute can be an eternity of happiness."

The quote resonates with Jared. That "life is a gift" is the reason he is talking to me day after day, after all, instead of passing away quietly in the relative isolation of his upstairs room. From the day of his diagnosis, and particularly from the terminal diagnosis one year later, every moment for Jared has been meaning-full. In Dostoevsky's words (and experience), every minute has been infused with eternal happiness. Even in moments of despair. Jared has never given up on his belief in life, and more life.

These thoughts are present as we begin our conversation. I'm feeling some guilt over my frustrations the previous day. And perhaps Jared is feeling different too because his demeanour is gentler than it was. He's more withdrawn, quieter. I'm struggling to hear him, even. But there's no defensiveness. No irritation. This is as authentic as I believe Jared can be. Death is present today. As near as Dostoevsky's riflemen. Jared can feel it. I can feel it. It stifles our discourse. Death is the greatest taboo of all because it's more than a topic of conversation—it's a force, a foe. The closer we come to it, the more I realise just how overbearing it is.

The New Normal

Jared begins by saying that he's still feeling out of sorts. I find it odd that a doctor can't isolate how he's feeling, but I know that this general feeling of unwellness is the way it's going to be. It's how the end will look. It has begun.

"I woke up early this morning," he says, wearily. "And I just had a sleep now for an hour and a half. I feel a bit better for having had a sleep. I'm not feeling nauseous; not feeling pain. It's really, really hard for me to put my finger on what it is that I'm feeling—I'm just feeling out of sorts. And I'm wondering whether it's just a progression of the illness really, more than anything else. It's kind of how I was feeling yesterday.

"I did say I wasn't feeling nauseous—but last night I had a big vomit. And was feeling quite unwell up until then. I felt a lot better after that. I lost pretty much everything I'd eaten from the day."

What I'm witnessing is true suffering. This is on my mind also, as Jared speaks. He's worn out, yet battling on. There's life there still. But this is what human suffering looks like. We can write about it, talk about it, teach on the subject of it. It is nothing compared to living it. Suffering has a colour—the colour of jaundice. They don't tell you that in the lectures.

I remind Jared that on the day we met he told me that he would know at the end of his first week at home how he was tracking—what the dying phase was likely to look like. I ask him whether how he's feeling today is an indication of it.

"I personally can't predict how this is going to go and whether I'm going to be well from one day to the next. There's no real way of knowing. And so I just wake up and I am the way that I am. And it might be that this is now the new normal for me, so…"

"Which I hear as fairly scary," I say. "The new normal could be this state of unwellness. If your body is dying surely that is what will happen. You're not going to feel fit then suddenly not be here, are you?"

"No, that's right—I'm going to progressively feel worse and worse, if that's how I'm tracking."

A Tunnel without a Light

When Jared fell out of bed, on the evening of the first day that our conversations began, he used the word "rehab" of his legs and the core strength that he hoped would return. It struck me at the time how unexpected it was that he was working to rehab anything, considering he had such a short time to live. I remind him of this, in this new context, and the ongoing refusal of his body to give up. I say that there doesn't seem to be any point where life meekly surrenders. It fights for as long as it can.

Jared refers me to a blog post he has written recently, in which he compares typical sickness to being like a train in a tunnel.

"You can see the light," he says. "Normally, when you get sick, you go into a tunnel and there's a light somewhere—whether it's really close or distant. But you're aiming for that light, and that's you getting better—coming out the other side of the illness.

"There is no light for me, so I'm just moving around, stumbling along in a tunnel. There is no obvious way that I'm getting better, and getting out of this tunnel. So…maybe I've just stumbled onto the next bit. I don't know."

The realisation of what happens to us, physically, as we deteriorate and die, is feeling particularly heavy, so I tell Jared this.

"It's no small thing, is it?" I say to him. It's a naive thing to say, but in the moment it's all I can think of.

"No. And I can see how, at some point, you get to a place where it becomes unbearable. And, of course, you can't control when you're going to die—which is where the whole discussion around euthanasia comes in.

And it's a conversation that, as a country, we haven't had yet. But we will have it eventually."

"Doctors seem to me to be more willing to have that conversation than others," I suggest. "Perhaps it's because you are confronted with it all the time."

"Well," says Jared, "they've done surveys of doctors versus lay people, in terms of end of life measures. They've asked them what they would like done, measures such as intubation and CPR, that kind of stuff—to keep you alive further. And doctors choose to opt out much, much sooner than lay people. Lay people would rather we do everything we can to keep them alive. Whereas, a doctor goes no, I've seen that—that's not necessarily the right thing and I would rather die sooner, thank you."

"What's your feeling?"

"Well, I think I would probably die sooner rather than later. I mean, we made the decision to go palliative based on that. We could have fought for longer. Could have. But that would have come at the price of quality of life. And I was never in this for quality of life, I was in it for length—and quality with Elise. But another two months' extra that I might get with her—if it's a miserable time then that's not two months of valuable time. And so..."

As Jared is speaking, I'm think that I, too, would want more time. It's another moment of realising how impossible it is to sit where Jared is right now and know how that feels. I say this to him.

"Yes—if you're really pro euthanasia you go, right, let's book an event, say Monday next week, get your friends along—if that's who you want to be there—and that's that. That's the end of your life. I don't know—I'm not saying that's necessarily what I agree with. In fact, I don't think that I do agree with euthanasia because as a Christian I struggle with upholding life. And as a doctor my job is to uphold life, and to suddenly introduce that component to it is a whole new can of worms. But I understand the reasoning, and why there's a conversation that probably will happen. Definitely."

"You would understand even more now, I would imagine?"

"Yeah, yeah. And even more so now. Yeah."

Jared of days past might have said this with some bombast, as if it was his obligation to inform me of the ethical issues related to death and dying. That much I have seen in him over the past week or so. But there is no bravado today. Only a sense of acceptance—and melancholy. The fragility of his voice today is in line with the leaden movements of his body. If our first couple of conversations felt like the beginning of something, this very much feels like an ending.

D-Day

In our conversations, the moment that changed Jared's life is always referred to as D-Day—diagnosis day. It's a day we are always mindful of, like a rock thrown in a pond—for the most part we talk about the ripples, not the stone itself, more concerned with the impact than the moment that caused it. But, on this day of honest reflection, we head back there. Back to the second week of November 2008, where D-Day is not a day as such, but several days—and, more critically, a two-week period that changed the plot-line of Jared's story and rewrote the ending—an ending that had taken all this time to play out.

"My guts had been playing up for a period of time," Jared starts. "For how long? Maybe at least a year leading up to diagnosis. I had been to India two years earlier and I got terrible Delhi belly over there. It never settled down, back to its normal—but it's quite normal for that to happen. It's called post-infectious irritable bowel—I self-diagnosed that. It's when you have such a terrible bout of food poisoning that your stomach and your gut lining just takes a couple years to settle down afterwards. And so that's what I assumed I had—just slightly less tolerant of fatty foods and high lactose foods.

"We were down in Dunedin having a pre-Christmas Christmas with Hannah's family, because we were about to go overseas and not have Christmas in the country. I just started to get stomach aches—I had a meal the night before and figured it was something I'd eaten that hadn't agreed with me. I had cramp pain and that would last for thirty-seconds to a minute—go for twenty minutes then come back again. Quite uncomfortable. So, I stopped eating, and what was unusual was that it progressively got worse over a couple of days. Then we flew back up to Auckland—this was the Tuesday before we were flying out, on the Friday. And the Tuesday night, about 1am, I started vomiting. And that was the point I thought, right, I need to go see someone because this could be semi-serious—especially if I'm going to get onto a plane in a few days' time."

"Did you have any thoughts what it could be? Any idea?"

"No idea at that point."

"You were still linking it back to the Delhi belly?"

"Still linking it back to that—possibly an appendicitis."

Jared then enters into one of the well-worn narratives that he is used to telling. He tells it without any emotional highs or lows, but with a sense of heaviness appropriate for what transpired. I get the feeling, though, that the heaviness is about his present situation, more than it is about the past. He speaks as your doctor might, but isn't detached from the story. It's more that he has a doctor's respect—respect for the patient (himself), but also respect for the disease and for the misery it can inflict.

"I came into hospital and I ended up having to wait ages to be seen. When I was finally seen about five or six in the morning, their conclusion was that it was probably an appendicitis, but they would sit and watch me conservatively—which basically means they won't do much, they'll just admit me and watch me. But I didn't get any better and it progressively got worse, and they thought maybe I was constipated—so they gave me some enemas. Which didn't do anything. I started to get really, really crook then, started vomiting—had to get a nasal gastric tube, my stomach blew up like a beach ball. So, they repeated the X-rays, and this time there were really obvious dilated loops of bowel, which was enough to make them want to take me into surgery. That was them basically going, you have a bowel obstruction of some description, we need to deal with it. And again, thinking the primary reason for it was appendicitis, as opposed to anything else of any significance. Because, I was twenty-seven. I didn't have any risk factors for anything else—no family history of anything to note."

Eventually, Jared was taken into surgery—the day he was meant to be flying out. He knew, of course, that a typical appendicectomy took forty-five minutes to an hour—but Jared was in surgery for three and a half hours. He woke up in the post-anaesthetic care unit, and Hannah, because she was staff and was given access to the PAC unit, was already there.

"I remember asking her was it my appendix," Jared says. "And she said no. And for whatever reason, the next thing that came to mind was, was it a tumour? And she goes, Oh, I don't want to tell you—I want the surgeons to tell you. And I said no, I want you to tell me. She said, yeah, they found a tumour in there—they found a growth, and it was obstructing everything, so they've taken it out. They did a right hemicolectomy—the right part of my bowel was taken out and rejoined together. We didn't know the nature of what that tumour was. And so as I slowly woke up out of my anaesthetic haze the idea of that began to sink in a little bit—what could this be? I guess we knew that to have a tumour would probably imply some kind of cancer. But you have to wait until the histology results come back to confirm that.

"The surgical team had their tails between their legs the next day on the ward round because of what they found. Six days later the histology came back and revealed that it was an adenocarcinoma of the bowel. It was staged as a T3 N2M1—a reasonably advanced adenocarcinoma of the bowel. You have a chance of being alive after five years of 40 per cent."

"So, a less than fifty-fifty chance?"

"Yes. That was when it really hit home. And that's when we had to cancel our trip and everything. It was like, yeah—I've got cancer."

Moments

The breeze is hitting Jared's hair again. Moments. Eternal happiness in every minute. I highlight it to Jared this time, and say that I've been watching how he interacts with time and space for the past week now, wondering how magnified these moments are in his consciousness.

"I think that they've been magnified in my consciousness for the last five and a half years, to be honest," Jared says, and refers me to a blog he wrote some years before about appreciating autumn in a whole new way. "I think I've been living the last four years in that context, of appreciating the now—knowing it could be the last time I get to appreciate it."

That post was titled "Colour," and was posted on May 9, 2010.

> One of the things I'm noticing these days, is that I am so much more aware of the beauty of life around me than I used to be... Knowing that this might be the last or second to last autumn that I ever experience has made me really appreciate the colours and the leaves, and just how beautiful the autumn season is.

Jared included a photo with the post. He had processed the picture to desaturate the background colours to highlight the richness of the leaves of autumn in the foreground.

"Life is like that I guess," he added. "We very rarely desaturate the background noise to notice the beauty."

I talk about Dostoevsky again, and tell Jared the story of his mock execution. Dostoevsky was among the second line of prisoners waiting their turn to be tied to stakes and shot, when a drum roll sounded signalling a stay of execution. But in the time it had taken for the first group to be tied up ready for the rifles to fire, it was like eternity had opened up for Dostoevsky and given him new eyes—a new appreciation for what it was to be alive.

"I would imagine the sip of the coffee, or holding a magazine, would take on more profound meaning in these days," I suggest to Jared.

"Yeah, some things more than others," he says. "But I think that's true. The things you take for granted in life, I'm less likely to take for granted. I think in the writing I've done, that's where a lot of people have drawn inspiration. They realise there's a lot of things we take for granted that we should be grateful for every day—but aren't. People have appreciated reading how grateful I am of just these little things. It puts into context their fears, their hopes, their desires, their dreams. And it makes them realise that, actually, this is just a little trivial thing. And, hey I'm still alive and I still get to breathe the fresh air and wake up in the morning and enjoy a roof over my head. And the fact that we live in New Zealand alone puts us in the top 10 per cent of the world's wealthy. Those are the things we take for granted."

I mention the movie *About Time*, which tells a story about a father and a son who are able to relive any day of their past life, to enjoy it again, or to enjoy it for the first time, in the event that the first time around wasn't that memorable. It reminds me of the Anaïs Nin quote: "We write to taste life twice, in the moment and in the remembering." The hero of the film eventually comes to realise that instead of living days twice, he only needs to live them well the first time around—to live them as if they were the second or third opportunity.

"I haven't seen that," Jared says. But he gets the point.

Shock of the Diagnosis

"You're a pragmatic guy," I say to Jared, "a faithful guy, a doctor—how did the news of your cancer hit home emotionally?"

"I guess it was being told you have cancer," he answers. "Nobody likes being told that. It is always a thing that hits you, to start with. But I think also, I was like, okay, 40 per cent chance—I can be that 40 per cent. And I resolved to be that 40 per cent rather than the 60 per cent. And the odds were still in my favour, basically—not greatly, but I still had a 40 per cent chance. They measure it to five years because, typically, if you get to five years you are going to survive onwards."

"Even so, the normal human responses would be fear and sorrow. Do they hit home as well?

"Yeah, they do. Because I had to go onto chemotherapy. After we claimed our travel insurance, we did two months around South-East Asia at the end of chemotherapy. I remember we were by a lake in northern Vietnam, just walking around it and just talking about what going back to New Zealand was going to be like, and the realities of it. And I remember I started crying, saying, 'I don't want to die of this.'"

Jared's throat tightens at this point and his voice thins out to a whisper.

"I'd been living with this uncertainty, but at this stage for all we knew it could have gone. I hadn't been diagnosed with any recurrence, but it was just like, I don't want to die of cancer. There's too much in life that I want to do. So, emotionally…I think those emotions were there the whole time. I just specifically remember that point."

"On the trip you could suspend those realities for a while?"

"Yeah. And when you are dealing with a 40 per cent chance, that's almost a form of denial that you live with. You live in that world of 40 per cent until you have reason not to. And I had been living in that 40 per cent world during the chemo, and afterwards—until I was told I couldn't any more."

Terminal

"So, you have your first six months of chemo—eight rounds of it, which you document in the blog. You have an overseas trip to South-East Asia, then come back. And they find something else."

"After a month of recovery, we travelled for two months around South-East Asia. Then they do a three-month follow-up CT scan. And that's the scan that showed the first relapse. And that was when everything changed. I went from being a five-year survival of 40 per cent to…well, when I spoke to the doctor, when I asked the oncologist what does this mean in terms of my survival, he said, "Well, we don't talk about five-year survivals any more—we talk about two-year survivals." And he didn't say that it was terminal, but that's basically what he was saying—generally speaking you don't survive this. This will kill you."

"What was the difference in your frame of mind between the second diagnosis and the first one?"

"I think this one is what changed everything, in terms of how you deal with it."

"What emotions were around that? Anger, frustration?"

"I was never angry. I think frustration. And just disappointment, more than anything else. You kind of just build your life up to be this thing that you want it to be, and it just gets shattered in front of you. And for me that was just sadness and disappointment, I didn't…I…" Jared pauses for a significant time. "I don't really know how else to describe it, but there is just a deep, deep sadness around…" He pauses again. He emphasises "deep, deep" with heart-rending force. "I guess how it's expressed at the time is disappointment. Hannah was at the appointment as well, so we both sort of just came home, talked about it amongst ourselves—we could process the information ourselves okay, actually. But it was when we had to ring our family and our friends, and tell them, that it really, really hit home. It was when I was telling my mum, for example, and she just started crying at the end of the phone, because she knew the implications of what everything meant. And so for me that's when I would start crying as well, when the family would start crying. You go through the emotional thing of hearing the news yourself, once, but every time you have to break it to someone else you relive it—you're reliving it through their eyes."

"So, you're grieving with them, over and over again, aren't you?"

"You're grieving with each person you tell, over and over again. I remember telling mum, and she was the one who told the rest of the family. I didn't go on to tell the rest—so she probably experienced the same thing when she had to tell them. But that was when all the tears came, when we sat down on the phones afterwards and started telling people that the cancer's come back, and what that would mean. And the fact there was no survival chance associated with it this time."

Jared's voice at this time has been reduced to a barely audible sigh, like a thin vapour.

"I can't imagine," I say.

"I don't think you can imagine until you are there. To be honest."

Reluctant Hero

I'm interested in what happens next. How does life just continue? What does it require for Jared, Hannah, their families, to pick themselves up and just carry on? My mind goes back to the story of Dostoevsky's mock execution. There's a character in the story who stands beside Dostoevsky, and after the execution is stayed he is not able to recover and suffers an emotional and mental breakdown. How does this not happen to Jared and Hannah—anyone who faces such bad news?

"I remember my parents came around that evening, just to hang out really. Just to be with us." Jared's story is laboured now, but it's not fatigue that's slowing him down. It's grief. "The day after that, you go and tell your concentric rings of family and friends. So, you spend the better part of a week telling people—which is partly why I used the blog. A lot of friends would want to come and hang out. But there's just this kind of, like a moroseness in the room, like a sadness. Melancholy. With whomever you are hanging out with. You know the reason you are hanging out is that I've just been told I'm going to die, from this cancer."

"You suddenly find yourself the central character of a story you don't want to be in."

"Yeah, you do, you do," he says, the analogy resonating with him. "Absolutely, in fact. You suddenly become the focus of attention, but you don't want to be the focus of that attention—the reasons being obvious. All of a sudden you find yourself playing the starring role."

Insignificance of Our Part

For the most part, we measure time relative to our own engagement with it. We experience time as the heroes of our own narrative, encountering other heroes along the way, characters who slip in and out of our stories like passengers getting on and off a train. No one else stays on our train as long as we do, from its starting point to its destination. And so we tend to think of ourselves as the hero of the story—here forever. But relative to the timeline of history, our stories are so insignificant. We enter the story for such a brief time. Sure, we can impact significant periods of the timeline during our moment in it, but we are rarely more than a blip, as Jared puts it.

I bring this up with Jared, and compare him to Joseph, the "father" of Jesus. He plays an integral role in the story, but disappears with no fanfare, and is never mentioned again. If someone of his importance exits the story so innocuously, what hope have we?

"The futurist side of me looks up at the stars and imagines the future and the sky and, you know, star travel and that sort of stuff," Jared says, in response. "But even beyond that. What I love about that is that it fulfils the science fiction, futuristic side of me, but it also gives me an understanding of just how huge the universe is. I do read a lot of science in general—what's been discovered in cosmology and all that kind of stuff. And we are so small and fleeting anyway, compared to all of creation. And you realise we are just this one medium-size sun that's in a solar system on the tip of a spiral galaxy, which is a medium-size cluster that's part of another galaxy cluster, part of a galaxy super cluster."

"So, spatially we are insignificant," I say. "And we are insignificant in terms of linear time. And yet here we are, in this moment, having these conversations about life and death—and the whole universe exists in this moment."

"As far as we can comprehend it, yeah. Our brains are limited."

"But your death has significance. It impacts a whole heap of people. And yet, who will be talking about you in a hundred years?"

"Well, hopefully they might read this book in a hundred and fifty years."

Missing Out on the Future

We begin to chat about what we would miss the most, if we died early—as Jared will some day soon. "I would be thinking about Liverpool Football Club," I admit. "I'd be thinking I'm not going to see the end of the football season. Or, the fact I'm not going to hold the iPhone 6—things like that."

This makes an instant connection with Jared, whose eyes flicker with excitement.

"All those things do cross my mind as well," he says. "I've often said when the iPhone 6 comes out, I'm going to buy it regardless of whether I'm a day out from dying or five—just because it marks the milestone that I survived long enough to get it. And then Hannah gets a good upgrade when I die." Jared laughs at his own comment, a short, sudden exhalation of breath.

"I think they're releasing it next week," I say. This is a week out from the September 9 Apple special event. These events are, for geeks like Jared and me anyway, as much markers of the passing of time as Christmas and birthdays.

"Yeah, they're announcing it next week," he says, fully aware of the hype. "The release date is to be announced."

I do a quick calculation in my head. I know that the phone will hit the stores later in the month, possibly later still in New Zealand. I work out the weeks remaining before Jared's own estimation of when he will die, and I realise it's unlikely he will see the new phone. I feel the finality of his life more acutely at this point, now that it's measured against something we both relate to so easily. We are both holding iPhones as we talk—Jared regularly checks his to see who has been messaging. They are a constant presence in our days together.

"Yeah, TV shows," Jared continues, picking up the pace. He is in his own groove now. "I remember early on in the piece, wondering whether or not I'd make it to the NZ Rugby World Cup. And I did, and I went to games there, and that was great. That was when we lived right next to Eden Park, which was great. But that was a goal to survive for. And then just certain...I don't know...they haven't even finished writing the *Game of Thrones* books yet, let alone the TV series. So, I'll never find out what happens at the end of that."

"And the author could die before he gets to the end anyway—so we all might miss out."

"Exactly."

"So, you've achieved some things. You have had these goals the whole way?"

"Yeah. I do remember before the third Batman movie came out, I really wanted to watch this one. And it was like, aargh, I need to stay alive long enough to watch the third in that trilogy. And I did."

"You'll miss out on the new *Star Wars* movie though."

"Yeah, I'm not sure if that's a tragedy or not."

Travel

Something new has happened for Jared and me today. Our pre-determined set of conversation topics has been set aside. There is no need for it. We've hit a new groove, relaxed into a way of being that feels more like friendship—and it sits well with both of us. Gone is the cautious circling around one another and the frustration and defensiveness associated with trying to encounter one another with authenticity. In its place is…well, authenticity.

"Where does your mind go," I ask Jared, "when you're sitting here alone?"

"Currently, not that far," he says, and I suspect for a second that he's about to shut down again. It's not arrogance that causes him to give up on a question—mostly the medication. But some questions require his mind to go to places that the drugs will simply not permit. "I think definitely with the drugs it influences things," he adds, as I'm contemplating that very point. "But my mind goes to all sorts of places. I have a reasonably good imagination. One of my strengths is that I'm a futurist—that idea of seeing the future and what it might be. That might be the future in my own life, but it might be the future on a bigger scale. I've always been into science fiction because of that. Science fiction is looking forward a hundred, two hundred, five hundred, a thousand years. But, of course, it's also having the future in your own life. One of the harder things that I've had to cope with is that future being taken away from me. I don't have a future in my own life now, but what helped drive me before was going, where will I be in twenty years, where will I be in ten years, in fifty years?"

Our sense of the future shapes who we are in the present, I say to Jared. We become what we are moving towards, actualising in the now what we hope for. But Jared has been without a trajectory like that for some time.

"Well, I've had where I would like to be and aimed for it blindly, I guess—but knowing that I'll never get there. The closer I've come to the end, the blinder I've been in terms of the stumbling around towards it. There's been less of a goal, less of a target."

"Back in the tunnel again?"

"Yeah, back in the tunnel again."

"So, does your mind go to stories? Does it imagine heaven?"

"It hasn't really done that to be honest," Jared says, and I am both surprised that he hasn't imagined an afterlife, but also relieved. It is consistent with the pragmatism he has applied to his life, and to his illness, faith and death.

"I would have thought somebody in my position would think a lot about what the next life might be," he adds. "I genuinely haven't done that. And that's because I know humanity's done that for so long and not really got anywhere on it." I laugh at this, enjoying the blunt response and the practical approach. "I don't really see the point in wasting my own time on it. I have an idea, and that's enough."

"You are incredibly pragmatic," I say. "And you clearly have always been that way."

"I think so. I would describe myself as pragmatic, yeah. And that's why I don't go there. At the moment, to be honest, a lot of times I just drift off and I just sleep."

This is typically the signal, the moment where I retreat from the next question, respecting the line he has drawn in the sand. So, I pause, wondering where to head next. And I'm surprised when Jared chooses to continue.

"I travel, in my thoughts," he says. "I go to the countries of the world that I haven't been to. I have adventures in that sort of way, because I'm a traveller at heart. Most of the world I haven't seen, and most of the world I've wanted to see. I've certainly had glimpses, with where I have travelled to, and what I've seen."

"Where would you like to have travelled to?"

"I would have liked to…I never got to Africa. So, there. To be honest, I often find myself going to places that are in current affairs at the moment. I don't know why. The Middle East would be one of them—I haven't been to the Middle East. We did have plans to go there, that was on the trip that got cancelled. We travelled to Peru three years ago and went trekking up into the Andes, into the highlands there. That was one of the best trips I've ever done. And I really, really want to get…" Jared stops himself here, and it's the one time I hear him slipping into the present tense. The slip is painful for him, I suspect, because he makes the slightest readjustment in his manner. There's no present tense for Jared, at least not one that anticipates a future, "…wanted to get to the Himalayas and do some tramping and trekking," he corrects himself. "And maybe get to Everest base camp, although, that's becoming a bit of a touristy thing to do these days. But yeah, just stuff like that would have been great."

And for once, I hear the emotion in Jared's voice. He says this last sentence quickly, rushing it out before his voice breaks, as though verbalising what he knows he will never have the opportunity to do is just all a bit too sad.

Fear of Death

It is in view of death that my reality becomes all the more real...

It is in view of death that I am able to celebrate life to a much greater degree...

It is in view of death that priorities change, and the true meaning of my life, the one God has blessed me with, becomes so much more apparent...

I find meaning in life by knowing that I am dying.

Through all of this, I ask, please don't tell me to stop talking about the fact that I am dying. If it is a reality you cannot face, please at the very least give me the permission to face it myself.

I am, after all, the one who is actually dying...and I have found a peace in all this that supersedes the natural, and can arguably be called the supernatural.

I don't like the fact that I am dying, but through the grace of God, I am okay with it, and I am at peace about it...

And that is more valuable than anything.

Jared Noel, The Boredom Blog
"Fear of death"
September 7, 2009

LIFE AND DEATH

Suffering Is Meaningless

I ask Jared about what he's concluded about suffering and its value.

Jared points out that when he's heard the topic discussed in terms of why do we suffer, there is rarely if ever a satisfactory answer. At the symposium on cancer and theology that he attended, he heard outlined four theological responses to suffering, from the Catholic, Protestant, prosperity doctrine and contemplative traditions. He says the frameworks aren't adequate for thinking about suffering, and perhaps we need to be asking a different question.

"I've been thinking about things differently," Jared says. "I would say, let's look at the question—let's go back to the beginning. Maybe the question is not why do we suffer, but how can we honour God. I think one of the prime directives we've been left is to build God's kingdom and honour him on this planet."

It's not a dissimilar position to that reached by the Servant, or at least the Servant as spoken of by the nations in Isaiah 53.

"We are animals that seek to find meaning in things," says Jared. "With suffering, the question that comes out of it is why do we suffer? And you can trace this back in evolution—you're a primate in Africa and you see the grass rustle, you quickly learn what the meaning of rustling grass is—it's a tiger about to attack you. Initially you don't know what the meaning of it is, but the tiger jumps out and you learn what the meaning of it is, to the point where you see the grass rustle and you run. You draw the conclusion without having to see the result. We do that in our lives all the time. It's called psychological bias—we have all these biases that allow us to draw meaning from things without having to go through all the steps to get to that meaning. But they also shortcut our way to actually, truly acknowledging whether we are drawing relevant information from a new and changing world. We impose categories on things and they're not necessarily correct."

One of those categories is the meaning we ascribe to suffering, I suggest.

"Yeah, we shortcut our thinking and jump to conclusions about suffering and about God that aren't always correct. So I would go back to the original question and say, let's rethink the original question, rethink the process from the very beginning. So now when we see the grass rustling, is it truly that there's a tiger there? Not necessarily. It may be wind or some other reason. Or it might be that grass has developed the ability to move."

I suggest to Jared that it sounds as though he's become quite satisfied with not having an answer to the question of why his calling was blocked by cancer. I know that according to what Jared believes, God could heal him if he wanted to.

"I haven't found a reason behind the question 'Why do we suffer?' I have looked, to a certain extent. What I'm saying is, maybe that's an irrelevant question. Maybe we can't find an answer to the question because it's the wrong one."

The question instead should be what?

"How can we honour God in our suffering?"

I ask Jared where that has taken him.

"It's a question that's very outward-focussed all of a sudden. It's a question that leads to it being a more constructive rather than contemplative question. It becomes much more constructive in its brief, and you find meaning in it. Instead of the question, 'Why does God allow me to suffer?,' if you ask, 'How can God use me in my suffering?,' what I begin to say is, 'Okay, what can I do to honour God in my suffering?' I could do this or that. Before long, I've found that the things I have done have created meaning in my suffering, and it becomes more of a creative process—rather than a contemplative process that doesn't really fulfil what I was looking for in the first place."

Jared says that ultimately what he's trying to say is that there is no meaning in suffering.

"Suffering itself is meaningless and so when we try to find meaning in it, we fail to find what we are looking for—because it's not there. The meaning is to be found in the creation of meaning in our suffering."

So, there's no meaning in suffering, it merely provides the context in which you can create it.

"Yes. There's a context in which to create meaning. I think that goes for many things in life. Whether that suffering is financial hardship or ill health, there is inherently no meaning in it to be found."

Jared is already five years on that journey of discovery. I ask him at which point he came to the conclusion that he wouldn't find meaning in the suffering itself.

"I think I've always been leaning that way," he says. "But I think when I was at that symposium and then realised that these are all questions that fall into frameworks that are trying to answer the question of where is the meaning in suffering. And I thought, well hang on a minute, maybe these frameworks aren't the problem—it's the question at the beginning. So, suffering in and of itself contains no meaning. That, of course, doesn't sit comfortably with everybody, because everybody grows up with different ideas of suffering. But I think if you try to find the meaning of your suffering, most people are not a hundred percent comfortable with their position, if they fall into one of those categories. Whereas I am. Suffering is meaningless. Therefore, how do I try and create in it? Fundamentally, our God is a creative God as well, and what I've done is, I've done through accident, really. But I've created meaning in the suffering that I have."

But even so, it didn't foreclose your sorrow, did it?

"I've still had to mourn," Jared says. "I've still had to deal with the issues around what it is that I'm going through. It hasn't stopped me crying, it hasn't stopped me from feeling my emotions. But it has allowed me to turn them into something creative. A consequence of it is that you've got peace. More or less. Maybe that's just me giving ambiguity to it. It does give me total peace about it."

"Do you feel fear?"

"No. I don't think so."

"Do you feel regret?"

"I feel regret in the things I can't do in the future, but the life that I've lived, I don't feel regret about."

The Antihero

"The anti-hero theme in your blog—where did that come from?" I ask Jared. It strikes a chord with me. Jared never tries to dress up his testimony as a potential miracle story. He knows he's going to die. Miracles aren't the point. Making the most of every opportunity to experience life is.

"It came out because someone told me that's what they thought of me," he said. "It was at a Promise Keepers concert. He said, 'Your story's interesting because in some ways you are not a hero of the Christian faith; you're an antihero, because we are celebrating your response in faith to not some great, glorious, miraculous healing, but in fact to what is going to be—hopefully not—but is likely to be an inevitable end. Instead of fulfilling the normal criteria of a hero, you're in fact the opposite of that. Yet you're being heroised for that.'"

I talk about the Suffering Servant, and the inherent contradictions in the life of the one who suffers but who also lives in a way that somehow testifies to God's goodness.

"The character of the antihero is an atypical experience," Jared says. "While embracing the position that I'm not actually going to be healed here, I'm still going to embrace faith and God and all that he has for me. It's a response that's not considered typical for our society and our time. We look for the salvation stories, the hero stories, where people overcome. Whereas in fact you won't overcome, you're likely to be destroyed, but you're still telling a story that is uplifting and faith-filling."

We talk about the narrative arc of Joseph Campbell's hero's journey— setting out on the quest, surmounting obstacles, overcoming. The antihero's arc is different. It seems from Jared's story that it's more about how to deal with life while you're being overcome by it.

"Yeah, that's happening to me right now," he says. "And this is the penultimate scenario really, where it will be the thing that actually gets me. But along the way, when that carrot gets dangled in front of you but is also cruelly removed…" Playing on Jared's mind is his second relapse, when the possibility of healing was held out to him, then cruelly taken away, "…and so you don't overcome that situation either, it's just another carrot that's removed from your story."

"This flipping around has been the character of your entire story," I suggest. "You're occupying the exact opposite of what your story was going to be."

"And also I'm the person who I wanted to help," Jared says. "That's the flip-side of it—I'm not just going to be overcome, but I was the person that when I was the hero in my mind, I would help overcome. So, not only am I not overcoming, I am also the person I was going to care for. It all just comes back to the situation that I'm in and I'm just at peace with it."

It's day 16.

Shades of Grey

Jared's in a bad way.

It's day 17. September 17, 2014. He's woken up before 5am, he tells me, feeling very ill and coughing a lot. The rest of his sleep was disrupted and the coughing has left him with sore airways. On top of all that Jared has becoming increasingly weary of an unspecified feeling of illness, a general deep fatigue that usually follows a day of more activity. He's had a big day the day before, and now he's paying for it.

"I just exhausted myself basically," he says. "Today I've just felt really, really, non-specifically unwell. I say non-specifically because I can't pin it onto any one thing. I can't say pain and I can't say nausea, although they have contributed."

I remind Jared that a week before he had complained of a similar thing. I realise as I'm saying it that this is what observing the dying of a man is, the steady decline of his life force.

"I think it's just the body's reserves are being used up, and when I have a day where I'm feeling well I've used up more than my quota."

I suggest to Jared that he can't avoid this now—the mortality.

"There's not really an escape from it," he agrees.

We're interrupted by Hannah and Elise, who Jared holds for a while.

"You know who daddy is," he says to Elise.

"That must take some getting used to," I say, when Elise has gone.

"That I can't escape it? I think I've got used to it over the last five years though. I've had five years of not escaping it and the highs and lows of it have been reminders of the ineffaceability of it. When I thought I might escape it with surgery, and then the relapse, that was a pretty harsh reminder that I haven't been able to escape it."

One of the major themes of Jared's blog, at least in the latter years, has been the call to live a fuller life, and never to take life for granted. We turn to that theme in light of how close his own mortality is feeling. I remind him that his bigger concern in the blog was not that people become desensitised to death, but that they become desensitised to life. I wonder out loud whether that has become more acute.

"I think my diagnosis from the very beginning has given me that awareness and that sensitivity," he says. "Right now I'm just as aware of it as I was before. Now I'm just more sensitive to the in-between of death and life, which is that unhealthy place in the middle. When you see people dying in hospital, you see that grey area. If white is alive and black is dead, the grey area in the middle is where I am at the moment. And that's not a pleasant area, depending on which shade of grey you are on."

"It's horrible," I say in response. "The shade is getting darker as you go."

"Yep, it's getting darker."

I point out that every relapse that I've witnessed over the past few weeks seems to have taken more out of him.

"Yep. I think what will happen is I will have these ups and downs and eventually one of them will be one that I don't come back from."

I've felt for some time in our conversations that it's not only Jared who's approaching death; it's almost like we're travelling there together, him to cross over and me to wave him off. But it's not like waving a friend off at the airport. In our case, it feels like long arms are reaching out from the other side to pull us both in, unaware that only one of us is sick. As it happens a few days later I'm in emergency suffering pancreatitis and a doctor looms over me in the darkness of my room to inform me of the high mortality rate from the disease. I think back to Jared's bedroom and the sense that the shadow of death is a predator, not a benign reality like I had imagined it; more like a hungry wolf prowling indiscriminately. All fanciful, of course, but in the moment, at the dying man's bedside, it all feels a bit too real.

"I feel that in our conversations we're walking hand in hand to the gates of Hell," I say to Jared. "To sit and look in the eyes of a man who's dying, that's how it feels."

"It's a depressing thought to be honest," Jared says, and I realise that I've made his day a whole lot worse. "I'd like to think I'm not walking towards that."

"Is there a sense to you that death is the enemy?"

"No, it's ultimately where all life comes to an end."

I point out that he's fought for the best part of a decade to prevent this very moment in the lives of others.

"And the last half of the decade for myself," he says.

"Some people view death as a portal to another life," I say. "Does it feel like a gateway to you, or as a finality? Is it a Harry Potter-type death where they pass through a curtain, or something more final?"

"I think I probably feel it as a finality," he says. "And then something happens afterwards. That's probably my take on it."

"And you have some relief about that?"

"I think there is a certain relief from suffering in death," he says. "Because there's that finality. There's the finality and then moving on into the next life, or whatever the next picture looks like. And for me, in some ways I don't see death as a terrible thing because of that; because there's something else, something beyond."

The Business of Dying

"You've spoken in recent months about 'the business of dying'. How satisfied are you now about how you've done the business of dying?"

"I've done pretty well," Jared says. "I've seen people that I need to see. I've always said that I want dying to be a faith-building process for people, not a faith-destroying process. I think I've achieved that."

"Has that been a wrestle as well?" I ask. "Have you hidden vulnerability and fears from people or have you been transparent?"

"I think I've been as transparent as possible."

"How close is God to you right now?"

"I don't know. But I presume he's as close as he can be. I'm not specifically feeling him, in this moment. But I believe he's here."

"What's uppermost in your mind?"

"Just a case of handling the now and the fatigue," Jared says. "Just trying to push through. To whatever's next. There is a point where I just move onto the next stage, the next phase."

Day 18.

Bearing Witness

I haven't seen Jared for a couple of days when I see him again on day 19. The lethargy is getting worse and the days are blurring, and he's finding it difficult to differentiate in order to give an account of what's been happening. Still, he wants to talk.

I mention an article that I've read before the visit, on Americans not thinking enough about death.

"I think the West doesn't accept death enough," he says. "Because we are shielded from it so well; our health system is so good."

I ask Jared what he would tell people about the dying process, now that he has gone through it.

"It's not an easy process," he admits. "It's been prolonged. It's different for everyone of course, depending on what your illness is. So it's hard to box me into a one-size-fits-all thing."

"Have you been surprised, by how hard it's been?"

"In some ways, in some ways not. I've been more surprised by the experience of it. What it's like to experience it is a very different thing to know about it. It's been hard to experience it. Whereas I kind of knew the process. But to actually experience it is difficult."

"What's been so difficult?" I ask him.

He says it's been hard on his mood, and his thinking. Despite being well supported.

We shift the conversation, to faith and doubt. I ask Jared what he would like his story to communicate to people of faith.

"Well, I think faith played a big and important part in my life and played an important role in painting what my life was going to look like, or did look like, or has looked like. And as a result we've seen what's occurred over the last five and a half years, which is this kind of God thread weaving through all the different opportunities and things that have played out and the impact it has had on Christians and non-Christians alike."

Most of that impact occurred because of his blog, which Jared started soon after his diagnosis in November 2008. In the subsequent six years it attracted three quarters of a million views.

I ask Jared what his story says about doubt.

"I've never really had the doubt," he says. "But there's too much stuff in the literature and from the pulpit that tells you how well your life will succeed if you're a Christian. And I think to a certain degree that's true—but I think it's crap for a lot of the time. And we get sold this false hope. There is hope in it, but the way our testimony-based system is set up is that we only hear about the good things that happen to people. And as a result we get this selection bias as to what we hear from the pulpit around the Christian message."

There's a sense out there that if you're part of a faith community, life will just work for you. Second Isaiah begins like that—with the community of Yahweh complaining that things have gone so badly.

"I want Christians to know that life still goes on," Jared says. "Life still has its ups and downs. And God's still there for you regardless. Faith's about the journey with God inasmuch as anything, in all aspects."

"Do you have a prayer that goes something like, 'Really God, can't it just be a little easier than this?'"

"Sometimes, yeah," Jared confesses. "For me I do, because I just feel like, after listening to all the feel-good testimonies, I never got to live that life."

Endurance Race

Jared's doctor has told him to think of dying as an endurance race. Break it up into parts. Work out how you're going to get through that particular day. Focus on each day as a new day. Don't think about what's ahead.

"Does that work for you?" I ask him.

"I don't know. It's the only way. That's probably the way I'm coping with it; the only way I know how to. I just start a day, wait to see how I feel on that day. Learn from previous days what makes me feel better, and what makes me feel worse."

It's day 20.

Goodbye

Love in the Noel house runs in crisscrossing lines of activity that greet you like a bus station full of people all running towards those they have missed the most. They come down the stairs and into the kitchen, or out the front door, or across past the dining table and into the lounge. Family, friends, hospice nurses, doctor. Brief visits, long visits, quick checks, serious consults. Bed washes, fresh clothes, pain relief, drainage checks, hot drinks, cool drinks. Some days a flurry, some days a calm. But always attention, crisscrossing attention, in Jared's direction, or Hannah's, or Elise's. People caring, people serving, people grieving, people checking in. But always people. There is no love without people. And Jared is surrounded by people, and by people who most definitely love.

Entering here during times of high activity is an intrusion, a disruption to the schedules drawn up by the requirements of love. They have to pause to let me in, for one thing. Then pause again to make the coffee. Some days the activity is there at the door as I arrive, as teams leave at the stroke of twelve, the signal that it's my turn, my time. On the odd occasion I sit at the dining table waiting for the activity to abate. For the talky doctor to wrap up his consult, for example. Or for mum to finish cleaning Jared up after a vomit. But mostly the activity parts, like the Red Sea at the command of Moses, and I get to have time with Jared that no one else gets. And this is the real intrusion, the real disruption. Love is more than service, and goodbyes, and moments of grief. Love is connection. It's conversation. It's an encounter, people discovering the otherness of the other and treasuring what they have discovered. It's working to sit where the other sits, travelling their timeline as they do. It's being there when the bravado cracks and the other reveals his heart, because he trusts that you can see how he sees his world.

There's no real obligation to let anyone into this space, to have these encounters, or to discover someone's otherness in this way. But love isn't about obligation. If it was, those crisscrossing lines of activity would not occur as they do. No. Love is always about grace. And in the Noel household, grace abounds—on day 21 as much as it did on our very first day.

How do you say goodbye to someone you have visited over the course of several weeks, listening to their story and their roller coaster of emotions and thoughts as they have journeyed towards their final moments? In a real sense, there's no end to the conversation I began with Jared. This much I know from my work on the Servant—the dialogically constituted hero remains open to fresh encounter, new dialogic, ongoing response. The very act of reporting Jared's conversations in order to present his story puts him in a similar category to that of the Servant, or Dostoevsky's polyphonic heroes.

Death is death, though. Suffering is suffering. The pain of the exilic community was real and scarring regardless of how the Servant responded to the call of Yahweh. And Jared has journeyed closer by the day to an actual death—one that, in the moment, I would rather not acknowledge.

Which is why, in our final moments together, on day 21, I prompt him to give me some (false) hope about the future.

"What are you saying to God these days, in your alone times?"

There's a long pause.

"Erm...I guess that I'm slowly welcoming him," he says, finally. "I don't necessarily feel that, but that's where I'm at. I'm ready to be embraced. It's a comforting feeling."

"Is there any distress in that for you?"

"The distress is just the day-to-day fatigue. Spiritually, and all that kind of stuff, I'm completely at peace with where I am and where I am going."

"Do you think about what comes next at all...about the 'resurrection' life?"

"No, not really," Jared answers. And he's surprisingly upbeat. "I'll pretty much take whatever comes. As far as I'm concerned, it's a mystery to me. And I'll discover what it is when I get there."

SELECT BIBLIOGRAPHY

Adams, J. W. (2004), 'Speech Act Theory, Biblical Interpretation, and Isaiah 40–55: Exploring the Use and Value of the Philosophical Notions of Speech Act Theory for Biblical Interpretation and Specifically for Isaiah 40–55', Fuller Theological Seminary, Pasadena.

Ådna, J. (2004), 'The Servant of Isaiah 53 as Triumphant and Interceding Messiah: The Reception of Isaiah 52:13–53:12 in the Targum of Isaiah with Special Attention to the Concept of the Messiah', in B. Janowski and P. Stuhlmacher (eds), *The Suffering Servant: Isaiah 53 in Jewish and Christian Sources*, 189–224, Grand Rapids, MI: Eerdmans.

Allen, R. B. (1980), 'עמל', *TWOT*, 2:675.

Allis, O. T. (1951), *The Unity of Isaiah*, London: Tyndale.

Alter, R. (1981), *The Art of Biblical Narrative*, London: Allen & Unwin.

Alter, R. (1985), *The Art of Biblical Poetry*, Edinburgh: T. & T. Clark.

Alter, R., and F. Kermode (1987), 'General Introduction', in R. Alter and F. Kermode (eds), *The Literary Guide to the Bible*, 1–8, Cambridge, MA: Belknap.

Anderson, B. W. (1989), 'The Holy One of Israel', in D. A. Knight and P. J. Paris (eds), *Justice and the Holy: Essays in Honour of Walter Harrelson*, 3–19, Atlanta, GA: Scholars Press.

Auld, A. G. (1980), 'Poetry, Prophecy, Hermeneutic: Recent Studies in Isaiah', *SJOT*, 33(6): 567–81.

Bakhtin, M. M. (1981). *The Dialogic Imagination*, trans. C. Emerson and M. Holquist, Austin: University of Texas Press.

Bakhtin, M. M. (1984), *Problems of Dostoevsky's Poetics*, trans. C. Emerson, Minneapolis: University of Minnesota Press.

Bakhtin, M. M. (1990), 'Author and Hero in Aesthetic Activity (ca. 1920–1923)', in M. Holquist and V. Liapunov (eds), *Art and Answerability: Early Philosophical Essays by M. M. Bakhtin*, 4–256, Austin: University of Texas Press.

Barré, M. L. (2000), 'Textual and Rhetorical-critical Observations on the Last Servant Song (Isaiah 52:13–53:12)', *CBQ*, 62: 1-27.

Barstad, H. M. (1989), *A Way in the Wilderness*, JSS 12, Manchester: University of Manchester Press.

Bastiaens, J. C. (1997), 'The Language of Suffering in Job 16–19 and in the Suffering Servant Passages of Deutero-Isaiah', in J. Van Ruiten and M. Vervenne (eds), *Studies in the Book of Isaiah: Festschrift Willem A. M. Beuken*, 421–32, Leuven: Uitgeverij Peeters.

Beauchamp, P. (1989), 'Le Quatrième Chant', in J. Vermeylen (ed.), *The Book of Isaiah— Le Livre d'Isaïe*, 325–55, Leuven: Uitgeverij Peeters.

Begrich, J. (1963), *Studien zu Deuterojesaja*, TBü 20, Munich: Chr. Kaiser Verlag. Orig. 1938, Stuttgart.

Bergey, R. (1997), 'The Rhetorical Role of Reiteration in the Suffering Servant Poem (Isa 52:13–53:12)', *JETS*, 40(2): 177–88.

Betz, A. (1992), 'Syene', *ABD* 6:250.

Betz, O. (1998), 'Jesus and Isaiah 53', in W. H. Bellinger Jr and W. R. Farmer (eds), *Jesus and the Suffering Servant: Isaiah 53 and Christian Origins*, 70–87, Harrisburg, PA: Trinity Press International.

Beuken, W. A. M. (1972), 'Mišpāṭ: The First Servant Song and its Context', *VT*, 22: 1–30.

Beuken, W. A. M. (1989), 'Servant and Herald of Good Tidings: Isaiah 61 as an Interpretation of Isaiah 40–55', in J. Vermeylen (ed.), *The Book of Isaiah—Le Livre d'Isaïe*, 411–42, Leuven: Uitgeverij Peeters.

Beuken, W. A. M. (1990), 'The Main Theme of Trito-Isaiah "The Servants of YHWH"', *JSOT*, 47: 67–87.

Blenkinsopp, J. (2000), *Isaiah 1–39*, AB 19, New York: Doubleday.

Blenkinsopp, J. (2002), *Isaiah 40–55*, AB 19A, New York: Doubleday.

Blenkinsopp, J. (2003), *Isaiah 56–66*, AB 19B, New York: Doubleday.

Bright, J. (2000), *A History of Israel*, Louisville, KY: Westminster John Knox.

Brueggemann, W. (1984), 'Unity and Dynamic in the Isaiah Tradition', *JSOT*, 29: 89–107.

Carpenter, E., and E. Nicole (1997), 'גזר', *NIDOTTE* 1:847–8.

Carr, D. (1993), 'Reaching for Unity in Isaiah', *JSOT*, 57: 61–80.

Ceresko, A. R. (1994), 'The Rhetorical Strategy of the Fourth Servant Song (Isaiah 52:13–53:12): Poetry and the Exodus-New Exodus', *CBQ*, 56: 42–55.

Childs, B. S. (1979), *Introduction to the Old Testament as Scripture*, Philadelphia: Fortress.

Childs, B. S. (2001), *Isaiah*, Old Testament Library, Louisville, KY: Westminster John Knox.

Childs, B. S. (2004), *The Struggle to Understand Isaiah as Christian Scripture*, Grand Rapids, MI: Eerdmans.

Chilton, B. D. (1987), *The Isaiah Targum: Introduction, Translation, Apparatus and Notes*, The Aramaic Bible 11, Collegeville, MN: Liturgical.

Claassens, L. J. M. (2003), 'Biblical Theology as Dialogue: Continuing the Conversation on Mikhail Bakhtin and Biblical Theology', *JBL*, 122(1): 127–44.

Clark, K., and M. Holquist (1984), *Mikhail Bakhtin*, Cambridge, MA: Belknap.

Clements, R. E. (1982), 'The Unity of the Book of Isaiah', *Interpretation*, 36: 117–29.

Clements, R. E. (1985), 'Beyond Tradition-History: Deutero-Isaianic Development of First Isaiah's Themes', *JSOT*, 31: 95–113.

Clements, R. E. (1998), 'Isaiah 53 and the Restoration of Israel', in W. H. Bellinger Jr and W. R. Farmer (eds), *Jesus and the Suffering Servant: Isaiah 53 and Christian Origins*, 39–54, Harrisburg, PA: Trinity Press International.

Clifford, R. J. (1984), *Fair Spoken and Persuading: An Interpretation of Second Isaiah*, Ramsey, NJ: Paulist Press.

Clines, D. J. A. (1976), *I, He, We, and They*, JSOTSup 1, Sheffield: JSOT Press.

Clines, D. J. A. (1980), 'Story and Poem: The Old Testament as Literature and as Scripture', *Interpretation*, 34: 115–27.

Clines, D. J. A. (1995), *Interested Parties: The Ideology of Writers and Readers of the Hebrew Bible*, JSOTSup 205, Sheffield: Sheffield Academic Press.

Clines, D. J. A., D. M. Gunn, and A. J. Hauser (eds) (1982), *Art and Meaning: Rhetoric in Biblical Literature*, JSOTSup 19, Sheffield: JSOT Press.

Coats, G. W. (1993), *The Moses Tradition*, JSOTSup 161, Sheffield: JSOT Press.

Cobb, W. H. (1882), 'The Integrity of the Book of Isaiah', *BSac*, 39: 519–54.

Combrink, H. J. B. (1996), 'The Rhetoric of Sacred Scripture', in S. E. Porter and T. H. Olbricht (eds), *Rhetoric, Scripture and Theology: Essays from the 1994 Pretoria Conference*, 102–23, JSOTSup 131, Sheffield: Sheffield Academic Press.

Conrad, J. (1996), 'נכה', *TDOT* 9:415–23.

Coppes, L. J. (1980a), 'נגש', *TWOT* 2:553.

Coppes, L. J. (1980b), 'נגע', *TWOT* 2:551–2.

Day, J., 1980, 'DA'AṮ "Humiliation" in Isaiah 53:11 in the Light of Isaiah 53:3 and Daniel 12:4, and the Oldest Known Interpretation of the Suffering Servant', *VT*, 30(1): 97–103.

de Waard, J. (1997), *A Handbook on Isaiah*, Textual Criticism and the Translator 1, Winona Lake, IN: Eisenbrauns.

Delcor, M. (1997), 'נגע', *TLOT* 2:718–19.

Domeris, W. R. (1997), 'דכא', *NIDOTTE* 1:943–6.

Dommershausen, W. (1980), 'הלל', *TDOT* 4:417–21.

Dorsey, D. A. (1999), *The Literary Structure of the Old Testament: A Commentary on Genesis–Malachi*, Grand Rapids, MI: Baker Books.

Driver, S. R., and A. Neubauer (eds). (1999), *The 'Suffering Servant' of Isaiah According to the Jewish Interpreters*, Eugene, OR: Wipf & Stock.

Duhm, B. (1892), *Das Buch Jesaia: übersetzt und erklärt*, HKAT, Göttingen: Vandenhoeck & Ruprecht.

Dumbrell, W. J. (1985), 'The Purpose of the Book of Isaiah', *TynB*, 36: 111–28.

Ekblad Jr., E. R. (1999), *Isaiah's Servant Poems According to the Septuagint: An Exegetical and Theological Study*, Contributions to Biblical Exegesis and Theology 23, Leuven: Peeters.

Elliger, K. (1978), *Deuterojesaja: 1. Teilband: Jesaja 40:1–45:7*, BKAT 11/1, Neukirchen: Neukirchener Verlag.

Emerson, C. (1997), *The First Hundred Years of Mikhail Bakhtin*, Princeton, NJ: Princeton University Press.

Evans, C. A. (1988), 'On the Unity and Parallel Structure of Isaiah', *VT*, 38(2): 129–47.

Exum, J. C. (1982), '"Whom Will He Teach Knowledge?": A Literary Approach to Isaiah 28', in D. J. A. Clines, D. M. Gunn, and A. J. Hauser (eds.), *Art and Meaning: Rhetoric in Biblical Literature*, 108–39, JSOTSup 19, Sheffield: JSOT Press.

Farmer, W. R. (1998), 'Reflections on Isaiah 53 and Christian Origins', in W. H. Bellinger Jr and W. R. Farmer (eds.), *Jesus and the Suffering Servant*, 260–80, Harrisburg, PA: Trinity Press International.

Fishbane, M. (1985), *Biblical Interpretation in Ancient Israel*, Oxford: Clarendon.

Fokkelman, J. P. (1997), 'The Cyrus Oracle (Isaiah 44:24–45:7) from the Perspectives of Syntax, Versification and Structure', in J. Van Ruiten and M. Vervenne (eds.), *Studies in the Book of Isaiah: Festschrift W. A. M. Beuken*, 303–23, BETL 132, Leuven: Uitgeverij Peeters.

Frank, J. (1990), *Dostoevsky: The Years of Ordeal, 1850–1859*, New Jersey: Princeton University Press.

Fretheim, T. E. (1997), 'כאב', *NIDOTTE* 2:575–6.

Frye, N. (1982), *The Great Code: The Bible and Literature*, London: Routledge & Kegan Paul.

Fuhs, H. F. (1978), 'דכא', *TDOT* 3:195-208.

Garrett, S. R. (1990), 'Exodus from Bondage: Luke 9.31 and Acts 12:1-24', *CBQ*, 52: 656–80.

Geller, S. A. (1995), 'Were the Prophets Poets?', in R. P. Gordon (ed.), *'The Place Is Too Small For Us': The Israelite Prophets in Recent Scholarship*, 154–65, SBTS 5, Winona Lake, IN: Eisenbrauns.

Gerstenberger, E. (2001), 'ענה', *TDOT* 11:230–52.

Gitay, Y. (1981), *Prophecy and Persuasion: A Study of Isaiah 40–48*, Bonn: Linguistica Biblica.

Gitay, Y. (1991), 'Rhetorical Criticism and the Prophetic Discourse', in D. F. Watson (ed.), *Persuasive Artistry: Studies in New Testament Rhetoric in Honour of George A. Kennedy*, 13–24, JSOTSup 50, Sheffield: JSOT Press.

Gitay, Y. (1996), 'The Realm of Prophetic Literature', in S. E. Porter and T. H. Olbricht (eds), *Rhetoric, Scripture and Theology: Essays from the 1994 Pretoria Conference*, 218–29, JSNTSup 131, Sheffield: Sheffield Academic.

Gitay, Y. (1997), 'The Projection of the Prophet: A Rhetorical Presentation of the Prophet Jeremiah', in Y. Gitay (ed.), *Prophecy and Prophets: The Diversity of Contemporary Issues in Scholarship*, 41–56, SBL Semeia Studies, Atlanta, GA: Scholars Press.

Gitay, Y. (2001), 'Prophetic Criticism—"What are they doing?": The Case of Isaiah—A Methodological Assessment', *JSOT*, 96: 101–27.

Goldingay, J. (1976), 'The Man of War and the Suffering Servant: The Old Testament and the Theology of Liberation', *TynB*, 27: 79–113.

Goldingay, J. (1984), *God's Prophet God's Servant: A Study in Jeremiah and Isaiah 40–66*, Exeter: Paternoster.

Goldingay, J. (1997), 'Isaiah 40–55 in the 1990s: Among Other Things, Deconstructing, Mystifying, Intertextual, Socio-Critical, and Hearer-Involving', *Biblical Interpretation*, 5: 225–46.

Goldingay, J. (2005), *The Message of Isaiah 40–55: A Literary-Theological Commentary*, London: T&T Clark.

Goldingay, J., and D. Payne (2007a), *Isaiah 40–55*, vol. 1, ICC, London: T&T Clark International.

Goldingay, J., and D. Payne (2007b), *Isaiah 40–55*, vol. 2, ICC, London: T&T Clark International.

Gordon, R. P. (1995), 'A Story of Two Paradigm Shifts', in R. P. Gordon (ed.), *'The Place Is Too Small For Us': The Israelite Prophets in Recent Scholarship*, 3–26, SBTS 5, Winona Lake, IN: Eisenbrauns.

Görg, M. (1975), 'גזר', *TDOT* 2:459–61.

Gottwald, N. K. (1992), 'Social Class and Ideology in Isaiah 40–55: An Eagletonian Reading', *Semeia*, 59: 43–57.

Green, B. (2000), *Mikhail Bakhtin and Biblical Scholarship: An Introduction*, SBL Semeia Studies 38, Atlanta, GA: Society of Biblical Literature.

Grisanti, M. A. (1997), 'נגע', *NIDOTTE* 3:22–4.

Habel, N. (1971), *Literary Criticism of the Old Testament*, Guides to Biblical Scholarship, Philadelphia: Fortress.

Hanson, P. D. (1998), 'The World of the Servant of the Lord in Isaiah 40–55', in W. H. Bellinger Jr and W. R. Farmer (eds), *Jesus and the Suffering Servant: Isaiah 53 and Christian Origins*, 9–22, Harrisburg, PA: Trinity Press International.

Harrison, R. K. (1997), 'חלה', *NIDOTTE* 2:140–2.

Harrison, R. K., and R. D. Patterson (1997), 'חבורה', *NIDOTTE* 2:4–5.

Hengel, M., and D. P. Bailey (2004), 'The Effective History of Isaiah 53 in the Pre-Christian Period', in B. Janowski and P. Stuhlmacher (eds), *The Suffering Servant: Isaiah 53 in Jewish and Christian Sources*, 75–146. Grand Rapids, MI: Eerdmans.

Hermisson, H.-J. (2004), 'The Fourth Servant Song in the Context of Second Isaiah', in B. Janowski and P. Stuhlmacher (eds), *The Suffering Servant: Isaiah 53 in Jewish and Christian Sources*, 16–47. Grand Rapids, MI: Eerdmans.

Hillers, D. R. (1978), '*berit 'am*: "Emancipation of the people"', *JBL*, 97(2): 175–82.

Hoffer, V. (1992), 'An Exegesis of Isaiah 38:21', *JSOT*, 56: 69–84.

Hofius, O. (2004), 'The Fourth Servant Song in the New Testament Letters', in B. Janowski and P. Stuhlmacher (eds), *The Suffering Servant: Isaiah 53 in Jewish and Christian Sources*, 163–88, Grand Rapids, MI: Eerdmans.

Hooker, M. D. (1959), *Jesus and the Servant: The Influence of the Servant Concept of Deutero-Isaiah in the New Testament*, London: SPCK.

Hooker, M. D. (1998), 'Did the Use of Isaiah 53 to Interpret His Mission Begin with Jesus?', in W. H. Bellinger Jr and W. R. Farmer (eds), *Jesus and the Suffering Servant: Isaiah 53 and Christian Origins*, 88–103. Harrisburg, PA: Trinity Press International.

House, P. R. (ed.). (1992), *Beyond Form Criticism: Essays in Old Testament Literary Criticism*, Winona Lake, IN: Eisenbrauns.

Hurtado, L. W. (2003), *Lord Jesus Christ: Devotion to Jesus in Earliest Christianity*, Grand Rapids, MI: Eerdmans.

Kessler, M. (1982), 'A Methodological Setting for Rhetorical Criticism', in D. J. A. Clines, D. M. Gunn, and A. J. Hauser (eds), *Art and Meaning: Rhetoric in Biblical Literature*, 1-19, JSOTSup 19, Sheffield: JSOT Press.

Kim, H. C. P. (1999), 'An Intertextual Reading of "A Crushed Reed" and "A Dim Wick" in Isaiah 42.3', *JSOT*, 83: 113–24.

Kleinig, J. W. (1994), 'Mother Zion—Mother Church', *Lutheran Theological Journal*, 28: 50–7.

Konkel, A. H. (1997), 'עצר', *NIDOTTE* 3:501–3.

Krašovec, J. (1992), 'The Source of Hope in the Book of Lamentations', *VT*, 42(2): 223–33.

Kuntz, J. K. (1982), 'The Contribution of Rhetorical Criticism to an Understanding of Isaiah 51:1-16', in D. J. A. Clines, D. M. Gunn, and A. J. Hauser (eds), *Art and Meaning: Rhetoric in Biblical Literature*, 140–71, JSOTSup 19, Sheffield: JSOT Press.

Laato, A. (1990), 'The Composition of Isaiah 40–55', *JBL*, 109(2): 207–28.

Laato, A. (1992), *The Servant of YHWH and Cyrus: A Reinterpretation of the Exilic Messianic Programme in Isaiah 40–55*, CBOTS 35, Stockholm: Almqvist & Wiksell International.

Leene, H. (1997), 'History and Eschatology in Deutero-Isaiah', in J. Van Ruiten and M. Vervenne (eds), *Studies in the Book of Isaiah: Festschrift Willem A. M. Beuken*, 223–49, BETL, Leuven: Uitgeverij Peeters.

Leske, A. M. (1998), 'Jesus and Isaiah 53', in W. H. Bellinger Jr and W. R. Farmer (eds), *Isaiah and Matthew: The Prophetic Influence in the First Gospel*, 152–69, Harrisburg, PA: Trinity Press International.

Lindsey, F. D. (1983), 'Isaiah's Songs of the Servant Pt 5: The Career of the Servant in Isaiah 52:13–53:12 (Concluded)', *BSac*, 140: 21–39.

Lindsey, F. D. (1985), *The Servant Songs: A Study in Isaiah*, Chicago: Moody.

Long, G. A. (1997), 'חלל', *NIDOTTE* 2:151–2.

Lowth, R. (1971), *Lectures on the Sacred Poetry of the Hebrews*, trans. G. Gregory, vol. 1, New York: Garland (originally published as Lectures on the Sacred Poetry of the Hebrews, 1787).

Markschies, C. (2004), 'Jesus Christ as a Man before God: Two Interpretive Models for Isaiah 53 in the Patristic Literature and Their Development', in B. Janowski and P. Stuhlmacher (eds), *The Suffering Servant: Isaiah 53 in Jewish and Christian Sources*, 225–323, Grand Rapids, MI: Eerdmans.

Martin-Achard, R. (1997), 'ענה', *TLOT* 2:931–7.

McConville, J. G. (1993), *Grace In the End: A Study in Deuteronomic Theology*, Grand Rapids, MI: Zondervan.

McKenzie, J. L. (1968), *Second Isaiah*, AB 20, New York: Doubleday.

Melugin, R. F. (1976), *The Formation of Isaiah 40–55*, BZAW 141, Berlin: de Gruyter.

Merrill, E. H. (1987), 'The Literary Character of Isaiah 40–55 Pt 1: Survey of a Century of Studies on Isaiah 40–55', *BSac*, 144(573): 24–43.

Mettinger, T. N. D. (1983), *A Farewell to the Servant Songs: A Critical Examination of an Exegetical Axiom*, Lund: CWK Gleerup.

Meynet, R. (1998), *Rhetorical Analysis: An Introduction to Biblical Rhetoric*, JSOTSup 256, Sheffield: Sheffield Academic Press.

Miller Jr, P. D. (1987), '"Moses My Servant": The Deuteronomic Portrayal of Moses', *Interpretation*, 41: 242–55.

Moltmann, J. (1974), *The Crucified God*, London: SCM.

Morson, G. S., and C. Emerson (1990), *Mikhail Bakhtin: Creation of a Prosaics*, Stanford, CA: Stanford University Press.

Motyer, J. A. (1993), *The Prophecy of Isaiah*, Leicester: IVP.

Mowinckel, S. (1959), *He That Cometh*, trans. G. W. Anderson, Oxford: Blackwell.

Muilenburg, J. (1956a), 'The Book of Isaiah, Chapters 40–66: Exegesis', *IB* 5:422–793.

Muilenburg, J. (1956b), 'The Book of Isaiah, Chapters 40–66: Introduction', *IB* 5:381–419.

Murray, J. (1988), 'Redeemer; Redemption', in G. W. Bromiley (ed.), *ISBE* 4:61–3, Grand Rapids, MI: Eerdmans.

Newsom, C. A. (1992), 'Response to Norman Gottwald, "Social Class and Ideology in Isaiah 40–55"', *Semeia*, 59: 73–8.

Newsom, C. A. (1996), 'Bakhtin, the Bible and Dialogic Truth', *Journal of Religion*, 76(2): 290–306.

Newsom, C. A. (2003), *The Book of Job: A Contest of Moral Imaginations*, Oxford: Oxford University Press.

North, C. R. (1964), *The Second Isaiah: Introduction, Translation and Commentary to Chapters 40–55*, Oxford: Clarendon.

North, C. R. (1956), *The Suffering Servant in Deutero-Isaiah*, London: Oxford University Press.

Norton, D. (1993a), *A History of the Bible as Literature: Volume 1, From Antiquity to 1700*, Cambridge: Cambridge University Press.

Norton, D. (1993b), *A History of the Bible as Literature: Volume 2, From 1700 to the Present Day*, Cambridge: Cambridge University Press.

Noth, M. (1981), *The Deuteronomistic History*, JSOTSup 15, Sheffield: JSOT Press.

O'Kane, M. (1996), 'Isaiah: A Prophet in the Footsteps of Moses', *JSOT*, 69: 29–51.

Orlinsky, H. M. (1977), 'The So-Called "Servant of the Lord" and "Suffering Servant" in Second Isaiah', in *Studies on the Second Part of the Book of Isaiah*, 1–133, VTSup 14, Leiden: E. J. Brill.

Oswalt, J. N. (1998), *The Book of Isaiah: Chapters 40–66*, NICOT, Grand Rapids, MI: Eerdmans.

Otzen, B. (2001), 'עמל', *TDOT* 11:196–202.

Patrick, D., and A. Scult (1990), *Rhetoric and Biblical Interpretation*, JSOTSup 82, Sheffield: Almond.

Raabe, P. R. (1984), 'The Effect of Repetition in the Suffering Servant Song', *JBL*, 103(1): 77–84.

Rad, G. von (1965), *Old Testament Theology, Vol. 2*, Louisville, KY: Westminster John Knox.

Reed, W. L. (1993), *Dialogues of the Word: The Bible as Literature According to Bakhtin*, Oxford: Oxford University Press.

Rendtorff, R. (1996), 'The Book of Isaiah: A Complex Unity. Synchronic and Diachronic Reading', in R. F. Melugin and M. A. Sweeney (eds), *New Visions of Isaiah*, 32–49, JSOTSup 214, Sheffield: Sheffield Academic Press.

Reventlow, H. G. (1998), 'Basic Issues in the Interpretation of Isaiah 53', in W. H. Bellinger Jr and W. R. Farmer (eds.), *Jesus and the Suffering Servant: Isaiah 53 and Christian Origins*, 23–38, Harrisburg, PA: Trinity Press International.

Robbins, V. K. (1997), 'The Present and Future of Rhetorical Analysis', in S. E. Porter and T. H. Olbricht (eds), *The Rhetorical Analysis of Scripture: Essays from the 1995 London Conference*, 24–52, JSOTSup 146, Sheffield: Sheffield Academic.

Rowley, H. H. (1965), 'The Servant of the Lord in the Light of Three Decades of Criticism', in *The Servant of the Lord and other Essays on the Old Testament*, Oxford: Blackwell.

Sawyer, J. F. A. (1989), 'Daughter of Zion and Servant of the Lord in Isaiah: A Comparison', *JSOT*, 44: 89–107.

Sawyer, J. F. A. (1996), *The Fifth Gospel: Isaiah in the History of Christianity*, Cambridge: Cambridge University Press.

Schökel, L. A. (1987), 'Isaiah', in R. Alter and F. Kermode (eds), *The Literary Guide to the Bible*, 165–83, Cambridge, MA: Belknap.

Schoors, A. (1973), *I Am God Your Saviour: A Form-critical Study of the Main Genres in Is. XL–LV*, VTSup 24, Leiden: E. J. Brill.

Schreiner, S. (2004), 'Isaiah 53 in the Sefer Hizzuk Emunah ("Faith Strengthened") of Rabbi Isaac ben Abraham of Troki', in B. Janowski and P. Stuhlmacher (eds), *The Suffering Servant: Isaiah 53 in Jewish and Christian Sources*, 418–61, Grand Rapids, MI: Eerdmans.

Schwertner, S. (1997), 'עמל', *TLOT* 2:924–6.

Schwienhorst, L. (1996), 'נגע', *TDOT* 9:203–9.

Seitz, C. R. (1988), 'Isaiah 1–66: Making Sense of the Whole', in C. R. Seitz (ed.), *Reading and Preaching the Book of Isaiah*, 105–26, Philadelphia: Fortress.

Seitz, C. R. (2001), 'The Book of Isaiah 40–66', *NIB* 6:309–552.

Seitz, C. R. (2004), 'How Is the Prophet Isaiah Present in the Latter Half of the Book?', *Word Without End: The Old Testament as Abiding Theological Witness*, 168–93, Waco, TX: Baylor University Press.

Seybold, K. (1980), 'חלה', *TDOT* 4:399–409.

Smith, J. E. (1980), 'גזר', *TWOT* 1:158.

Smith, P. A. (1995), *Rhetoric and Redaction in Trito-Isaiah: The Structure, Growth and Authorship of Isaiah 56–66*, VTSup 62, Leiden: E. J. Brill.

Snaith, N. H. (1977), 'Isaiah 40–66: A Study of the Teaching of the Second Isaiah and its Consequences', *Studies on the Second Part of the Book of Isaiah*, 135–264, VTSup 14, Leiden: E. J. Brill.

Sommer, B. D. (1998), *A Prophet Reads Scripture: Allusion in Isaiah 40–66*, Stanford, CA: Stanford University Press.

Spieckermann, H. (2004), 'The Conception and Prehistory of the Idea of Vicarious Suffering in the Old Testament', in B. Janowski and P. Stuhlmacher (eds), *The Suffering Servant: Isaiah 53 in Jewish and Christian Sources*, 1–15, Grand Rapids, MI: Eerdmans.

Spykerboer, H. C. (1976), *The Structure and Composition of Deutero-Isaiah: With Special Reference to the Polemics against Idolatry*, Meppel: Krips Repro B.V.

Steck, O. H. (1992), *Gottesknecht und Zion: Gesammelte Aufsätze zu Deuterojesaja*, FAT 4, Tübingen: J. C. B. Mohr (Paul Siebeck).

Stenning, J. F. (ed.). (1949), *The Targum of Isaiah*, Oxford: Clarendon.

Stolz, F. (1997), 'חלה', *TLOT* 1:425–7.

Stuhlmacher, P. (2004), 'Isaiah 53 in the Gospels and Acts', in B. Janowski and P. Stuhlmacher (eds), *The Suffering Servant: Isaiah 53 in Jewish and Christian Sources*, 147–62, Grand Rapids, MI: Eerdmans.

Stuhlmueller, C. (1970), *Creative Redemption in Deutero-Isaiah*, Analecta Biblica 43, Rome: Biblical Institute.

Swart, I., and P. J. Nel (1997), 'נגש', *NIDOTTE* 3:27–9.

Sweeney, M. A. (1988), *Isaiah 1–4 and the Post-Exilic Understanding of the Isaianic Tradition*, BZAW 171, Berlin: de Gruyter.

Sweeney, M. A. (1997), 'The Reconceptualisation of the Davidic Covenant in Isaiah', in J. Van Ruiten and M. Vervenne (eds), *Studies in the Book of Isaiah: Festschrift W. A. M. Beuken*, 41–61, Leuven: Uitgeverij Peeters.

Todorov, T. (1984), *Mikhail Bakhtin: The Dialogical Principle*, trans. W. Godzich, Theory and History of Literature 13, Manchester: Manchester University Press.

Trible, P. (1994), *Rhetorical Criticism: Context, Method, and the Book of Jonah*, Minneapolis: Fortress.

Tull Willey, P. (1997), *Remember the Former Things: The Recollection of Previous Texts in Second Isaiah*, SBL Dissertation Series 161, Atlanta, GA: Scholars Press.

Tull, P. K. (1999), 'Rhetorical Criticism and Intertextuality', in S. L. McKenzie and S. R. Haynes (eds), *To Each Its Own Meaning: An Introduction to Biblical Criticisms and their Application*, 156–80, revised ed., Louisville, KY: Westminster John Knox.

Tull, P. K. (2006), 'One Book, Many Voices: Conceiving of Isaiah's Polyphonic Message', in C. M. McGinnis and P. K. Tull (eds), *'As Those Who Are Taught': The Interpretation of Isaiah from the LXX to the SBL*, 279–314, SBLSP 34, Atlanta: SBL.

Unterman, J. (1992), 'Redemption', *ABD* 5:650–4.

Van Dam, C. (1997), 'נכה', *NIDOTTE* 3:102–5.

Vriezen, T. C. (1970), *An Outline of Old Testament Theology*, Oxford: Blackwell.

Wagner, J. R. (2003), *Heralds of the Good News: Isaiah and Paul in Concert in the Letter to the Romans*, Leiden: Brill.

Watts, J. D. W. (1987), *Isaiah 34–66*, WBC 25, Waco, TX: Word.

Watts, J. D. W. (2005a, *Isaiah 1–33*, WBC 24, rev. ed., Nashville, TN: Nelson Reference.

Watts, J. D. W. (2005b), *Isaiah 34–66*, WBC 25, rev. ed., Nashville, TN: Nelson Reference.

Watts, R. E. (1990), 'Consolation or Confrontation? Isaiah 40–55 and the Delay of the New Exodus', *TynB*, 41: 31–59.

Webb, B. G. (1990), 'Zion in Transformation: A Literary Approach to Isaiah', in D. J. A. Clines, S. E. Fowl, and S. E. Porter (eds.), *The Bible in Three Dimensions*, 65–84, JSOTSup 87, Sheffield: JSOT Press.

Westermann, C. (1969), *Isaiah 40–66: A Commentary*, trans. D. M. G. Stalker, Old Testament Library, London: SCM Press.

Westermann, C. (1991), *Basic Forms of Prophetic Speech*, trans. H. C. White, Cambridge: Lutterworth.

Whybray, R. N. (1975), *Isaiah 40–66*, Grand Rapids, MI: Eerdmans.

Whybray, R. N. (1983), *The Second Isaiah*, Sheffield: JSOT Press.

Wiklander, B. (1984), *Prophecy as Literature: A Text-Linguistic and Rhetorical Approach to Isaiah 2–4*, CBOT 22, Uppsala: CWK Gleerup.

Wilcox, P., and D. Paton-Williams (1988), 'The Servant Songs in Deutero-Isaiah', *JSOT*, 42: 79–102.

Williams, D. W. (2015), *Message to My Girl: A Dying Father's Powerful Legacy of Hope*, Auckland, NZ: Allen & Unwin.

Williamson, H. G. M. (1994), *The Book Called Isaiah: Deutero-Isaiah's Role in Composition and Redaction*, Oxford: Oxford University Press.

Williamson, H. G. M. (1998), *Variations on a Theme: King, Messiah and Servant in the Book of Isaiah*, Carlisle, UK: Paternoster.

Williamson, H. G. M. (2006), *Isaiah 1–5*, vol. 1, ICC, London: T&T Clark International.

Wilshire, L. E. (1975), 'The Servant-City: A New Interpretation of the "Servant of the Lord" in the Servant Songs of Deutero-Isaiah', *JBL*, 94: 356–67.

Wilson, A. (1986), *The Nations in Deutero-Isaiah: A Study on Composition and Structure*, ANETS 1, Lewiston: Edwin Mellen.

Wilson, M. R. (1980), 'נכה', *TWOT* 2:577–9.

Wiseman, D. J. (1980), 'חלל', *TWOT* 2:288–9.

Wolf, H. (1980), 'דכא', *TWOT* 1:188–9.

Wright, D. P., and J. Milgrom (2001), 'עצר', *TDOT* 11: 310–15.

Wuellner, W. (1987), 'Where Is Rhetorical Criticism Taking Us?', *CBQ*, 49(3): 448–63.

INDEX OF REFERENCES

Index of Authors

Lightning Source UK Ltd.
Milton Keynes UK
UKHW021842241120
374029UK00003B/128